Military System of East India Company

Military System of East India Company

Edited by

Dr. Raj Kumar

Commonwealth

Military System of East India Company

First Published : 2004

ISBN 81-7169-861-1

Published by.:

Ajay Verma
***for* COMMONWEALTH PUBLISHERS**
4831/24, Prahlad Street,
Ansari Road, Darya Ganj,
New Delhi - 110002
Ph. : 23272541, 23257835
Fax : 91- 011- 23257835
e-mail : campusbooks@hotmail.com

Laser Typesetting by :

Arjun Computers
Delhi - 110051

Printed at :
Roshan Offset Printers
Delhi

PREFACE

The British East India Company came as traders. As soon as they started their factories, they began to keep armed personals for their protection. As their trade increased their defence requirements also multiplied. This ultimately required the military system.

Object of this compilation is to see how the conquest of India by the company was organized and managed during almost two hundred years of the rules. What defence organization and administration they created in India during the above period?

Authorities consulted and the sources used have been varied and many. I am deeply obliged .

Friends at the U.S.I. have been very kind and helpful. I am grateful to them.

Librarians and staff members of institutions and universities have extended to me every possible co-operation. I am thankful to them.

My publisher, his staff members at publishing and printing levels have worked hard. I thank them all.

Raj Kumar

PREFACE

Contents

1 Introduction

The first Indian troops of the British period were the watch-keepers employed by the Honourable British East India Company to protect its trading stations. Established as a purely trading organization, the Company soon acquired territorial jurisdiction and emerged as an expanding administrative authority. The watch-keepers were gradually decked out in uniform at first as much to satisfy the vanity of the Company officers as for any other reason. Later they were trained and drilled for more serious tasks than guarding the Company caravans and storehouses. Ultimately, they developed into three Presidency Armies of Madras, Bengal and Bombay.

Presidency Armies

The Bengal Army took precedence of the Madras army and the latter, of Bombay. East Presidency was separated, for at least two hundred years, from the other by hundreds of miles of trackless jungles or of independent States, and for many years had even no common Governor-General and, therefore, no coordinated policy. For all practical purposes, they were entirely separate countries dealing with widely different people. Their armies, were in many ways different, through from time to time, the Company issued regulations governing the main organization with a view to making them similar in their broad lines. In 1748, they were, for the first time, placed under the Commander-in-Chief, the first 'Father' of the *Army in India,* being major Stringer Lawrence. From his appointment onwards, the Presidency Armies showed continued all-round development and his appointment constitutes the first link in the long chain of consolidation of the *Army in India.* The year 1745 saw the arrival of the first Royal troops in India. The arrival introduced into the *Army in India* a new element. It was hereafter divided into King's Troops, Company's European Troops and Company's Indian Troops. This arrangement continued for more than one hundred years.

First General Reconstruction

During the constant war with French, Mysore and the Maharathas, the Presidency armies grew and developed. In 1793, the fall of Pondicherry ended the power of the French in India. When this struggle came to an end, Lord Cornwallis undertook to put some organization and system into the mass of troops that had grown up during the war years. In 1795, when the general reconstruction on a definite principle throughout the three armies came, there were 13,000 European troops (King's and Company's), and some 24,000 native troops in Bengal and Madras respectively with 9,000 in Bombay (according to Gen. MacMunn). The reoragnization took the accepted form of collecting artillery companies into battalions, cavalry troops into regiments and forming the infantry into two battalion regiments. This meant renumbering the whole of the battalions in each of the three armies except the first half and incurring the usual dislike of Corps for a change of the number under which they had won fame. The uniforms of the Corps were more strictly assimilated to those of the King's troops and a regular army came into being. The result of the reorganization was as under :

Bengal

European artillery—Three battalions of five companies each. European Infantry—Three battalions of ten companies each. Native Cavalry—Four regiments. Native Infantry—Twelve regiments to two battalions.

Madras

European Infantry—Two battalions of ten companies each, with fifteen companies of lascars. Native Cavalry—Four regiments. Native Infantry—Eleven regiments of two battalions.

Bombay

European Artillery—Six companies, European Infantry—two battalions of ten companies. Native Infantry—Four regiments of two battalions and a marine battalion. ('Native' was the term generally used for Indian troops in the service of the Company).

Marquis of Wellesley, his Wards and his Medals

In 1798, Lord Mornington, later the Marquis of Wellesley..... 'The Great Marquis' became the Governor-General and launched his general offensive to wipe out the French ruling authority and the authority of the Indian ruling chiefs, who had a large number of Europeans (other than the British) in their services and whose armies, trained on European model, were fast growing into a mortal threat. The armies of Marquis broke the power of Scindia in two pitched battles and a dozen of successful sieges and assaults. In order to commemorate the victories and the glorious deeds of the 'Sepoy Army,' which was evolving itself in the school of experience as an army of the line, in battle and march and siege, earning much fame in the process, the Marquis of Wellesley instituted a medal with the inscription. "To the Army of India," Its tally clasps included the wars of 'Assaye', 'Argaum', 'Ghawilghur', 'Asserghur', 'Laswarrie', 'Allighur', 'Battle of Deig', 'Capture of Deig', 'Battle of Delhi', 'Defence of Delhi.'

The Imperial Role

During the earlier years of the nineteenth century, the *Army in India* fulfilled an essentially imperial role. The overseas expeditions, and the power to commence expeditions from a self-supporting base, was considered a great strategical asset to the British. More important of the expeditions during the period and which would merit serious study were :

In 1792, an expedition composed of Madras troops took part in the war with Spain by capturing Manila. In 1795, an expedition of troops from Madras and Bengal captured Ceylor from the Dutch and the French. In the same year, an expedition from Madras captured Amboyna and the Spice Islands from the Dutch. In 1801, a force from India under Sir David Baird proceeded to join the British force in Egypt. In 1808, a force of volunteers from the Bengal Army proceeded to occupy Macao with a view of forestalling the French. In 1810, the depredations of the French privateers on British Commerce demanded the capture of Mauritius (Ile de France) Bourbon and Rodrigues. An expedition of troops from Bombay and Madras accomplished the task. In 1811, a naval and military force proceeded to capture the Island of Java from the Dutch and the French. The troops included several battalions from Bengal and some horse artillery and pioneers from Madras. In 1814, the war with Nepal broke out wherein Indian troops participated and distinguished themselves in service. In 1817, in India, the Sepoy Army pitched against the Pindaris who, according to Sir MacMunn, 'were enormous bands of free lances who, seizing strongholds and forming centres wherever they pleased, scourged the country round, swept and raided where they listed and brought half of India to the State of Europe in the days of Wallenstein and Tilly". The battles during the period were commemorated by additing 'To the Army of India', new claps of 'Kirkee', 'Poona', 'Kirkee and Poona', 'Seetabuldee', 'Nagpur', 'Seetabuldee and Nagpur', 'Mahidpoor', 'Corygaum'.

Minor Mutinies and Reorganization

It must not be supposed that in all these years of alien rule and the natural consequences that flow from it, there had not been any mutinies. A large army, controlled by a foreign trading company with large ideas on the subject of profits, was bound to have passed through periods of well-founded grievances. The first serious mutiny was of Vellore in 1806. Again in 1824, the corps ordered to march to Arakan refused to move. In 1824 therefore, a general reorganization of the armies was undertaken. They were renumbered, double battalion regiments were abolished and the line in each army was renumbered from I upwards. The army of 1824 was composed as follows :

Bengal

Three brigades of horse artillery of four troops each, of which one troops was native : Five battalions of artillery of four companies each; A corps of sappers and miners, with a cadre of 47, engineer officers, and a corps of pioneers; 2 battalions of European infantry; 8 regiments of light cavalry (regulars); 5

regiments of irregular horse; 68 battalions of native infantry ; several local corps and legions. *Madras* :— Two brigades of horse artillery, one European and one native; 3 battalions of foot artillery of 4 companies each, with 4 companies of lascar attached; 3 regiments of light cavalry ; 2 corps of pioneers ; 2 battalions. *Bombay*:— 4 troops of horse artillery ; 8 companies of foot artillery; A corps of engineers and pioneers; 3 regiments of light cavalry ; 2 regiments of irregular horse; 2 battalions of European infantry; 24 battalions of native infantry.

Campaigns Again

After the close of Pindari Wars, the expedition to Burma in 1824, the capture of Bhurtpore by a formidable force of cavalry and infantry, backed by half the heavy guns in India, and the Afghan war, were the immediate military commitments. In 1840, an expedition was sent to South China. The major portion of the force were troops of the Madras line. An aftermath of the Afghan wars, was the trouble with Scindia, which resulted in a short and famous campaign in which three Bombay cavalry and two Bombay infantry regiments tool part with the 22nd foot. The domains of Scindia were annexed.

In 1845, the most serious trouble that had threatened for many years came to ahead. Maharaja Ranjit Singh had died and the Khalsa Army crossed Sutlej in large numbers near Ferozepore. The British Indian troops that took the field were entirely from Bengal. The Second Sikh War broke out in the early summer of 1848. The British committed to battle a huge force of four brigades of cavalry and three divisions of infantry..

It has been admitted by the British themselves that the Khalsa Soldiery proved to be the toughest foe encountered by them in India. The brunt of the heavy fighting in these two wars fell on the Europeans and the losses sustained by them were extremely severe, far more than any portion, especially the native infantry, had been accustomed to experience for many years. The gainful result to the British, however, was that they could and they did recruit the disbanded Khalsa soldiery into their own armies and formed the world-famous Punjab

Frontier Force and laid the true foundations of the *Army in India* which later earned renown in numerous theatres of war throughout the world.

The troops of the *Army in India* also fought in the Crimean War, Second Burma War and the Persian Expedition, before the Great Mutiny broke out in 1857.

The Great Revolt (1857)

It was in 1757 that Clive scored one of the greatest victories at the Battle of Plassey. The battle lasted just one afternoon and the total casualties suffered by the British were twenty-three killed and nineteen wounded. Whole of Bengal lay prostrate and thus were laid the foundations of the British Empire in India. However, prophecy had it said that the British power in India would last just one hundred years. The prophecy may be said to have been true inasmuch as the Great Revolt of the Sepoy Army....the first clash on a national scale in battle that had run on ever since, spreading across oceans from India to Africa, to America and then back to East again; the growing rift of hatred between white and coloured people ... broke out in 1857.

Indian View-Point

Some Indian historians have been at pains to describe the Great Mutiny of 1857 as "The First War of Independence'. However, commentators of the calibre and capacity of the late Maulana Abdul Kalam Azad and the great author Surendra Nath Sen, have not shared their viewpoint. Commenting upon the nature and character of the Revolt, the late Maulana said : "some Indians have written on the struggle in the early years of this century. If the truth is to be told, we have to admit that the books that they have written are not history, but were propaganda to present the uprising as a planned war of independence...... after reading the various accounts, we are forced to the conclusion that the uprising was not the result of careful planning, nor were there any master minds behind it". Writing on the same subject, Surendra Nath Sen, said : "on all accounts, the movement of 1857 was not pre-planned it was not engineered by any political party in India or any foreign power hostile to England... The only feature which could give to the rebellion the character of the war of Independence, is that the mutineers of Meerut placed themselves under the King of Delhi and a section of the landed aristocracy and civilian population declared themselves in its favour."

British View-Point

The British commentators have generally considered the uprising of 1857 as a "mutiny pure and simple". In their opinion, the uprising did not have the support even from a substantial body of Indian sepoys. The outsiders, who joined hands with the rebels, had no national or patriotic considerations and certainly had no plan whatsoever to set up a national government. However, some British Commentators have admitted that 'the mutiny was no hasty thing, touched of spontaneously by the celebrated incident of issuing cartridges to sepoys' who believed that they were greased with cow's fat and pig's lard. This was a link into the chain of events, but certainly not the most important. It caught the imagination of the public of the day and by its acceptance, the mutineers were relieved of any obligation to dig deeper for the roots of the trouble. The roots of the unrest in India were deep indeed, and could be traced back over the years to 1,600 when the East India Company was founded."

The Causes

According to Bacon, 'the causes and motives for sedition were innovations in religion, taxes, alterations of laws and customs , breaking of privileges, general oppression, advancement of unworthy persons, strangers, disbanded soldiers, factions grown desperate, and whatsoever in offending people joineth and knitteth them in a common cause'. Not all these basic impulses to mutiny were strong in India bur certainly many were and the two acts, above all others operative were, the abolition of suttee and the annexation of Oudh. Among other causes operative to a lesser extent were, the forced participation in the Afghan War and the Burma Wars of the sepoys, who considered journey across the dark seas contrary to the terms of agreement and religious usage.

Storm Centres

Commentators and historians have not found it easy to compute the exact strength of the mutineers. Roughly speaking, some 30,000 are claimed to have remained loyal upto the end, a like number are claimed to have disarmed or deserted. Some 70,000 are claimed to have joined the revolt at different times. The storm centres of the revolt were Meerut, Delhi, Kanpur, Benaras, Allahabad, Oudh, Gwalior, Bithur, Fatehgarh, Lucknow, Patna, Jhansi, Ajmer, Nasirabad, Nimach, Aligarh, Lahore, Govindgarh, Jullundur, Kangra, Peshawar and Ferozepore.

Consequences

Every city had to suffer untold miseries twice. First, when the mutineers murdered, looted, plundered and pillaged and when English repeated the process with vengeance.

Of Delhi alone, it is said, : "The occupation of Delhi by the English was completed, but the cost was enormous. On the British side alone, 3,837 men and Officers were killed, wounded or missing. How many sepoys laid down their lives in the defence of Delhi will never be known.

The strength of Sepoy Army at the Imperial city has not yet been correctly computed. Wilson calculated the rebel strength at 40,000. The more vivid imagination of Hodson magnified the figure to 70,000. The British solders had heard to the butchered children, dishonoured women and comrades burnt alive. They were thirsting for vengeance and even Christian priest found nothing unworthy in righteous retribution, Ghalib the famous Urdu Poet, who was at Delhi at the time mournfully wrote :

'God alone knows the number of persons who were hanged. The victorious army entered the city along the main road, Whomsever they met on the way was killed.'

2
Naval Strategy in Historical Perspectives

Scholars analysing maritime strategy begin with Mahan. *The Influence of Sea Power Upon History*, 1660-1783, by Rear-Admiral Alfred Thayer Mahan of the US Navy, is a pioneering work in understanding geo-strategy of maritime power.

Though the study of theoreticians is essential in understanding the current maritime aspirations of great powers, their relevance needs to be reexamined in the context of formulation of maritime strategy of regional powers. For those who are seeking to evolve a maritime strategy for South Asian states, AD 1660, the starting point of the study of Mahan, is too 'contemporary.

South Asian region has been primarily influenced by the development of events in the Indian Ocean region, specially after the entry of the Portuguese by the end of the fifteenth century and more so with the policies of the British East India Company. It was their maritime strategy in the Indian Ocean region and its adjoining waters that has left the deep imprint upon the Indian mind.

There are three reasons for this formulation. Though the Portuguese and the English (EIC had links in Europe, both developed a strong and autonomous regional base. Both employed regional resources, even naval, to expand their power base. Both had a very clear perspective of the Indian Ocean as a unified geo-strategic region and not as a mere trade route for commerce as was the case earlier or as it is today. The Portuguese sought to influence the policy in the Indian Ocean region by establishing strong military bases that were also politico-economic centres in strategically located points in the Socotra (Red Sea), Hormuz (Persian Gulf), Malacca (South East Asia) besides a chain of major and minor bases along the coast of South Asia) besides a chain of major and minor bases along the coast of South Asia including present day Sri Lanka. The EIC followed the footsteps of the Portuguese. It is this Anglo-Portuguese perception of the Indian Ocean as a composite neighbourhood maritime entity that influenced and continues to influence Indian maritime strategic perception.

Naval strategy, at the conceptual leval, has been a hotly debated issue, especially in the countries of the developed North. It is still a relatively new subject in the South. As a result of the colonial legacy and continuing academic inputs from the North, experts in the South too tried to borrow concepts and theories from the North. However, over the years, not only circumstances indigenous to the South but also experiences of the past five decades have enabled them to evolve their own concepts and theories that are more approiate to their requirements. These, in turn, have influenced their naval strategy. In South Asia alone, while India has opted for what can be broadly called a sea control strategy, Pakistan, especially after the 1971 war, has preferred to focus in sea denial. Sri Lanka, thanks to its singular experience, has been forced to fashion its naval strategy that is geared to combat maritime insurgency along its coast. Thus, even in South Asia, objective situations have led to the evolution of three distinct models of naval strategy.

It is also important to underline that naval strategy cannot be delinked from the overall maritime strategy of a given state. Maritime strategy, as one understands it today, is a recent concept and has evolved over a period of last four centuries or even less. It is the result of a combination of developments since the sixteenth century in ship designing and construction, improved sailing and navigational techniques and finally, the use of artillery as the main weapon. It led to voyages of discovery which gave a new turn to the thrust of seabased colonial and imperial policies of the Europeans. Though this phase started with emphasis on trade and commerce, it soon revolutionized the then existing world order by using sea as a medium not only for trade and commerce but also for power projection in far away lands. It forced open continents that were earlier unapproachable for Europeans. It led to a spurt in conquest and rapid colonization which was unprecedented in history. It also became the basis for a new type of rivalry at the global level in which control over the sea was as important or sometimes even more important than control over the land. That struggle for supremacy is still going on, despite the advance of the space age.

This development in maritime affairs was neither purely naval nor commercial but was the product of their interaction. According to an Indian scholar, "Maritime strategy is the total response of a nation to the oceans around it for which sea power is required to achieve economic, political and military goals at sea".[1] Thus, the concept of maritime power or sea power is not confined to naval ships or naval aircraft operating by themselves. It is a combination of many factors but above all"... it means a flourishing mercantile fleet, a sea-faring community, a commerce-minded people and a Navy capable of defending the shipping at sea".[2] This interaction between civilian and military dimensions of maritime of sea power is also highlighted by an Indian diplomat as follows : "Sea power then is the totality of a nation's fishing fleet, merchant fleet, scientific fleet, military fleet, the sophistication and efficiency of its communication systems, and finally the R&D apparatus accompanying all these".[3]

Broad parameters of maritime strategy would, therefore, encompass the following variables : safeguarding the freedom of passage on the high seas, especially keeping open the sea-lanes of strategic importance, promoting and protecting national efforts towards the exploitation of maritime resources, both living and non-living, and also preventing their exploitation by unauthorized persons, promoting sea-borne trade and commerce, and finally, protecting not only the coast and the immediate hinterland but also the islands and artificial installations like oil and gas platforms in the national maritime zone from threats directed by the adversaries *via* the maritime frontiers of the country.

Naval strategy is thus only a part of the broader maritime strategy. The navy, with its primary emphasis upon war fighting, is basically one aspect of the triad consisting of the army war fighting, is basically one aspect of the triad consisting of the army, navy and air force. It has to act in concert with them except when it is used independently for force projection beyond the normal reach of the army and the air force. Maritime strategy, on the other hand, is a broader concept and aims at enabling the state not only to exploit maritime resources but also to use the sea to reach beyond one's frontiers for improving social, economic and political relations. In the case of the archipelagic states or states whose major components are separated by sea, maritime strategy even becomes a major component of the over-all nation-building process. Thus, maritime strategy covers the civilian facets that naval strategy does not. Moreover, the effectiveness of naval strategy is tested only in times of military confrontation while the success of maritime strategy is judged not only in times of war but more so in times of peace. In fact, an effective maritime strategy becomes the bedrock for an effective naval power.

This interaction of civilian and military aspects of maritime strategy is witnessed more in the industrialized North than in the developing South. Though some of the states in the South might boast of a strong navy, few of them have a strong maritime base or a coherent national maritime strategy. The North is far advanced in the field of ship-designing, ship-building and repairs,, merchant marine and even fishery. Fishing fleets of these states sail to far away places, including the Indian Ocean, to catch fish, especially tuna, in the deep sea while the littoral states are content to fish mostly in their in-shore waters despite exclusive fishing rights in their respective exclusive economic zone (EEZ) under the provisions of the UNCLOS III. No wonder, these states allow the non-regional maritime powers to dominate them even in their own waters not only in times of war but also in times of peace.

Two examples will help to underline the lack of maritime strategic thinking in the South. Domestic politics of pre-1971 Pakistan illustrated the absence of maritime thinking. Its two wings were separated by India, an adversary power especially since the war of 1965. Only sea could have integrated the two wings of Pakistan but the ruling elite of Pakistan failed to evolve a suitable maritime strategy since its very creation in 1947. Its strong merchant marine would have acted as a bringing factor in times of peace and as a source of power in times of war. The eastern wing was neglected even in terms of naval strategy with disastrous consequences in 1971.

In the Gulf, especially in its Arab littoral, where the economy is primarily dependent upon export of oil and oil products, states have failed to strengthen their maritime base. They have no ship-building facilities. Their ship repair facilities are also limited. Their merchant marine is too small. Because of inadequate tankers and other ships, their sea-borne trade is largely in the hands of non-regional powers. Even their naval capability is lopsided. While the naval strategy of these states relies heavily upon the deterrence posed by surface and air-launched long-range anti-ship missiles, they do not have adequate surveillance and C_3I capability. Moreover, this narrow area, that is always saturated with oil tankers and cargo ships, lacks even the basic mine counter-measure capability as was obvious during the Iraq-Iran War after 1986. No wonder, the North Atlantic Treaty Organization (NATO) dominates the Gulf.

Maritime Thinking in the South

Why do the states of the South lack an effective maritime strategy? Is it a lack of resources, or a lack of maritime culture, or is it the result of long years of colonial dominance when "others" managed their maritime affairs. Possibly, it is a combination of all three. Some states are indeed small and weak and cannot afford to project a credible maritime power. But not all states are small or poor. Moreover, some of these constraints could have been overcome if these states had combined to evolve a regional maritime policy. But, newly acquired state sovereignty was too zealously guarded to encourage such a regional cooperation at that time. May be the time is now ripe for the evolution of such a policy.

Is the lack of so-called maritime culture responsible for this neglect? There are divergent views on this question. Some scholars like K.M. Panikkar argued that Indians were not geography conscious and hence India never had a foreign policy till the British established their authority over it. " We were neither maritime nor continental in our outlook."[4] Another renowned Indian historian, K.A. Nilkanta Sastri, holds the contrary view and blames the imprint of British colonial education upon Indian historical thinking in this regard. According to him, the British text-books of the nineteenth and the early twentieth centuries propagated the myth of an isolated India, cut-off by mountains and sea from the rest of the world but somehow always open to invasions and conquests from the Northwest until the end of the fifteenth century when Vasco da Gama came by sea followed by intruders from other European nations along the same route. According to him, that myth was a sub-conscious creation of the colonial epoch. Reality was that India had played an important and active part throughout long centuries in maintaining a brisk intercourse with her neighbours and mutually beneficient interchange of goods and ideas.[5]

Despite this debate one point will have to be noted. While the coastal region of the Indian subcontinent was always interacting socially and economically with other areas in the Indian Ocean and even beyond, the direct involvement of the hinterland power in such an interaction was always small unless the hinterland and the coast were under one strong power and trade and commerce were closely monitored by the central authority. Earlier, the Chola Empire was such an exception in South India when the state not only encouraged maritime affairs but also sought to project its naval presence *vis-a-vis* the Sri Vijay Empire in Southeast Asia. At the time of the Portuguese arrival, the Sultanate of Gujarat was one such state. Not only did it try to resist the Portuguese on its own but it also sought the help o the Mamluk Sultans of Egypt and, after they were defeated by the Turks, of the Ottoman Sultan, in confronting the Portuguese. But the countries-old neglect of science and technology, especially in the rapidly evolving field of naval warfare, led to the Europeans acquiring and retaining an upper hand.

None of the rulers in the South, be it the tottering Vijaynagar Empire or the states of the ex-Bahmani Sultanate, had the maritime vision to evolve a strategy to confront the newly emerging maritime threat. The Mughals, who had started consolidating their power in the North and were reaching the seas by the time the Portuguese were acquiring footholds on the Indian coast, could not even conceive of suitable maritime countermeasures. One possible explanation for this apathy, primarily based upon ignorance of maritime affairs, was that their primary focus of attention, be it economic, political or military, was on land. Whether it was the question of land revenue or commercial activities or political and military challenges; they all seemed to emanate from the land. Hence, as against that immediate urgency, the long-term maritime threats were ignored. In Sri Lanka also, before the fourteenth century, when the centre of power was in the hinterland at Anuradhapur, the coast and the associated maritime policy was neglected. In the Malabar region, maritime trade and shipping was entrusted to a sea-faring community with pan-Indian Ocean linkages but with limited interaction with the hinterland. That was also one of the factors inhibiting the hinterland from evoloping a viable maritime policy.

Another point that is often debated is the role of the colonial or the imperial power. Was the lack of development of maritime consciousness due to a deliberated policy of colonial powers? If control over maritime power was central to their policy of colonialism and imperialism, one would not expect them to help the colonized people to undermine their power base by encouraging maritime consciousness and by promoting maritime activities in those areas. Thus, the 'myth' of India as a traditional 'land power' could have been deliberately cultivated thereby leaving maritime affairs to Britain. Moreover, as a part of the larger policy of keeping India insular, maritime activities were discouraged. During the colonial rule, especially of the British crown, the flourishing ship-building industry of India was allowed to decay. Also, Indians faced stiff opposition in carrying on ship-borne trade even in the coastal waters. The British sought to retain their monopoly over the sea-borne trade of India. The EIC had tried to organize some sort of navy and the marines but after the British Government took over the administration of India after 1857-58 that navy was allowed to lapse while the army was expanded. And, when the navy was recreated under the threat of impending Second World War it was small and ill-equipped and acted as an adjunct to the Royal Navy. The British did nothing to encourage fishing in the adjoining waters away from the immediate coast.

Thus, whether South Asia had or did not have a maritime tradition in the past, one thing that emerges clearly is that the British colonial policy positively discouraged the development of even maritime consciousness, leave aside maritime capability, in South Asia. That aspect of the European colonial policy was true in other areas of the Indian Ocean region as well . Such a policy left its imprint upon the slow pace of growth of maritime consciousness in the post-colonial period also.

The Civilian Aspect of Maritime Strategy

As noted earlier, maritime consciousness was the outcome of interaction of civilian and military dimensions, especially in Europe, since the fifteenth century, if not earlier. In the civilian sector, the growing emphasis on deep-sea fishing and sea-borne trade was the cause and also the effect of rapid improvements and innovations in the field of ship designing and ship building, sailing, navigation, port and dockyard facilities etc. By the middle of the fifteenth century, fishermen had started venturing out into the stormy waters of the North Atlantic and the North Sea. Ships were designed to face the rough sea conditions. Sailing also improved which enabled ships to sail in contrary wind conditions. Long sea voyages for fishing prepared ordinary sailors both physically and psychologically to be out-of-sight of land for days. Improved navigation techniques and cartography enabled them to sail more boldly into unknown waters.

These developments, mosly in Europe, might have allowed the more adventurous to discover lands unknown to them and to trade there but would not have allowed them to conquer and colonize them. It is interesting that developments in the civilian sectors of maritime affairs also coincided with rapid growth in the use of artillery as the main weapon on board the ship. While in the initial period the same ship that carried commercial cargo also doubled up as a fighting vessel, gradually, the growing sophistication in the use of artillery separated the sea-going vessels into two clear roles : commerce and fighting. This role continues even today. But both were interlinked in the past, as they are today, in the broader context of maritime strategy.

Very often this interrelationship between the civilian and the military dimensions of maritime power is ignored. The great naval strategic thinker, Alfred Mahan, while analysing the rise of England as a sea power in the eighteenth century and onwards, said that it was not merely due to the navy, because France too had a navy in 1580s, nor because of prosperous commerce, because, the Dutch were equally good at it, but it was a result of the combination of the two. "It was in the union of the two, *carefully fostered*, that England made the gain of sea power over and beyond all other states; and this gain is distinctly associated with and dates from the War of Spanish Succession. Before that England was one of the sea powers, after it she was the sea power, without any second. This power she held alone, unshared by friend and unchecked by foe".[6] Another historian also underlines this alliance of government and commerce. In a sort of division of labour, merchants and merchant-shipping were to pursue their tasks unrestricted by government or by war-like necessities, while the government represented their interests and the Royal Navy protected them against foreign interference.[7]

Till the end of the fifteenth century, this evolution in shipping and also in armament was in the context of intra-

European, and more so intra-Mediterranean, contest for maritime supremacy. It resulted in the evolution of maritime strategy which aimed at acquiring absolute monopoly not only over the trade but as over the sea-routes. The Europeans, beginning with the Portuguese, who burst into the Indian Ocean by the end of the fifteenth century, brought this maritime strategy in an area which was totally unprepared for it at that time.

Contrary to the practice in Europe and in the Mediterranean, states in the Indian Ocean region normally followed the policy of freedom of trade and of navigation. While the navy might have been used as an adjunct of the army in the nearby coastal battle or across a short distance as between parts of Southern India and Sri Lanka, by the Arabs from the Gulf when they first conquered Sindh, or the Gujarat coast and north Konkan, it was rare that naval power was used for force projection across the high seas. Thus, the Chola naval expedition against the Sri Vijaya Empire was an exception, probably the only exception of long distance naval operation in the Indian Ocean region.

That probably was one major reason why the states of the Indian Ocean region did not evolve a credible navy to buttress the trade. Naval duty was primarily confined to checking local pirates in the adjoining waters, and not in far away areas. Such was the primary objective of the Mughal navy even during its most glorious days. It was not good enough even for that limited objective. Mughal warships patrolled the coastal waters of Bengal, while pirates looted the prized possession of Aurangzeb, the *Ganj-e-Sawai*, in distant waters. Even the Mughal pilgrim ships on the *Haj* voyage were not escorted by the Mughal navy. Often, they were escorted by the Portuguese and later on by the English vessels. Mughal ships even paid the tax and obtained *cartaz* from the Portuguese to sail from the home ports. The only possible explanation for such utter neglect of maritime affairs was the grand obsession to subdue the 'land'. The defence of the maritime interests was left to the Marathas who were confronting not only the Portuguese, the

Dutch and the British but also the Mughals as represented by the Sidis of Janjira.

This basic difference in the attitude towards the maritime strategy of Europe and the Indian Ocean region, *i.e.* Europe's objective of acquiring monopoly not only were trade and commerce but also over the sea lanes, has to be kept in mind while analysing the wave of maritime colonization and imperialism after the sixteenth century.

Europeans 'discovered' and colonized far-away continents like the two Americas, Australia, Africa and Asia. In areas where the indigenous population was unable to resist massive and sustained waves of immigration from across the sea, Europeans 'claimed' entire continents as their property. In areas where they were confronted with established order, they still sought to rule the land under their imperial authority. Never in the history had such large-scale migration, colonization and establishment of imperial dominance occurred in such far away places across the sea. To say the least, that was possible largely due to the spurt in the evolution Europe's maritime capability coupled with an aggressive and monopolistic maritime strategy. This would not have evolved nor could it have been sustained without the conscious enter-meshing of civilian and military aspects like ship-building, port facilities and sea-borne trade and commerce besides emphasis upon specialized fighting vessels. It would not be wrong to say that civilian efforts buttressed the naval aspect of the over-all maritime capability. Developments in science and technology also contributed to its success. Countries of the South, including those of South Asia, were left far behind in this race.

The Military Dimensions of Maritime Strategy

While not underplaying the civilian aspect of maritime strategy, one can ignore the military dimensions at one's own peril. One of the glaring lessons of the history of the Indian Ocean region since the end of the fifteenth century is that though a region might boast of the best of the civilian facets of maritime affairs; ship building, port facilities, maritime trade and commerce etc., all that can be lost unless these are buttressed by an appropriate naval capability. Thus, military dimensions of maritime strategy cannot be ignored or downplayed.

The naval capability needs to be abalysed in the context of two main requirements. The first is the role that the navy is required to play as a part of the triad of the fighting force comprising the army, the navy and the airforce. The other is when the navy is asked to act as an independent variable in projecting maritime power in areas where the army and air force cannot be expected to operate effectively. This capability of the navy to project force over a long distance has been a major factor in shaping world history. It has prompted naval historians and strategists from Mohan to Gorshkov to look at the navy from the perspective of its global role; a role that could not have been possible without the maritime development since the sixteenth century. Prior to that, the navy could at best play only a regional role as in the Mediterranean Sea, the Baltic Sea or the Bay of Bengal.

The navy has been acquiring increasing sophistication specially since the end of the nineteenth century. The development of subsurface capability during the First World War and of the sea-based air capability during the Second World War has given the navy a three dimensional role that the other two arms of the triad cannot acquire. The army can be air-borne and the air force can hit targets on sea but neither of them can acquire the degree of independence of operation over long distances from home bases as the navy can. It is the capacity of the navy to operate independently for long periods far away from the base that has given real substance to the term 'command of the sea'. Since the sixteenth century, maritime powers have been striving to acquire and to retain it. The Portuguese were able to acquire that in the context of the Indian Ocean in the sixteenth century. That was challenged by the Dutch, the French and the British. USA emerged as the sea power after the Second World War. Its command over the seas was sought to be contested by the Soviet Union, since the mid-sixties but because of the disintegration of the Soviet Union, USA has remained the single undisputed sea-power with near absolute command over the sea at the global level. Thus, a glance at the recent world history would reveal that very often changes in the position of world leadership are associated with the shift in the distribution of sea power.[8]

This capability acquired a new strategic dimension when submarine-launched ballistic missiles (SLBM) were introduced in 1962-63. Till then the navy had limited role in nuclear strategy. But the SLBM gave the navy a role comparable if not superior to land-based ballistic missiles and manned bombers. One could even argue that the capability of a nuclear-powered submarine to travel long-distance while submerged and thus remain undetected from the space, and the range and accuracy of the missile, offered the navy advantages that the land-based nuclear weapon delivery systems, be they manned bomber or Inter-continental Ballistic Missiles (ICBMs), could not achieve.

The navy has another edge over the army and the air force in the sense that it can be, and is, often used very effectively as an instrument of state policy even in times of peace. The classical use of sea power in times of peace has been defined by a scholar as : " To back up friends, to warn potential enemies, neutralize similar deployment by other naval power, to exert influence in ambiguous situations, to demonstrate resolve through a deployment of palpable force—all these are tasks that naval power is uniquely able to perform. For these purposes the advantages of naval power over land or air power are clear."[9] According to Vice-Admiral R.B. Suri, naval power is that element of military power associated with forces, ships, submarines, aircraft, naval marines, free standing mines—that operate primarily on, under, over, or from the sea. Land attack nuclear—armed submarines are also included.[10]

Admiral Gorshkov, the theoretician and one of the chief architects of the Soviet Navy, while analysing the role of the navy, said that during times of peace it possesses the capability to vividly demonstrate the economic and military might of a country beyond its borders. According to him, "... because of that quality, the imperialist states have used it to deter or suppress the intentions of potential enemies as well as to support friendly states." He adds, "While representing a formidable force in war, it has always been an instrument of policy of the imperialist state and an important support for diplomacy in peace time owing to its inherent qualities which permit it to a greater degree than other branches of the armed forces to exert pressures on potential enemies without the direct employment of weaponry".[11]

Despite the oft-quoted statement of Cromwell that man-of-war was his best ambassador, warship has certain assets and also certain liabilities as instruments of diplomacy. Its assets are its versatility, controllability *i.e.* the capability to escalate or to withdraw, mobility, force projection capability, access potential because of the freedom of the high seas, symbolism of national sovereignty on the high seas, and endurance. Its liabilities are its relatively slow mobility which influences the time factor in response, potential for initiating hostility if seen as gunboat diplomacy, its inability to bring results on its own and hence its limited scope of action. Even in the context of coercive diplomacy, it cannot produce the impact of massed troops across the frontier especially against the immediate neighbours.[12] There is no doubt that in spite of its limitations, "...Ocean going warships provide the government with an extra tool, a set of lazy tongs, an extended reach. Their utility is likely to last as long as violent peace".[13] In this context, it needs to be underlined that the peace time role of the naval power, especially as an instrument of diplomatic coercion has been analysed by the strategists primarily in the context of great powers who have a credible naval force projection capability even in an adverse political environment. That role cannot fit the navies of small and medium states especially in the developing world. Hence, it is necessary to concentrate upon the non-coercive aspects like goodwill mission, joint exercises as a part of confidence building measure, and as a first step in the direction of evolving a regional maritime strategy.

The navy's real capability is assessed in times of war. The debate over the primacy of sea power or land power continues unresolved. Now, space power is also considered in that context. Arguing for sea power, Sardar K.M. Panikkar quotes Khaireddin Pasha, the Turkish admiral in the Mediterranean who was confronting the Christian world in the fifteenth century, as saying, "He who rules on the seas will shortly rule on the land also."[14] While a strong land power can always defy the sea power on land it is unable to deny the adversary control of the sea and hence of the sea lanes, maritime commerce and even certain areas of the coast over which the sea power can exercise immediate jurisdiction from the sea. Thus, while France was a major land power in the eighteenth century, England's dominance over the seas enabled it not only to effectively blockade the coast under the French dominance but also facilitated British support to anti-French forces on land. Nearer home, the Siddis of Janjira, a major local naval power on the Arabian Sea coast of India, could not be evicted from their coastal zone, leave aside their island fortress, by the Maratha land power. Similarly, the whole history of European penetration and subjugation of Asia and Africa illustrates the dominance of sea power over land power

There are several reasons why sea power, and that includes naval-air-power now, can dominate over land power per se. Among other things, sea power is ubiquitous. The sea, unlike the land, knows no barriers. Distances are no real bar to expansion and consolidation of sea power. According to Prof. Hedley Bull, sea power has several advantages like flexibility, visibility and universality or pervasiveness.[15] A naval force can be sent and withdrawn, the activities varied, with a higher expectation that it will remain subject to control than is possible when ground forces are committed. It has high visibility. When on the high seas or even in a foreign port, a navy can convey threat, provide reassurance or even prestige in a way that troops and aircraft in their home bases cannot do. The universality is guaranteed because the high seas, in contrast to the land and the air space, are an international medium and allow naval vessels to reach distant areas independent of nearby bases. It makes a state possessing sea power virtual neighbours of any other state that is accessible by sea.

Commenting upon this, Admiral S.N. Kohli said that sea power is ideal in that it is flexible. It has none of the potential provocation of a territorial military commitment, and it has historical acceptance in the area. It can give valuable aid in times of disaster and can provide a visible sign of interest by the flag power. It can deter harassment and blackmail by enemies, and provide a safe means of evacuating civilians in times of crisis. It gives its owner a wide spectrum of roles to choose from. It can command the respect of enemies and stiffen the confidence of friends. What matters is its existence, rather than the purpose for which it was built." He adds, "In the Navy, a nation has a uniquely useful and versatile tool which can be applied overtly or covertly, directly or indirectly, but always effectively, in whatever may, at the moment, be in the national interest."[16]

Determinants of Naval Strategy

Wartime role of navy has acquired a more complex character today. Before the First World War, the navy largely depended for operations upon surface vessels and shore installations supporting them. Now, the navy has become a three-dimensional force-surface, sub-surface and air. It operates a naval-air wing which is both sea-bases and land-based, as well as the marines. Marines were a part of the navy earlier but unlike the marines in the past, which were armed with light weapons only, today the marines have the capability to fight independently since they have their own armour force, air force and an effective ground-based area defence capability. Thus, several of the roles of the navy overlap those of other arms, despite the fact that navy is itself a part of the triad consisting of the army, navy and the air force. Hence coordination between the three arms demands a greater sophistication now as compared to the past when their roles could be demarcated more sharply.

Navies have often been defined as blue, green or brown water navies. Vice-Admiral R.B. Suri has, however, defined their operational roles as follows. All states expect at least that their navies would deter or defend against encroachment or attack on their territories and maritime economic zones. Some aspire to regional or global prestige and expect their navies to operate further out. A few—most enterprising ones—wish their navies to be ready for undertaking sizable and far distance offensive operations.[17]

The navy's tasks during war can be described as defensive, offensive or a combination of the two depending upon the capability and the requirements at a given time. Among the tasks that are primarily defensive in nature can be listed the protection of ports, coastline and immediate hinterland, off-shore installations etc., and protecting maritime trade by keeping the sea-lanes open, conducting mine counter-measure operations and by escorting merchant vessels against threats posed by submarines, surface vessels and enemy aircraft. Its role in offensive operations consists of blockading the adversary's coast and ports, shore bombardment, amphibious landing, evacuation operations and so on. Normally, the navy is asked to perform a mix of both types of operations though the major thrust may vary from time to time and from country to country.

Each state evolves its naval strategy based upon its threat perception and its military capability as conditioned by political, economic and military constraints. Threat perception and military capability are not always static. They reflect the changing regional and international environment and the response of the ruling elite at different times.

Naval strategy can be analysed in its three main broad facets, though the policy makers might choose a mix that they feel is appropriate to the national requirement. These three facets are sea denial, sea control and force projection both on sea and on land. These three facets are also influenced by two other variables: the focus of operation and the range of operation. These are qualitatively different variables because while the one denotes the specific area, the other deals with the distance that the naval strategy wishes to influence. In several cases, naval force projection need not always be in far off lands or sea but can also be a part of the overall military strategy *vis-a-vis* the immediate neighbourhood. Increasingly. The navy is faced with the challenge of evolving an appropriate strategy against low intensity maritime threat.

There is some controversy about the terms in-shore, off-shore or coastal and high seas. I would prefer to equate them with the three well recognized terms of international law dealing with maritime affairs; and contiguous zone, territorial waters EEZ and the seas beyond the jurisdiction of any sovereign state *i.e.* the high seas. Thus, in-shore waters would include the territorial sea and the contiguous zone, coastal or off-shore waters would include the extent of the EEZ, and the high seas would be beyond it. Such a definition would be handicapped while defining the sea area where the territorial sew and EEZ are reduced because of close proximity of two or more maritime neighbours. But, by and large, 24 n. miles and 200 n. miles can be used to determine the basic characteristics of the in-shore and the off-shore or coastal waters in the context of defining maritime strategy.

The capability of a state to fulfil its strategic objectives rests, among other things, upon its military capability which, in turn, depends upon the weapons that it possesses. Thus, it is possible to speculate fairly accurately on the possible strategic thinking of a state at a given time as well as to evaluate the changes in strategic thrust over a given period by analyzing its weapons acquisition programme in the light of their designed roles. In this context, it is also important to underline the fact that strategic thrust and operational performance are two different things. A state may possess excellent weapons but its battlefield performance can be poor. Operational performance will depend upon factors like the degree of weapons assimilation in the national armed forces, level of training and maintenance, and lastly, the capability of the adversary. Hence, while it is relatively easy to speculate on the possible thrust of naval strategy, it is more difficult to evaluate the naval capability of a given state at a given time.

While trying to assess the main thrust of naval strategy through the analysis of a combination of available weapons system and the weapons in the pipe line, it is important to note that specific weapons are best tailored for their designed roles. Thus, while the submarine, armed with guided torpedo, and now with long-range cruise missiles with conventional warhead, can be used as a part of a task-force for force projection, it is best suited for the sea denial strategy. Similarly, the fast patrol boasts or the corvettes armed with anti-ship missiles are best suited for the sea denial strategy for in-shore and off-shore zones, yet under favourable conditions they can also be used for force projection over a limited range of operations, as was done during the India-Pakistan War in 1971.

It is possible to evaluate the main thrusts of the naval strategy of a given power at a given time by analysing the capabilities of the weapon systems that it possesses or which are in the popeline, as well as the possible combinations based upon them. *Table 1* dealing with the weapon systems and their main strategic roles provides a pointer in that direction. While each weapon has a specific capability, a combination of these weapons will point to the likely strategic thrust at a given time. If that thrust is recognized, it is possible to analyse the interaction of strategy and weapons more correctly and to make a fairly accurate assessment of the likely naval strategy a country is capable of adopting and is likely to adopt.

The main thrust of sea denial strategy is "to prevent the navy of the hostile power from maintaining requisite naval supremacy."[18] It also aims at refusing the use of a given area to the adversary in times of war and need not necessarily mean that the party that is adopting the sea denial strategy would like to control that area. The classical example of that strategy was the use of submarines by Germany during the two World Wars when it sought to deny to its adversary the use of the high seas for strategic purposes.

Sea denial strategy would be influenced by the range and the specific area of operation. These can also be broadly sub-divided as in-shore, off-shore or coastal and the high seas as noted in Table 1. Sea denial in the in-shore zone can be based upon shore-based guns and anti-ship missiles and fast patrol boats (FPB) and corvettes as well as aircraft armed with anti-

Table 1
Naval Weapons and their Main Strategic Roles

Weapons	*Sea Denial*		*Sea Control*		*For Projection*			*COIN*	
	Inshore	*Offshore*	*High Seas*	*Inshore*	*Offshore*		*High Seas*	*On Seas*	*On Land*
(1)	*(2)*	*(3)*	*(4)*	*(5)*	*(6)*		*(7)*	*(8)*	*(9)*
Warships									
Aircraft carrier	-	-	*	-	*	*	*	*	-
Submarine	-	*	*	-	*	*	*	*	-
Cruiser	-	*	*	-	*	*	*	*	-
Destroyer	-	*	*	-	*	*	*	*	-
Frigate	-	*	*	-	*	*	*	*	-
Corvette	*	*	-	*	*	-	-	-	*
Fast Patrol Boat, Missile	*	*	-	*	-	-	-	-	-
Boat, Gun	*	-	-	*	-	-	-	-	*
Boat, Torpedo	*	-	-	*	-	-	-	-	-
Minesweeper Ocean	-	*	*	-	*	*	*	-	-

(Contd...)

(Contd...)

(1)	*(2)*	*(3)*	*(4)*	*(5)*	*(6)*		*(7)*	*(8)*	*(9)*
Coastal	-	*	-	-	*	-	*	-	-
Inshore	*	-	-	*	-	-	-	-	*
Landing Ship	-	-	-	-	-	-	-	*	*
Landing Craft	-	-	-	-	-	-	-	*	*
Fleet Repl.									
ship.....	-	-	-	-	*	*	*	*	-
Naval-Air Arm									
Shipborne aircraft									
fixed wing									
and helicopter....	-	-	-	-	-	*	*	*	*
Land based :									
fixed-wing....	*	*	-	*	*	*	*		*
helicopter	*	*	-	*	*	-	-	-	*

Note : * indicates the role of the weapon.

ship missiles. FPBs armed with guns are increasingly being used now for coast guard, customs and fishery protection duties. Modern long-range anti-ship missiles that can be mounted on FPBs, corvettes and helicopters have offered to the small and medium powers an efficient weapon system for the sea denial strategy, especially in the in-shore and the off-shore or coastal zones. In these cases, air power for maritime reconnaissance, anti-submarine warfare (ASW) and anti-ship operations can also be projected from land bases. This strategy is generally followed by those states that cannot afford or do not wish to incur the heavy cost of a big naval programme.

The sea denial strategy for the coastal waters would need inputs of heavier vessels, at least at the destroyer/frigate level, to add endurance and heavier fire power. Moreover, a helicopter on board the vessel geared or ASW or anti-ship role adds substantially to that punch. Some states have started using submarines for that role too, especially when the adversary is compelled by geography to use their coastal waters. That was especially true in the Baltic Sea, the North Sea, the Mediterranean and the North Pacific. These were the areas from where the Soviet vessels, including the nuclear powered submarines, armed with SLBMs, had to break out to reach the designated zones in the oceans so as to target USA. Thus the small, shallow water submarines of West European states and Japan, armed with conventional torpedoes were also designed for a sea-denial role against the Super Power's nuclear strategy.

Sea denial strategy for the high sea depended heavily upon submarines whose range and endurance would depend upon geopolitical considerations. For states whose naval strategy is governed by considerations of shallow sea and limited range of operation, as in the Baltic Sea, the Mediterranean, the Arabian Sea etc., small or medium size submarines with limited range and endurance are more suitable. For countries whose naval strategies are oriented more towards deep waters and long distances, larger long-range ocean-going submarines are more suitable. Nuclear-powered attack submarines (SSN) have added greater punch to that capability. Submarines are a potent weapon not only for the sea denial strategy but also as an instrument of strategic ambivalence. Thus, even in the hands of a small state, it can project a massive threat which can even be seen as provocative unless it fits within the larger strategic framework of that country.

Sea control strategy, as opposed to the sea denial strategy, has a more positive thrust. That strategy aims at gaining and maintaining general naval supremacy with a view to controlling vital sea lanes in order to protect lines of communication and commerce by ensuring local superiority in an area of naval operations.[19] Admiral Kohli is more precise in defining the term. According to him, the ability to control the sea means denying the enemy the use of the seas while asserting one's own use of them.[20] According to him, sea control is an offensive maritime strategy. It demands a substantial naval force to render the threat posed completely ineffective. An inadequate force level would lead to a stalemate leading to sea denial by both sides, but with neither side being able to use the sea for their own advantage.[21]

The weapons mix for sea control strategy is bound to be different from that of sea denial strategy though in some areas nearer the shore the two combinations might appear to be similar, as seen from Table 1. The main thrust of weapons mix for sea control strategy is to neutralize the sea denial capability of the adversary, whether it be subsurface, surface or air. Thus, heavier surface vessels with ASW and anti-air capability are essential for the sea control strategy especially in the off-shore waters and on the high seas.

The weapons mix would also be affected by factors like range, endurance, and the area of operation. If it is in-shore, it will get support from shore-based facilities for anti-surface, anti-sub-surface and anti-air operations. Shore-based naval-air operations can also be extended to parts of off-shore waters in certain cases. But aircraft carrier would prove necessary to provide the necessary air support in areas that are beyond the the effective and timely reach of shore-based aircraft even in off-shore waters. Thus, destroyers and cruisers, capable of providing heavy fire power, and aircraft carrier to provide immediate air support become essential for an effective sea control strategy, especially on the high seas. Submarines, in the hunter-killer role, are proving to be useful and are often included as a part of the naval task force. The task force, if used in sea control role on the high seas, which might mean long endurance, has also to have support facilities like oilers, supply vessels and fleet replenishment vessels. The long-range sea control strategy is mainly employed by major naval powers who have that capability.

Force projection is conceptually different from that of sea denial or sea control though it might use some of the weapons designed for these two roles. Force projection is primarily an offensive strategy in that force is projected far away from the home ports to serve a specific politic-military objective. Force projection at short-range can also be carried out as a part of a combined land-sea operations. But if such an amphibious operation has to be effective, it will need to be linked up to land-based military operations as early as possible unless the expected opposition is small enough to be neutralized by the navy and the marines on their own.

Force projection can be divided into two main sub-heads : force projection on the high seas to search and destroy the enemy's naval capability, and on the land for purposes of destroying the military capability of the adversary or for the purpose of acquiring and consolidating the beach-head there. While the weapons mix of the first may be the same as that of the sea control on the high seas, the weapons mix for the other will include additional inputs tailored specifically for amphibious operations like the landing ship/craft, vertical lift capability, marines etc. Logistics and force level requirements will be determined by the distances involved and the degree of resistance expected at the point of confrontation. Few developing countries possess the capability for force projection in that sense.

Arms Transfer and Naval Strategy

Very few among the developing countries have the capability to manufacture highly sophisticated weapon systems that constitute that constitute the backbone of a modern navy. Hence, they acquire them from the states of the North. Arms transfer is conditioned by politico-military factors. Sophisticated equipment are not easily acquired from an open market. These weapons are often acquired as a grant or under concessional terms within the pattern of an over-all strategic relationship between the donor and the recipient state. Even when a state wishes to buy these weapons, the transfer reflects the pattern of strategic relationship between the two. Hence, if weapons determine the strategy, arms transfer and weapons acquisition programme would indicate the strategic options not only of the recipient but also of the donor state.

In this context, arms transfer and weapons acquisition policies have to be seen from three different angles. In the first case, the state seeks to acquire weapons that it feels are essential within the framework of the strategy that it wishes to adopt. It is another matter whether it can successfully overcome the political, economic and technological constraints involved in arms transfer. But, the initiative rests primarily with the recipient state which exercises a degree of autonomy in determining its naval strategy. For example, Pakistan's determined efforts since the mid-sixties to acquire modern submarines from France falls under that category. It signified Pakistan's thrust on acquiring a credible sea-denial capability.

In the second case, the donor transfers weapons not as per the strategic requirements of the recipient state but within the broad framework of the strategic requirements of the donor state in that given region. In other words, arms transfer itself becomes an extension of the strategy of the donor state in that particular area. In this case, the initiative rests primarily with the donor state. Hence, an analysis of arms transfer over a given period, within this framework, might also reveal the patterns of political and strategic interests of the great powers in a given region.

The Anglo-American arms transfer to South Asia till the early sixties were conditioned by their strategic considerations in the Indian Ocean within the over-all framework of the

Commonwealth naval strategy. In this broad strategy, the three maritime states of South Asia—India, Ceylon (Sri Lanka) and Pakistan—were entrusted with the role of limited sea control and escort duty on the major sea lanes of the region. As per the requirements of that strategy, heavy surface vessels like frigates, destroyers and cruisers as well as minesweepers were transferred to these three states. Under that strategy, India was to be transferred two light aircraft carriers to provide sea-borne air cover during long-range escort operations. Only one was transferred by the time the British withdrew from the Indian Ocean. The Americans replaced them. The British never transferred submarines to South Asia. Even the Americans gave only one World War Second vintage submarine to Pakistan in 1964. The year 1965 was a watershed in the history of naval arms transfer in South Asia. While India began to look towards the Soviet Union, Pakistan opted for China and France for its weapons supply.

The third case is where the donor-recipient relationship might not necessarily be governed solely by politico-military considerations, yet arms transfer affects the strategy of the recipient state in an indirect manner. Till the late sixties, each of the great powers had definite strategic thrusts, like sea denial, sea control and force projection as far as their individual conventional naval strategies were concerned. Their weapons were, therefore, designed primarily keeping in view their own roles in mind. Since the Anglo-American naval strategy was geared towards sea control and force projection they had a weapons mix primarily tailored for those roles. Thus, when they transferred weapons like frigates, destroyers, cruisers and aircraft carriers, they were in fact offering to the recipient state a mix of weapons suitable for sea control strategy.

The Soviet Union and China, on the other hand, had sea denial as the primary objective of their naval strategy, at least till the late sixties. Hence, their weapons were tailored to meet that requirement. Therefore, when these powers transferred their weapons to others they indirectly influenced the strategy of the recipient state also because of the characteristics of the weapons that they transferred. Till the seventies, the Soviet Union transferred weapons like submarines, frigates and missile boats, basically a sea denial mix. It influenced the naval strategy of the recipient states unless they already possessed or were able to acquire weapons suitable for other roles.

India was lucky in the sense that it could combine the weapons from England and from the Soviet Union to evolve a combination of a balanced naval force with sea denial, sea control and force projection capability. Pakistan could not do so because the Chinese could transfer only a small surface fleet and Pakistan did not have the financial resources to purchase heavier surface vessels. Hence, it opted for acquiring a few modern submarines from France. This combination gave Pakistan a limited sea denial capability in the seventies till circumstances were once again favourable and Pakistan began receiving havier surface vessels like frigates and destroyers from USA in the context of the new Cold War and also the US strategy of Rapid Deployment Force (RDF) towards the Gulf. Hence, directly and indirectly, arms transfer influences, in many ways, the naval strategy of the recipient state unless it has options for diversifying its sources and enough economic and technological resources to keep its options open.

Thus, it can be said that the evolution of maritime strategy in its comprehensive framework is conditioned by multiple factors like the geographic location, historical experience, development of civilian facets of maritime affairs, development of the navy in the context not only of the triad of the armed forces, and as a component of the larger maritime security of the state but also in the context of the policy of arms transfer. Awareness of affairs maritime had influenced the thinking, both civilian and military, in the North for centuries. In certain cases, it had dominated even the main strategic thinking like in Britain in the nineteenth century and in USA in the post-Second World War era.

The concept of maritime strategy has still to be understood in its wider perspective in the South, even though maritime affairs are going to be increasingly important in the light of global integration at the level of trade and commerce if nothing else. Till the end of the eighteenth century, the states of the South could remain insular of the forces that were operating across the oceans. The Mughal Empire, the Persian Empire and the Chinese Empire could be land powers and could even hope to survive politically, economically and militarily. Not any more. The growing importance of overseas trade, investment, even of exploitation of maritime resources has compelled the states of the South, most of whom are littoral states, to give a greater thought to their overall maritime strategy. Granted that some of them are too small to evolve an effective autonomous maritime capability but regional cooperation can overcome some of those constraints. Unless these states reorient their strategic thinking, they will continue to be dominated, as they have been since the sixteenth century, by the countries of the industrialized North which are also the maritime powers.

REFERENCES

1. Rai, Ranjit, *A Nation and Its Navy at War.* 1987. Lancers International; New Delhi, p. 44.
2. Chatterji, A.K., in *The Hindu* 11 December 1966, quoted by Raju G. C. Thomas, Politics of Naval Rearmament, 1962-1974, *Pacific Community* (Tokyo). April 1975, 6(3) 462-63.
3. Rasgotra, M.K., India's Security and the Sea, *Strategic Analysis,* December 1991, 14(9) 1035.
4. Panikkar, K.M. *Geographical Factors in Indian History,* 1969 (3rd ed.) Bharatiya Vidhya Bhawan; Bombay, p. x.
5. Nilankanta Sastri, K.A. *South India and South-East Asia, Studies in Their History and Culture,* Geetha Book House; Mysore. 1978, p. 90.
6. Mahan, Alfred, *The Influence of Sea Power Upon History,* 1892. Sampson Low; London. p. 225.
7. Padfield, Peter, *Tide of Empire : Decisive Naval Compaigns in the Rise of the West,* 1481-1645. 1979. Routledge & Kegan Paul; London; pp. 184-85.
8. Modelski, D. G. and Thompson, W.R., *Sea Power and Global Politics,* 1494-1793. 1988 London, Macmillan, pp. 16-17, quoted by Uday Bhaskar, Role of the Indian Navy, *Strategic Analysis,* 14(7) October 1991, 796.

9. Richardson, Elliot L., Power Mobility and the Law of the Sea. *Foreign Affairs.* Spring 1980. Reproduced in *Strategic Digest.* July 1980, 10(7) 456.

10. Suri, R.B., *Shape and Size of the Indian Navy in the Early Twenty-first Century.* New Delhi. May 1998.

11. *Proceedings of the US Naval Institute,* October 1974, 9(859), p. 59. (Translation of the article by S.G. Gorshkov in *Morski Sbornik,* November 2, 1972.

12. Booth, Ken, Warship and Political Influence, in McGwire, Michael and McDonnell, John, Eds. *Soviet Naval Influence, Domestic and Foreign Dimensions.* 1972. Praeger, New York. pp. 465-68.

13. Cable, James, *Navies in Violent Peace.* 1989. Macmillan. p. 111, quoted in Uday Bhaskar, Role of the Indian Navy, *Strategic Analysis.* October 1991, 14(7) 800.

14. Panikkar, K.M., *India and the Indian Ocean : An Essay on the Influence of Sea Power on Indian History.* 1945. London. p. 7.

15. Bull, Hedley, Sea Power and Political Influence. *In Power At Sea, I,* The New Environment. Adelphi Paper No. 122. Spring 1976. IISS; London. p. 6.

16. Kohli, S.N., *Indian Defence Review.* January 1989, p. 46.

17. Suri, R.B., *Shape and Size of Indian Navy.* 1998. New Delhi, pp. 20-21.

18. Tellis, Ashley J., The Naval Power in the Indian Sub-Continent, *Asian Survey.* December 1985, 25(12) 1200.

19. *Ibid.,* p. 1197.

20. Kohli, S.N., *Sea Power and the Indian Ocean, with Special Reference to India.* 1978. New Delhi. pp. 26-27.

21 Kohli, S.N., Maritime Strategy and Force Level, *Chanakya Defence Annual.* 1976, pp. 133-34.

3
Establishment of East India Company

In 1600 Queen Elizabeth I issued a Charter to the company of Merchants of London for trading to the East Indies. This Company was granted the monopoly of all trade between England and all lands from the Cape of Good Hope as far east as Cape Horn, except for any place in the possession of a Christian prince, whose own subjects might trade with England as he wished. The monopoly was not, however, intended to be in restraint of trade, but to promote and regulate it, and to provide for its protection by arms if necessary.

The purpose of arrangements which placed trade in the hands of a particular group was to ensure the exclusion of individuals who, in search of a quick profit, might alienate local authorities on whose goodwill a regular prosperous trading system depended. A company which held the monopoly could be relied upon to govern the activities of its members and servants with a view to the long-term interests of itself and the nation of which it became, in its chartered area, the representative.

It was hoped that a body of merchants, who generally speaking find peace more profitable then war, would be particularly anxious to avoid occasions of dispute. On the other hand, as the East Indies were a vast area, a year away from orders or help from home, the East India Company was empowered to arm its ships and servants for their own protection, and to make laws, not repugnant to the laws of England, for their regulation.[1]

The constitutional right to establish trading stations or

'factories', where their local factors would do any necessary business between the arrival of one annual voyage and the next, and to fortify or garrison them, was also dependent upon individual characters, granted by the rulers in whose domains these lay. The first such station on the Indian subcontinent of South Asia was established on the west coast, at Surat, by authority of a grant from the Mughal Governor of Gujarat. On the east coast a factory was set up at Masulipatam around 1620, and the Company's first fortifications were built at Armagaon in 1625. The first grant of land, with the right to construct defence works and collect revenue was made in August 1639, when the Company's factor on the Coromandel coast obtained a grant from the local representative of the Raja of Chandragiri. This monarch, the vestigial successor of the Hindu empire of Vijaynagar, destroyed by the Muslim Sultanates of southern India after the battle of Talikota in 1565, thus played his part in the foundation of a new empire that would become paramount in India. The fort, named in honour of England's patron saint, and builtùdespite the objections of the East India Company's home authorities to the financial implications—was Fort St. George, the official title of what subsequently became the Presidency of Madras.[2]

In 1661 the Portuguese settlement at Bombay was ceded to the English Crown as part of the dowry of Charles II's queen, Catherine of Braganza. A battalion of 400 troops, the first element of the British army to serve in India was sent to take possession, but, as a result of opposition by the local Portuguese officials, and a refusal by the Mughal authorities to allow it to disembark at Surat, it did not succeed in doing so until 1665, having lost 75 percent of its numbers to tropical or other illnesses. Reinforcements were subsequently sent, and the whole garrison, together with the rest of the Bombay establishment, was handed over the Charles II to the East India Company in 1669.[3]

The charter granted to the Company by Charles II on his restoration in 1661 took account of the existence of permanent British possessions in India. It empowered the Company to maintain warships as well as the armed East Indiamen which it chartered, and to recruit men as regular soldiers, with whom it could lawfully make war against any non-Christian prince. When the charter was renewed in 1683, the Company's right to maintain local fleets and armies, subject to ultimate Royal authority over their employment, was further confirmed.[4] It was with forces raised under the provisions of this charter that the Company began its first war against an Indian power, a campaign in 1688-90 against the government of the Mughal Emperor Aurangzeb.[5]

The charter of 1661 establishment the London East India Company as a permanent joint stock corporation. Major stockholders could summon and vote in a general court, which determined company policy and appointed an executive body made up of twenty-four committee men, headed by an elected Governor and Deputy Governor. The same charter empowered the Company to appoint governors and councils to rule over its major settlements and execute the directions they received from their masters in London. Their right to exercise martial law was specified in the charter of 1669 handing over Bombay to the Company, and extended in that of 1683, which authorised the Company's governors and factors to 'execute and use within the said Plantations, Forts and Places, the Law called the Martial Law, for the defence of the said Forts, Places, and Plantations, against any foreign Invasion, or domestic Insurrection or Rebellion.'[6] By granting this right to the Company, the Crown recognised that the Company's holdings in India had become rich enough and large enough to attract military threat and merit military defence.

The East India Company's first regular troops were those taken over, with Bombay itself, from the Crown in 1669. Most of the original contingent of royal troops which had landed four years previously had succumbed to the effects of the climate, drink and disease, but replacement drafts from England, and locally recruited mercenaries of European descent (mostly Portuguese with a few Frenchmen) gave the East India Company a Bombay Regiment of two companies and a total strength of 5 officers, 139 European other ranks, and 54 Indian Christians or 'topasses' so-named from the Persian word 'top' or gun. An additional company under command of Captain Shaxton arrived in 1671, and Shaxton was appointed by Governor Aungier as member of the Bombay Council and Deputy Governor.[7] It was to this company that three years later fell the unenviable distinction of committing the first of the numerous acts of mutiny that disfigure the record of British arms in India. As with so many mutinies, the grievance was a financial one, the troops objecting to the losses they suffered when their notional pay was exchanged into local currency, and to what they did receive being further diminished by stoppages to pay for their uniforms. One mutineer was hanged, Shaxton was sent back to England, and Aungier was ordered that in future his Council should be drawn only from the Company's factors, not its military servants. The Council of the Company's settlement at Surat, to which Bombay was subordinate, recorded its view that soldiers were a 'querulous ungrateful people, and never satisfied'.[8]

After the Glorious Revolution of 1688, the East India Company, which had been patronised by James II, received little sympathy from William III or the Whig majority in Parliament, and the latter resolved in 1691 that a new East India Company should be founded. Lavish bribes by its own directors secured a fresh charter for the original or London Company in 1693, but the new Company of Merchants of England trading to the East Indies was itself granted a charter in 1698.[9] These disputes in England led to difficulties in India, where the Mughal authorities found it difficult to distinguish between two sets of English merchants, each traducing the other as thieves and pirates. In November 1701 Aurangzeb placed an embargo on trade with both of them, and on all other European companies, pending the payment of compensation for losses inflicted by pirates, and the provision of anti-piracy patrols.[10] By a compromise effected in 1702 by Lord Godolphin the two rival East India Companies were combined into a single body, known from 1709 until 1833 as The United Company of Merchants of England trading to the East Indies. This company inherited the powers of both its predecessors in England and India. Its government was vested in a Court of twenty-four Directors, including a Chairman and Deputy Chairman, generally referred to as 'The Chairs' to be elected by the general court composed of major holders or 'proprietors' of the Company's stock. The Directors were also empowered, according to the English company's charter of 1698, to appoint and remove governors and officers, and to 'raise', train, and muster such military forces as shall or may be necessary' for the defence of their forts and factories.[11] In India, the Company legitimised its position by obtaining a charter or *farman* in 1716 from the Mughal Emperor Farrukhsiyar, a great-grandson of Aurangzeb, and the third emperor to come to the throne since the latter's death nine years earlier.[12]

At the time of the War of the Austrian Succession in Europe, the 'country powers' (the various South Asian states) certainly seemed strong enough. The Mughal empire was the mere shadow of a great name, but its successor states had large and well-practised armies at their disposal. In the south, the *suba* of the Deccan was ruled by Asaf Jah, once the Wazir (or finance minister) of the whole empire, but who had since his resignation from this post in 1724 established himself as a virtually independent ruler. Although still technically *Subadar*, or Governor, he adopted the honorific title Nizam-ul-Mulk, or Sovereign of the land, and , from the name of his capital city, became known to the British as the Nizam of Hyderabad. Though defeated by the Marathas in 1738, he and his generals had twenty years of active campaigning to their credit. Much the same could be said of Anwar-al-Din, appointed by the Nizam in 1744 to be Nawab of Arcot, from which city the territory of the Carnatic was governed.[13] This included the Coromandel coast, in which were situated the English factories of Fort St. George, at Madras, and Fort St. David, at Cuddalore, a few miles from the factory established in 1683 by the French East India Company, at Pondicherry.[14]

Anwar-al-Din, in response to a request from the French, warned both European companies not to make war within his dominions. Governor Morse of Madras replied that he had neither the means nor desire to make war, but pointed out that he had no power over the Royal Navy, which had begun to make valuable prizes of French East Indiamen off the Coromandel coast. When in 1746 the British naval squadron moved to the Bay of Bengal, a group of French ships appeared off Madras, with a regiment of regular infantry from the French army, supported by locally raised Indian troops led by Joseph Dupleix, Governor of Pondicherry. The garrison of Fort St. George put up only a token resistance, and Governor Morse and his council surrendered in anticipation of being able to pay a ransom, a proceeding then as common in European as in Indian conduct of war. It then became clear, however, that Dupleix had no intention of conforming to this agreeable convention, but planned to hold the place indefinitely.[15]

This episode had profound military and political consequences. Fort St. David was left as the only British trading station on the coast. The Company's authorities there hastened to strengthen its fortifications and raise 2,000 peons, while the Bombay government hurried a force of European and Indian soldiers round from the west coast and recruited additional local levies for their own defence. When the news of the fall of Madras reached London, the Directors appointed the first soldier to be Commander-in-Chief of all their forces in India. This was Major Stringer Lawrence, the father of the Indian army, an experienced infantry officer who had been a captain in the British army before accepting this appointment from the East India Company.[16] In addition to his position as C-in-C, he was appointed a member of the Madras Council, third in seniority, but was not to rise above that position. The British government, alarmed at the sudden prospect of losing the trade of southern India to the French, sent twelve independent companies of infantry and reached Fort St. David in July 1748. The question of a Company's officer having command over these royal troops was avoided by the appointment of Admiral Boscawen as C-in-C of all British naval and military forces in the East Indies.[17]

Anwar al-Din's reaction to the French seizure of Madras was that, as the town lay within his dominions, it should revert to him. When Dupleix refused to hand it over, a conventionally organised Mughal army, commanded by Anwar al-Din's son, Mahfuz Khan, laid siege to it. A sally by French infantry and field guns demonstrated that Mughal cavalry could be defeated by the rapid artillery and musketry fire of a well-drilled western army. Further encounters between French and Mahfuz Khan's troops had a similar result. Although the style of fighting practised by European armies in the mid-eighteenth century was not unknown to Indian generals, it had not previously carried all before it. English attacks, often in conjunction with the forces of Indian states, against pirate strongholds on the west coast had had limited success. As recently as 1739 the Portuguese had been defeated by the Marathas, losing Bassein, their last remaining major fortress in India.[18] Anwar al-Din himself, surprising the French when they first reached Fort St. David, proved that European troops were not invincible. The ease with which the French defeated Mahfuz Khan owed at least as much to the indiscipline of the Mughal troopers as to the discipline of the French infantry, and to the faulty tactics of the former as to the superior technology of the latter. The French victories nevertheless had a psychological effect on the great princes of southern India, out of all proportion to the number of men involved, and created the impression that European troops, or Indian troops drilled, armed and disciplined in the European style (raised first by the French and then the English) could have a decisive effect.

The War of the Austrian Succession ended in 1748. In India Dupleix had failed to take Fort St. David, and the English, despite Stringer Lawrence's men, the twelve British companies and Admiral Boscawen's battle fleet, had failed to take Pondicherry. Madras was restored to the East India Company at the peace treaty of Aix-la Chapelle, but despite this treaty, English and French soldiers continued to find themselves on opposing sides in Indian campaigns. The rival Companies made alliances with Indian rulers or with those who wished to become Indian rulers, since there were by this time disputed claims to the thrones of Hyderabad (following Asa Jah's death in 1748) and Arcot (following Anwar al-Din's death in battle in 1749). The rival European Companies had at their disposal what was, in Indian warfare, a new weapons system, well-drilled flintlock musketmen and field artillery. Their local representatives were happy to put them to work as mercenaries in the service of any Indian prince who could pay for them with cash, and in the long term, promises of trade concessions.[19] Although the ability of European infantry to defeat much larger bodies of Indian cavalry (once the initial surprise factor of their novel tactics had worn off) could not be taken for granted, their presence on one side or the other might be enough to tip the balance. Thus if one army had a European contingent, its opponent needed to have one as a counter to it. The Directors of the English East India Company, as their military changed from being a local defence force into a field army, had to give up their old policy, of having no 'gentlemen' in their employment, and replaced the superannuated subalterns and volunteer civil servants on whom they had previously relied, with experienced officers, available from British regiments reduced at the end of the War of the Austrian Succession.[20]

This different class of officer turned up to be spirited not only in the field, but in their attitude to their civil superiors, especially over financial questions. The rates of pay of the Company's troops were fixed on the assumption that they would serve only in the Company's fixed defences on the coast. Once they were required to go into the field, they incurred additional expenses, including the cost of transport, hire of tentage, and the purchase of all kinds of personal supplies which they would not have otherwise needed, and therefore they were compensated by the issue of *batta* or foreign service allowance. Officers in garrison at Fort St. George and Fort St. David were given free rations until Lawrence arranged for this to be replaced by a messing allowance which was continued to be paid in addition to the service *batta*. In 1749, Anwar al-Din's illegitimate son Muhammad Ali, whose claim to the throne of Arcot was supported by English troops, paid an additional allowance to the officers in recognition of the expense, and attendant risks, of carriage of articles of European origin from the coast to the theatre of operations inland. He subsequently discontinued this payment, as he had granted *jagirs* to the

Madras government, which provided the funds to pay the military contingents provided for him by the English. The Madras government, however, chose to regard this allowance as an act of personal generosity by the Nawab; which, it told the aggrieved officers, they could expect to see renewed when he was again in full possession of his dominions. The officers' further remonstrances were greeted with accusations of mutiny. Officers were recalled to the coast in ones and twos on the pretext of relief, to prevent the whole corps refusing to do duty, and three were arrested as ringleaders.[21]

Every officer was needed at this period as British military power in India was built up. Companies of German and Swiss mercenaries were sent out by the Directors, though the latter caused difficulties by insisting on maintaining their own separate codes of discipline, and were moreover inclined to desert to the French, or any country power which might offer better wages.[22] The passage of the Mutiny Act in 1754 replaced the old Articles of War as the basis of military discipline in British India, though strongly opposed in Parliament because it had the effect of allowing regiments of the British army to be sent to India. The French government, however, had sent its own troops to India in support of the interests of the Compagnie des Indes. These troops were therefore, within months of the passage of this act, matched by the arrival at Madras of the 39th Foot. Their commanding officer, Colonel Adlercron, outranked Stringer Lawrence (though the latter was simultaneously granted a royal commission as Lieutenant-Colonel), and so assumed command over all land forces in Madras. Supreme command was taken by Admiral Charles Watson, whose squadron had escorted the East Indiamen which brought the troops. The Mutiny Act also provided that officers of the British army were to have seniority over officers of the Company's service in the same rank, much as was the relative position of regular officers to militia, or colonial forces. This arrangement, though in itself reasonable enough, was later to become a source of grievance in India, just as it was already becoming in the American colonies, since it took no account of seniority within each rank.[23]

The major innovation of the period was the gradual replacement of the peons by a new kind of Indian soldier, the sepoy. The name, derived from the Persian sipahi, a regular soldier as distinct from a quasi-feudal retainer, was applied to Indians who were armed, trained, and, to a large extent dressed, in the European style. Equally importantly, at least when it came to raising recruits, they were promised pay in the European style, in cash at the end of each month. No great skill was required to load and fire a flintlock musket, while the battlefield drill of eighteenth-century armies could, under efficient officers and sergeants, be learnt in a matter of weeks, as its greatest exponent, Frederick the Great, freely asserted. Not only were sepoys easier to recruit than Europeans, but they were also cheaper to maintain, and less likely to succumb to the tropical diseases and intemperance which carried off the European soldiers with such regularity. Sepoys were formed into companies on the European model each commanded by its own subedar. As the success of this innovation, first introduced by the French, and then adopted by the British, became apparent, it was taken up by the country powers, and by 1760 a sepoy contingent formed part of the standard order of battle of all major Indian armies.

The great majority of these sepoys came from the plains of Hindustan, particularly from the eastern (*purabi*) region between Bihar and Agra. This gave them the name 'easterners' (*purabiya*) or, as the British called them 'poorbeahs'. They were also known as Baksaris or 'buxerries' from the name of the city, Baksar (Buxar) which was their most prominent recruiting centre. Centuries of warfare in northern India had encouraged the development of a society in which everyone of the slightest consequence carried weapons. Swards and spears were readily available, and even muskets were to be found in private hands. During the Mughal period, the most influential Rajput groups, desirous of maintaining their own status, had introduced new forms of genealogical orthodoxy, and created a more narrow Rajput identity, virtually confined to their states in Western India, or Rajasthan. The Rajputs of the east, mostly living in peasant agricultural groups, were excluded from this group and thus were denied the opportunity of serving as troopers in the contingents supplied to the imperial armies by the great Rajput princes. They were still, however, inspired by the Rajput ideal of *naukari* or service. Their culture was still one in which young men sought honourable and profitable employment as soldiers for a few years before returning to their villages to set up as respected and prosperous peasant proprietors.[24] A new outlet for this spirit opened with the arrival in the military environment of the matchlock musket, which was most effective in the hands of practised infantrymen. From the middle of the seventeenth century, therefore, the great majority of the matchlockmen serving with the Mughal forces in the Deccan campaigns were Purabiyas recruited at Baksar. They were organized into permanent companies, and provided an element of stability in the predominantly cavalry armies of the time. In the best-managed Mughal armies, regular shooting tests had been conducted, with the musketeers classified, according to the results, into one of three grades, and their pay adjusted accordingly. Just like the gentlemen troopers, the matchlockmen were described in detail on the muster rolls, to prevent impersonation. One Ganga Ram, for example, was listed on 24 September 1646 as 30 years of age, the son of Khanna, a Rajput, with blue eyes, several scars and three moles on his face, a resident of Baksar, and due to be paid five rupees *per mensem*.[25]

No Indian army maintained any central recruiting system. Instead reliance was placed upon intermediary agents. In the sixteenth century this function had been performed mostly by zamindars, who not only collected the revenue, but raised warbands from among those who lived in their district. By the late Mughal period, zamindars, although they continued to employ armed retainers, no longer acted as either recruiters, or leaders of fighting men, and had been replaced in these roles by jemadars (*jama'dar*, the holder of a group or collection), the military embodiment of the labour contractor or jobber, a figure long established in Indian custom. 'Jemadar' was for long a rather nebulous term in respect of the size of the 'gang' or company which such officers produced and led, and corresponded to the early use of the English word 'captain' to mean a military commander rather than the holder of a particular rank. Some commanded as few as fifty, others a thousand or more. Jemadars selected recruits on the basis of their past and future good character, and their general acceptability. As the main purpose of military service was to enhance the prestige and the income of the individual and his family, such patronage was a valuable asset, the future possession of which was not to be risked by introducing anyone likely to be a bad soldier. The system therefore was geared to producing the kind of recruit who would be acceptable in terms of physique, spirit, and social background to the other members of the war-band, and who would in short 'fit in', an ability which has an undeniable military value in maintaining the cohesion of small groups during the stresses of active service.

When the British first began to raise Indian troops for the defence of their trading stations, it was to the jemadari system that they turned, as the normal local way of finding soldiers. The first such men were a company of Rajputs, commanded by their own officers and armed with their own weapons, raised at Madras in 1664. Similar Rajput companies were raised in Bengal in 1682 and at Bombay in 1684. [26] The precise areas from which these men were recruited is not easy to determine, but all three presidencies were employing Purabiyas by the middle of the following century. The duties, drills, and conditions of service of musketeers in the new European-style sepoy battalions were not so different from those in the companies of Mughal matchlockmen as to inhibit Purabiya recruitment, and the East India Company found no difficulty in raising its Indian infantry. Although two-thirds of the sepoys who fought in Clive's army at Plassey in 1757 had been raised in Madras, and only one-third in Bengal, the Madras troops were of Purabiya descent, if not of actual birth. Their commander Kesher Singh, was a well-known Baksari jemadar, and their agent at Madras, Parbat Singh, himself had a Purabiya name.[27] Indian officers when recruiting naturally gave preference to members of their own families and would have been thought by members of their own society, to have behaved disgracefully had they acted otherwise. Thus it was that Purabiya soldiers continued to be employed in the expanding British Indian armies, especially that of Bengal which was stationed nearest to their home area. Although Rajputs or even Brahmans formed the majority of recruits so raised, Muslim peasant-warrior communities also contributed their share.

In 1756, after fifty years, war came to Bengal. A new young Nawab, styled Siraj al daulat ('Sir Roger Dowler' to the British) was alarmed at the dominance which the European Companies had achieved by their military intervention in the affairs of the Deccan and the Carnatic. He was, moreover, aggrieved by the loss to his revenues resulting from the English claims to exemption from transit tolls. Although his predecessors had authorised the construction of fortifications at Calcutta against Afghan raiders in 1697 and against Marathas in 1742, a British proposal in 1756 to improve these defences (in case the French might take Calcutta as they had Madras) was answered by the Nawab marching upon first the East India Company's factory at Kasimbazar which fell without a struggle, and then Calcutta itself which put up only a brief resistance. The senior officials escaped in the Company's ships. Their juniors were taken prisoner and put in the fort's detention cell or 'black hole' where most died of heatstroke. This incident was caused mostly by negligence on the part of the captors but subsequently passed into British folk lore as an example of deliberate cruelty.[28]

The reinforcements that Pitt had sent from England to counter the French arrived to find that they were needed against the Nawab of Bengal. Joined by five companies of Europeans and 1,200 sepoys from Madras, they picked up the surviving two companies of Bengal European Infantry, and seventy volunteers from those of the company's civil servants who had escaped from Calcutta and its outstations. Calcutta was recaptured by a *coup de main* six months after if had fallen. The constitutional position was a complicated one and a dispute arose between on the one hand Admiral Watson who appointed Captain Eyre Coote, of the British army, to be commandant of Fort William, and on the other hand Lieutenant–Colonel Clive, who as well as holding a senior rank to Coote in the British army, was the senior military officer present of the company's service. Against this could be argued that he was under the orders of the President and Council of Madras, not those of Bengal, and that the two Presidencies were quite independent of each other. Watson threatened to bombard the fort, with Clive in it, if Coote's authority was not recognised. Clive defied him and only yielded when Watson landed in person, and acting as supreme commander, handed over control to President Drake of the Bengal Council.[29]

News of the outbreak of the Seven Years War spread the conflict in Bengal. The Nawab at first offered his protection to the French factories in his territories, but then withdrew it, with a view to settling his differences with the British and obtaining their aid against Ahmad Shah, the victor of Panipat, the master of Delhi, and the possible next invader of Bengal. At the end of March 1757 Chandarnagar, the base of French trade in Bengal was captured by the British. Clive then marched against Siraj al-Daulat, reaching Plassey (Palasi) on 23 June. Against 1,000 European and 2,000 sepoys, Siraj al-Daulat had an army of 50,000, but as many of these were led by Mir Jafar, a nobleman whose own aspirations to become Nawab Clive had secretly agreed to support, only about 12,000 came into action. Once again European-style discipline, musketry, and field guns were able to defeat a largely cavalry army in what came to be recognised as being—although a mere cannonade by comparison with other engagements fought upon Indian soil—one of the decisive battles of South Asian history. A grateful Mir Jafar, on becoming Nawab of Bengal, not only paid over vast sums, which his treasury could ill afford, to Clive and the members of the Bengal Council, but granted to the East India Company the right to collect the revenue of twenty-four parganas or districts around Calcutta, the first major British territorial holdings in Bengal.[30]

With Bengal secure, the British were able to restore their position in Madras. The French were defeated by Eyre Coote at the Battle of Wandewash on 22 January 1760, and his subsequent capture of Pondicherry, after a siege lasting from 16 November 1760 to 16 January 1761, brought the French Indian empire to an end. The last involvement of Indian troops in the Seven Years War was the successful expedition sent from Madras in 1762 to capture Manila in the Spanish Philippine Islands, the earliest demonstration that troops from British India might have a part to play in imperial as well as local power politics.[31]

In Bengal, Nawab Mir Jafar found himself unable to cope with the problems of government. His western districts were raided by Marathas claiming to collect a share of the revenue on behalf of the Mughal Emperor, and by the army of the new Mughal Emperor, Shah Alam II, collecting on his own behalf. His eastern districts failed to produce the revenue on which his British friends counted for the payment of their troops, and indeed for all their other expenses in India. British authorities at Calcutta persuaded him, in August 1760, to retire in favour of his son-in-law, Mir Kasim, who assigned the revenues of further districts to the British in return for troops for the defence of what remained of his state. When he tried to restore his depleted treasury by challenging the Company's claim to exemption form inland trading tools the British sent these troops to arrest him in July 1763. This attempted coup failed and several hundred men, Europeans as well as sepoys, were taken prisoner. The British then declared war on Mir Kasim though their initial movements against him were hampered by a mutiny first of their European troops, and then of their sepoys, over arrears of pay and prospects of prize money. Order was restored by a mixture of cajolery and threats, but the commander of Bengal forces, Major Carnac, was replaced by Major Hector Munro, a stern disciplinarian. Another incident, considered by him to be mutiny, and desertion with intent to join the enemy, was according to the conventions of the Baksaris, nothing more than the attempted renegotiation of their contract in favour of another employer. An entire battalion decamped, but was pursued and captured. Twenty-four men were put to death by the conventional Mughal punishment for mutineers being blown away from the muzzles of guns.[32] Mir Kasim fell back with his army into Awadh, the heart of Hindustan. There the Nawab of Awadh, and Wazir of the empire, Suja al Daulat, then in company with the Emperor Shah

Alam II, had mustered a combined force, to exact tribute due from the neigbouring region of Bundelkhand. Mir Kasim joined them in this expedition, and they in turn marched to restore him to his place in Bengal, still constitutionally a province of the Mughal empire.

They were met by Munro, at Baksar, on the Awadh-Bengal border, on 23 October 1764. Against the allies' 50,000 men including a sepoy brigade in Mir Kasim's service (led by a German mercenary, known locally as 'Samru', who had murdered Mir Kasim's 200 European prisoners of war at Patna), the British mustered 900 Europeans and 7,000 sepoys and 20 field guns. In their hardest fought battle in India thus far, the British lost over 800 men, before the allied army gave way, leaving 2,000 dead on the field. Mir Kasim fled, to die in poverty. Samru and his sepoys found employment with the Nawab of Awadh who made peace with the British. In return for an undertaking that he would receive his long unpaid share of it, Shah Alam granted to the East India Company the land revenue of Bengal, Bihar and Orissa. In practice this placed the government of that province under British control and the last Nawab of Bengal, Mir Jafar's son Najm-al-Daulat, retired on a handsome allowance.

In 1764, recognising that they now had a standing army that had increased in size ten-fold in ten years, the Directors changed their method of appointing officers. Those in the British regiments then being recalled from India were still permitted to transfer to the Company's service when their units returned to Europe. They thus, except in the artillery where this system did not apply, realised a substantial sum by the sale of their commissions, though accepting permanent service in India. All other appointments to commissions were to be made from candidates sent out to India as cadets.[33] Cadets did duty as private soldiers in European units, occasionally in combat, forming elite sections for special tasks. Promotion for all was by seniority in each army, unlike the British line, where the senior in each rank could in normal circumstances succeed to a vacancy only in his own regiment, and only by payment of a substantial sum for his new commission so that those who could afford it might purchase promotion, over the heads of those who could not. The seniority principle, intended to avoid the probability of corruption, was also applied to all ranks in the sepoy companies, with the seniority being that within each company. Any exceptions to this rule if the next in line for promotion were considered unfit to hold higher rank, required the approval of the local government. The first subedars and jemadars, men of independent means who had produced their own companies in the traditional Indian way were, in the course of time, succeeded by those who had come up through the ranks. The Military disadvantage of this was compensated for by the political benefit of phasing out a body on independent contractors who, in the unsettled conditions of eighteenth-century India, might use their troops, paid and armed by the British, for their own purposes. A notable case was that of Subedar Yusuf Muhammad Khan, who for his distinguished services in the Carnatic was appointed commandant of all the Company's sepoys in the Madras army, and granted an extensive *Jagir* by the Nawab Muhammad Ali ('Subedar' by now meant 'Indian captain'). He subsequently attempted to use his own troops to establish an independent state in alliance with Haydar Ali (who had come to power in neighbouring Mysore by just such a means) but was eventually hanged by the Nawab as a rebel.[34]

In the space of a single decade the position of the military in British India had changed, more radically than it had in the first century and a half of the East India Company's entire existence. A few companies of ill-led Europeans, retained for the local defence of a few coastal trading stations and supplemented in emergency by war-bands obtained from Indian military contractors, had been replaced by a standing army of European and Indian regulars. Instead of being financed out of the profits of the company's trade, they were funded by the revenues of the territories which they had conquered. The infantry sepoy had emerged as the most effective type of South Asian soldier. Nevertheless the institutions and authorities under which the military operated remained essence the same. The Company's very existence as a body depended upon the grant (and periodic renewal), of its charter from the British Crown, voted by a majority in Parliament. The Company's Governors and councils in India were subject to the court of Directors, and the Company's military was subordinate to the local Governors. A new element had emerged in the arrival of British army troops, but the Mutiny Act of 1754 had ensured that all came under the same operational command locally. In South Asia the position of the Company continued to derive from Mughal imperial grants. Like the other South Asian powers, the Company had the authority to collect revenues and apply them to the maintenance of troops on which in theory the Mughal government could call when required. In practice, the British, like any other South Asian powers who could do so with impunity (by 1764, all of them) provided the troops for whose maintenance the revenues had been alienated only when it suited them, and ultimately used them to overthrow the power of their nominal overlords or that of rival powers. For the time being, however, the British government was content to exert its power over British India through the East India Company, and the Company was happy to leave the task of ruling the provinces whose revenues were in its hands, to the princes who were themselves nominally agents of the Mughal Emperor, but whose possession of their thrones was actually dependent upon British military support.

REFERENCES

1. W.A.J. Archbold, *Outlines of Indian Constitutional History,* London, 1926, pp. 10-12.
2. H.H. Dodwell, *The Cambridge History of India, Vol. V. British India 1497-1858,* Cambridge, 1929, pp. 88-9.
3. J. Keay, *Honorable Company,* London, 1991, pp. 132-4.
4. Archbold, *op. cit.,* p. 15.
5. V.A. Smith, *The Oxford History of India,* Oxford, 1958, pp. 426-7.
6. *Cit.* in Archbold, *op. cit.,* p. 33.
7. P. Cadell, *History of the Bombay Army,* London, 1938, pp. 23-4.
8. *Cit.* in Cadell, *op. cit.,* p. 24.

9. Dodwell, *op. cit.*, p. 98.
10. Keay, *op. cit.*, p. 187.
11. *Cit.* in Archbold, *op. cit.*, p. 23.
12. V.A. Smith, *op. cit.*, p. 33
13. Dodwell, *op. cit.*, p. 119.
14. V.A. Smith, *op. cit.*, p. 456.
15. *Ibid.*, p. 459.
16. W.J. Wilson, *History of the Madras Army*, Vol. 1, Madras, 1882, p. 25.
17. *Ibid.*
18. Dodwell, *op. cit.*, p. 14.
19. P.J. Marshall, 'The Seventeenth and Eighteenth Centuries', Ch. 1, *The Raj*, ed. C.A. Bayly, London, 1990, p. 21.
20. Cadell, *op. cit.*, p. 51.
21. W.J. Wilson, *op. cit.*, pp. 34-5.
22. *Ibid.*, p. 64.
23. R. Callahan, *The East India Company and Army Reform 1783-1798*, Cambridge, Mass., 1972, pp. 35-6.
24. D.H.A. Kolff, *Naukar, Rajput and Sepoy. The Ethno-history of the Military Labour Market in Hindustan 1450-1850*, Cambridge, 1990, *passim*.
25. *Cit.* in Kolff, *op. cit.*
26. *The Army in India and its Evolution*, Calcutta, 1924.
27. Kolff, *op. cit.*
28. Smith, *op. cit.*, p. 479.
29. Keay, *op. cit.*, p. 308.
30. Archbold, *op. cit.*, p. 44.
31. Wilson, *op. cit.*, p. 161.
32. A. Broome, *History of the Rise and Progress of the Bengal Army*, Calcutta, 1850, p. 458.
33. Wilson, *op. cit.*, p. 217.
34. *Ibid.*, p. 386.

4
The East India Company's Army

EVOLUTION

The scope of this chapter is limited to the evolution of the artillery arms of British and Indian powers from the Battle of Plassey (1757) to the revolt of 1857. In order to look at the evolution of the British artillery from 1748 onwards, however, it is relevant to examine, very broadly, the evolution of the British army as a whole, as its organisation, tactics, equipment, weaponry and political compulsions influenced not only the artillery but the other two combat arms, the infantry and the cavalry as well.

1. Organisation 1748-1795

Progress upto 1785: Due to the historical background, distances and lack of good communications, the three Presidencies developed their own armies and there was very little in common between them upto 1785. Their establishments were devised to serve local requirements and the directors in England issued orders separately to each Presidency regarding policy and organisation. Some sort of central coordination was attempted in 1748 when Major Stringer Lawrence was appointed as commander of all forces of the East India Company. At the same time, a Director of Artillery or Inspector General of Artillery was appointed in 1747 to coordinate the artillery of the three Presidencies. Despite such instructions, for all practical purposes, the three armies remained separate entities under their respective Governors and Commander-in-Chief who had powers both for political and military affairs.

In time of need, however, troops from one area were switched or reinforced with those from another, as happened in the case of the Battle of Plassey where the artillery force consisted of gunners from Bengal, Bombay and Madras, and also from the navy.

Reorganisation of 1785 : In 1785, the East India Company was made a subordinate department of the English government and placed under a Governor General and a council of three with its headquarters at Calcutta and with the three Presidencies under the Governor General for all questions of war, revenue and diplomacy. Each Presidency had a separate military board under its respective Comander-in-Chief with a number of military officers including the senior artillery officers as one of its members.

The troops of the Company comprised the following :

(a) Royal troops from England to man all three arms.

(b) European troops for all three arms.

(c) Native troops for cavalry and infantry and later for artillery, from 1777 onwards.

(d) Subsidiary troops. Raised and paid by Indian chiefs but trained and disciplined by British officers and in some cases commanded by them also.

(e) Irregular native troops for cavalry and infantry. Artillery was never irregular except for a very brief period.

(f) Hyderabad contingent of all arms.

(g) Punjab Force of cavalry and infantry only.

(h) Singh and Bengal Police; the former were foot and horse borne, whereas the latter also had guns. These police forces were mainly army forces.

Lack of cavalry : It is significant that for almost the first 50 years, the army was composed mainly of artillery and infantry arms and the British inflicted major defeats on the Moghuls and Marathas with these two arms alone even though their enemies had overwhelming cavalry. Commenting on this, Wilson writes :

> Whatever the reason may have been, the fact remains that in our first and second wars with Hyder, our force

consisted entirely of artillery and infantry and the services rendered by that force cannot be properly estimated unless it be borne in mind that they were performed without assistance from cavalry, against an enemy principally of that arm.

The Company in fact started raining their cavalry in strength only from 1803 onwards. Thus, for all their initial conquests, they dependent mainly on European dominated artillery and disciplined native infantry led by British officers.

Financial considerations : The size and composition of the army was dictated by political and security requirements but finance was invariably a major limiting factor; in fact military expenditure had a major share of the budget as indicated by the following :

Receipts (million of rupees)		*Expenditure*	
Land	14:25	Military	11:75
Custom	2:00		
Salt	1:25	Civil	4:75
Opium	2:50	Interest Debt	2:50
Miscellaneous	6:00	Miscellaneous	7:00
	26:00		26:00

Financing native troops was, of course, much cheaper. The average of maintaining a soldier was £185 in England and £36 in India. One European cost as much as three natives. The troops of the Royal forces were even costlier. On arguments of safety alone, it would have been better to have Europeans only but safety had to be balanced with economy. A compromise had to be arrived at. We will see later that whereas this compromise was done to the maximum extent in cavalry and infantry, it was kept to a minimum in artillery.

Uniformity in Presidencies : During 1785, the Directors laid down instructions for having some sort of uniformity in the three arms of the Presidencies and instructed that "Corps should be formed to enable them to take the shortest notice, and to act with effect whenever they shall happen to be united."

To achieve that, they laid down the following :

(a) Establishment of each sub unit of all the arms was fixed and ordered to be the same in all three Presidencies so that the complement of officers and men in the sub units of artillery, cavalry and infantry stayed the same.

(b) Whenever each Presidency had to increase its army over what was laid down, complete sub units were to be added without any alteration in the number of officers and men, whether they were companies of artillery, regiments of cavalry, or battalions of European or native infantry.

Strength in 1785 : As a result of major reorganisation and attempts at uniformity, the force level of the armies of the three Presidencies was fixed as under in 1785 :

(a) Bengal

(i) European artillery — 3 battalions
(ii) Native artillery — Nil
(iii) Native cavalry — 2 tps
(iv) European infantry — 6 battalions
(v) Native infantry — 36 battalions
(vi) Lascars — 30 companies

(b) Madras

(i) European artillery — 2 battalions
(ii) Native artillery — Nil
(iii) European cavalry — 1 regiment
(iv) Native cavalry — 5 regiments
(v) European infantry — 4 battalions
(vi) Native infantry — 36 battalions
(vii) Lascars — 36 Companies

(c) Bombay

(i) European artillery — 1 battalion
(ii) Native artillery — Nil
(iii) European infantry — 2 battalions
(iv) Native infantry — 12 battalions
(v) Lascars — 10 companies

Native artillery units had been raised in 1777 but disbanded soon after. In 1785, therefore, there were no native artillery units at all. The total strength of the army was 73,000 with the native portion forming the largest part as is evident from the figures below:

	European	Native	Total
(i) Artillery battalions	6	—	6
(ii) Cavalry regiments	1	5½	6½
(iii) Infantry battalions	12	86	98
(iv) Lascar companies	—	76	76

Progress from 1785 to 1796 : The above organisation remained almost unchanged till 1796, except minor internal changes in the composition of units. During this period, the army tool part in wars in Mysore (1790-92).

From the overall strength, it is apparent that the British, in spite of their wars in the south against Tipu Sultan, continued to depend mainly on their European artillery and native infantry, the latter being almost 86 percent of overall strength. It is also to be noted that the strength of the cavalry was very small, taking into account the cavalry of Indian powers. For example, the strength of British forces at Seringapatam in January, 1792, against Tipu Sultan was as under :

(a) Artillery		
(i) European	—	1145
(ii) Native	—	Nil
(iii) Lascars	—	3077
(b) Cavalry		
(i) European	—	404
(ii) Native	—	702
(c) Infantry		
(i) European	—	4482
(ii) Native	—	11,133

The artillery had 86 guns including siege guns. These were exclusive of the guns held with the European infantry battalion and native infantry battalions of the Bengal Army (guns from native infantry battalions of the Madras Army were withdrawn in 1770).

2. Reorganisation 1796-1857

By Pitt's Act of 1784, the Governor General was made

responsible for all affairs, civil and military: Under him were three Commanders-in-Chief; one for each Presidency. The Commander-in-Chief of Bengal was termed 'Commander-in-Chief' India. Strictly speaking, he did not command all three armies as they were independent for all purposes but when he visited the other two Presidencies he assumed command of all forces there.

Indeed, right upto 1857, the identity and distinct features of the three armies were maintained and no effort was ever made to unite them as it was felt that this would be politically unsafe. Even later in 1824, when the armies were being reorganised, the directors felt that it was useless to unite them. After the reorganisation of 1858, it was remarked by some senior officers that 'no attempt should be made to assimilate the three armies and they should be kept as separate as possible.

The three armies however, despite their distinct entities, were required to fight together as one homogenous body. To simplify this problem, in 1790 Lord Cornwallis laid down the relative precedence of the troops of the armies. In war, Bengal troops were always to be on the right; Madras and Bombay were to take the right of each other in their own Presidency; but when they met on neutral ground, they were supposed to draw lots for the post.

In addition to the three armies, there were other forces which reinforced the regular armies.

(a) Hyderabad contingent

This was raised in 1798, when the Nizam came under British protection. It was commanded by British officers and controlled by the British government. In 1853, its strength was as under :

(i) Artillery
4 field batteries

(ii) Cavalry
5,000

(iii) Infantry
8 battalions

(b) *Punjab force*

This force was raised in 1849. It had only infantry and cavalry with Sikhs forming the majority in the force. In 1857 there were 70,000 Sikhs on the pay roster. It was directly under the Bengal Commander-in-Chief and not under any Presidency.

(c) *Irregular forces*

The British raised a large number of irregular forces as these were economical and could be disbanded when they were no longer required. These were mainly in the cavalry and infantry arms and some of these units were kept embodied for as much as over 50 years. The artillery was never irregular. For a short period, however, irregular artillery units of golandaz were formed in 1805 composed of 137 men who had come over from Maratha service. These were gradually absorbed in regular companies.

The gradual expansion in territories of the Company, as well as war in the south Tipu, and the Maratha and Sikh wars brought great increase in the strength of the armies. The increase was :

(a)	1796	—	70,000	
(b)	1805	—	1,54,000	
(c)	1813	—	2,00,000	
(d)	1826	—	2,70,000	
(e)	1830	—	2,23,000	
(f)	1849	—	3,00,000	(with 400 guns)
(g)	1856	—	3,23,000	(with 516 guns)

European versus native manpower: The strength of natives in the army was invariably more than European troops particularly in the infantry and cavalry as can be gauged by the following :

(a) *1796*

Europeans	—	13,000
Natives	—	57,000

(b) *1805*

Europeans	—	24,000
Natives	—	1,30,000

(c) *1856*

Europeans	—	48,319
Natives	—	2,75,304

The Bengal army by itself formed more than half the strength of armies. Its composition in 1827 and 1857 (given below) reveals the relative proportion of Europeans and natives in the main arms :

1827

(a) *Artillery*	*Europeans*	*Native*	*Total*
Horse	1086	330	1416
Foot	2250	2062	4312
Gun lascars	—	1224	1224
(b) *Cavalry*			
Bodyguards	183	—	183
Regiments	260	4980	5240
(c) *Infantry*			
European units	781	—	781
Native units	1776	55648	57424

1857

(a) *Europeans*		
Royal artillery	—	2,686
Royal cavalry	—	2,962
Royal engineers	—	200
Royal infantry	—	37,888
Company's troops	—	15,750
Total	—	59,486
(b) *Natives*	—	1,70,000

Over the period, the strength of the Queen's troops from England increased considerably. Here we have over 43,000 such troops against the Company's own European troops (only about 16,000), notwithstanding the fact that the Queen's troops were more expensive than European troops of the Company to maintain. Thus economy at this stage had second priority, paramount being the consolidation of the Empire as by this time, all Indian powers had been subdued.

Officering of armies : All units of the Company's forces were commanded by the European commissioned officers. Throughout the regime of the East India Company, there was no case of a native commissioned officer. The highest appointment for a native was a Subedar, which was upgraded to Subedar Major on 28 October 1817. Speaking of native soldiers and their command, Sir Thomas Munro remarked :

> Native troops are quite orderly and easily managed; the native officers are well acquainted with their duties. They conduct almost all the interior details and leave but little for the European officers to do. They are however apt to grow insolent and careless when left to themselves and European officers are therefore absolutely necessary to direct them but not many. One to a Company is quite enough for a useful purpose.

The above observation is not really startling and the sentiments reflect the universally recognised statement of Napoleon, that there are no bad troops but only bad officers and that the morale and efficiency of a unit is a reflection on their officers. Indian soldiers have, of course, always been first rate; in fact better than most countries, as not only did they have a tradition of fighting for centuries but their morale was also high as the fighting class in India had a very high social status. In the battles between British and Indian powers, even when both sides had Indians as soldiers, the British were invariably the victors, as their armies were led by professional and dedicated offices as against amateurs and the self-centred leadership of the armies of Indian powers.

3. Conclusion

The reasons for the British armies being composed mainly of Indian soldiers and yet overwhelming the armies of native powers despite being outnumbered themselves make a fascinating study. The armies of the East India Company, notwithstanding internal problems, struggles between military and civilians, mutinies of units and frequent dissatisfaction of officers and men, stood the test of time. Within 110 years of creating regular armies, although greatly outnumbered, they established the largest components of their Empire mainly by the clash of arms.

The role of the army was summed up by Sir T. Metcalfe, Governor General, in the following minutes :

> Is it no proof of efficiency that it has conquered all India? Is it no proof of efficiency that India in more universally tranquil owing to our Indian Army than it ever was under any native Government or Governments that we read of? If our Indian Army be so expensive, why do we not employ Europeans troops alone to maintain India? Why, but because Europeans are so much more expensive that we could not pay a sufficient number. If our Indian Army be so inefficient, why do we incur the expense of making soldiers of the natives? Why do we not entertain the same number of undisciplined people who would cost much less? Why, but because then we should lose the country from the inefficiency of our native force.

Notwithstanding the above observations, it is nonetheless true that the British ensured that their artillery arm was kept predominantly European for reasons of political safety and security.

PROGRESS AND DEVELOPMENT

Despite attempts at standardisation in the three armies, both the organisation and equipment of the artillery and the other arms varied a great deal. Standardisation was achieved for the first time in 1785, when it was ordered that the establishment of units in all three armies will be the same. This applied only to the establishment within an artillery company; a number of companies kept varying according to local needs, the dictates of the economy and other factors. For example, the establishment of an artillery company in Bengal and Madras in 1768 varied as under :

	Bengal	*Madras*
Captain	1	1
Captain Lieutenant	1	—
First Lieutenant	1	2
Second Lieutenant	1	—

Lieutenant fireworkers	3	3
Sergeants	6	4
Bombardiers	10	6
Corporals	6	4
Gunners	20	20
Drummers	2	2
Fifers	2	—
Matrosses	40	40

In 1785, the establishment of an artillery company was fixed as under for all three presidencies, although the number of companies in a battalion or battalions in an artillery brigade varied. The establishment of a European company was as under :

Captain	1	
Lieutenants	2	
Lieutenant fireworkers	2	
Sergeants	4	
Corporals	4	
Gunners	8	
Matrosses	56	
Drummers and fifers	2	
Pukhalies	2	(watermen)

As and when there was a requirement to change the manpower of a company, instructions were issued to all the three armies to implement the changes. The actual implementation took its own time.

The progress of the raising of artillery units varied considerably in the three armies due to the operational tasks assigned to them. For this reason, the Bengal and Madras armies always had priority and the Bombay Army acted mainly as a reinforcing army, although it had its own role in looking after the western areas. After the defeat of Tipu Sultan in 1799 and the end of the Anglo-Maratha wars, the focus shifted to the Bengal Army, whose paramount assigned role was the conquest of the northern territories in which the Madras Army also played a significant role.

1. Artillery of Bengal Presidency

The court always gave priority to Bengal where the "Company had so much at stake". The first artillery company was raised in 1749, the greater part of it (about 45 men) perished in the so-called "Black Hole on 20 June 1756." The remnants joined the artillery (which had arrived from Madras and Bombay) under Clive and took part in the Battle of Plassey in June 1757. The second company was raised on 19 September 1758 and the armament authorised to it is interesting from a historical point of view. It had the following guns :

(a) 6 x 6 pounders
(b) 1 x howitzer
(c) 4 x 24 pounders]
(d) 4 x 18 pounders] Battering train
(e) 1 x 8 inch mortar]
(f) 2 x 5 ½ inch mortars]

The normal armament of a foot artillery company in those days was six pounder guns and light howitzers. The inclusion of heavy guns then known as 'battering trains' and later as 'siege artillery', leaves no doubt that the British had assigned to themselves the role of conquest and not merely that of defenders of their trading interests, as some historians tend to project.

A third company was raised on 17 September 1763, followed by a fourth on 4 August 1765. The artillery then became a distinct corps an all companies were placed under a battalion. In 1768, the strength of the Bengal Army was fixed as under :

(a) Artillery
1 battalion of 4 foot companies

(b) Infantry
3 regiments of 7 companies each

(c) Cavalry
Nil

Native artillery : As brought out earlier, three companies of artillery or golandaz units had been raised in 1777 in Oudh and in the same year were transferred to the service of the

Company. Immediately thereafter, three battalions of golandaz with eight companies were raised.

Formation of artillery brigade : Thus in 1778, there were three battalions of native artillery and one of European artillery. These were formed into a brigade of artillery and this is the first mention of an artillery brigade showing the importance being attached to this arm. The pattern was the same as in infantry, *i.e.* 3:1 of native and European troops. However in 1779, all the native battalions were disbanded and artillery companies were grouped with infantry brigades.

Re-raising of native artillery : During 1780/1782, five companies of golandaz artillery were raised again but gradually disbanded during 1784-85, as the number of native units would exceed those manned by Europeans and this was unacceptable to the Directors who wrote a strong directive again, objecting to the raising of native artillery The full text of the order issued in 1785 was under :

> It is moreover the express orders of the Honourable Court of Directors that all establishments respecting native artillery or golandaz shall cease, and that the officers and men of these corps shall be incorporated into the sepoy battalions or into the sepoy battalions or into the lascars attached to the artillery. It is likewise their express orders that none of the natives from the interior country of Hindustan shall henceforth be taught the exercise of artillery, and that none shall be enlisted for the corps of artillery lascars, but such as are actually seamen or boatmen settled within the limits of the different Presidencies.

Reorganisation of 1785: Based on the experience of various operations upto 1785, it was decided to reorganise all three armies. Apart from many other changes like attempts at standardisation of units and assimilation of all three armies as far as possible, orders were issued for complete Europeanisation by giving the command of native units to European officers and by disbanding the native artillery, although the armies were allowed to have native infantry and cavalry units.

The all European artillery was authorised as under :

(a) *Bengal*	3 battalions	(15 companies)
(b) *Madras*	2 battalions	(10 companies)
(c) *Bombay*	1 battalion	(5 companies)

It is interesting to note that in 1785, at the time of reorganisation, the army of the East India Company was 73,000 strong with the native portion forming the largest share. The establishment of an artillery battalion was fixed as under :

(a) *Headquarters*

Lieutenant colonel	—	1
Major	—	1
Adjutant	—	1
Quartermaster	—	1
Surgeon	—	1
Mate of surgeon	—	1
Sergeant Major	—	1
Quartermaster sergeant	—	1
Drill sergeant	—	1
Drill corporal	—	1
Drum major	—	1
Fife major	—	1
Total	—	12

(b) *Company* (each)

Captain	—	1
Lieutenants	—	2
Lieutenant fire-workers	—	2
Sergeants	—	4
Corporals	—	4
Gunners	—	8
Matrosses	—	56
Drummers and fifers	—	2
Pukhalies	—	2
Total		81

Interestingly, all artillery units, whether European or native manned, had large number of lascars attached to artillery companies. The normal attachment was one lascar company per artillery company but sometimes as many as three lascar companies were provided. In 1785, the establishment of a lascar company was 1 Serang, 2 First Tindals, 2 Second Tindals, 56 Privates and 1 Pukhalie.

The allotment of lascar companies to their armies was :

(a)	Bengal	—	30
(b)	Madras	—	36
(c)	Bombay	—	10

Raising of mixed artillery units : Subsequent to 1785, due to wars in the south and the planned requirement for expansion of territories in the north, the army had to be expanded. To raise pure European manned artillery units in the absence of the availability of such manpower was difficult. To raise pure native units was contrary to policy. To overcome the problem, it was decided that native artillerymen be attached to European units of which they were to form a part. This experiment started in 1798 but did not last long. Cardew terms it 'faulty and unsuccessful."

The experiment may have had its flaws, as the deployment of artillery in battle and the firing of guns required a very high standard of fire discipline, drill in deployment and battle procedure. There were also fairly major problems in administration and actual operations due to ethnic and language problems. It does, however, appear that the mixed units were really not given a fair chance and trial, and that they were disbanded too quickly probably due to the inherent prejudice among the British about Indians. The experiment could have been a great success as proved in the war fought later between the British and the Rajah of Travancore in 1809 (Section-2). In Bengal, mixed artillery units were disbanded in 1802.

Reorganisation of 1796 : Major changes were made in all three armies after the reorganisation of 1796. The Bengal Army and the artillery in particular, was increased for the protection and tranquility of Oudh. The major changes were :

(a) An officer of the rank of Colonel was authorised to command the Bengal Artillery with a Brigade Major as his staff officer.
(b) In 1797, an Experimental Horse Artillery was formed.
(c) In 1802, a Stud Department was opened to provide horses for horse artillery and cavalry.
(d) In 1806, native artillery units were raised again.
(e) In 1815, Rocket Artillery was introduced.

Re-raising of native artillery : Again, the problem faced by the Directors in increasing their artillery arm was the same, that is, how to compromise the requirements of expansion and security. Since they were not too happy with the experiment of mixed artillery, during a high level meeting in 1799, it was decided that the only way to preserve the artillery arm was to raise native units again.

In 1806, five companies were raised and thereafter there was no looking back. The schedule of raising and expansion was as under :

(a) 1806 — 5 companies
(b) 1809 — 2 companies
(c) 1812 — 3 companies
(d) 1814 — 4 companies
(e) 1818 — 1 company Total 15 companies
(f) 1824 — 5 companies Total 20 companies
(g) 1827 — Reorganised into 2 battalions of 8 companies each
(h) 1842 — Reorganised into 2 battalions of 10 companies each
(i) 1845 — Reorganised into 3 battalions of 6 companies each

Horse and rocket artillery : The horse artillery was first raised in Madras in 1805. In Bengal, the first raising was in 1811 when a troop of native artillery was formed for service in Java but reduced on return. In 1817, three troops were raised. Major raisings were, however, carried out in 1825. In Bengal, the rocket artillery troop was raised in 1815 but disbanded in 1821.

Reorganisation of 1824 : No major changes in the overall military organisation and system were made or planned. Some internal changes were made in the establishment of units of the three arms. These were mainly needed because of financial reasons and in order to achieve further uniformity in all three armies. It was laid down that the number of officers will be the same in the combat arms as under :

(a) *Foot artillery* (European)
Each battalion to have 4 companies.
Total 20 officers.

(b) *Foot artillery* (native)
Not yet organised into battalions. In Madras in 1818, one battalion of 10 companies was raised but it had a separate establishment.

(c) *Horse artillery*
Each brigade to have 4 troops.
Total 16 officers.

(d) *Cavalry*
Each regiment to have 6 troops.
Total 20 officers.

(e) *Infantry*
Each battalion to have 5 companies.
Total 20 officers.

Each horse artillery brigade, cavalry regiment, artillery regiment and infantry battalion thus had 20 officers (16 for horse artillery). Among these the rank structure was the same, *i.c.* number of majors, captains and junior officers. This helped in removing some of the anomalies in the promotion of officers in the three arms. To further help in career planning, the commander of each unit could either be a colonel or lieutenant colonel depending upon his seniority in rank.

Thus in 1825, the Bengal artillery had :

(a) *Horse artillery*
3 brigades of 4 troops each; each brigade having 1 native troop.
Total 12 troops.

(b) *Foot artillery* (European)
5 battalions of 4 companies each.
Total 20 companies.

(c) *Foot artillery* (native)
20 companies.

The ratio of European and native units works out as under :

	European	*Native*
(a) Horse artillery troops	9	3
(b) Foot companies	20	20

Reorganisation of 1827: The expansion carried out in 1825 was to meet the increased commitment of operations in the north and was a significant landmark in the evolution of the artillery arm, in that there was parity in the strength of native and European manned artillery (foot) despite the clear policy of the Directors on the subject. This was a far cry from the earlier days when natives were not even entrusted with two guns held with native infantry battalions.

In 1827, the native portion of the artillery was reduced to 16 companies by forming them in two battalions of eight companies each. The numerical strength was as under :

	Europeans	*Natives*
(a) Horse artillery	1086	330
(b) Foot artillery	2250	2062
(c) Lascars (20 companies)	—	1224

Another major change made in 1827 was the conversion of some foot companies, both European and native, into light field batteries, *i.e.* drawn by horses instead of bullocks. Cardew gives the number thus converted as eight European and four native. These light field batteries were found to be extremely useful during the Anglo-Sikh wars, operations in Afghanistan and on the frontier, as these gave much greater mobility to foot artillery.

Artillery division : A significant event in the evolution of the British artillery was the formation of the artillery division in 1825. The British force, which moved against Bharatpore in 1825 under the Commander-in-Chief, Lord Combermere, on 5 December, had the following :

(a) Cavalry division

(b) First infantry division

(c) Second infantry division

(d) Artillery division (Brigadier A. Macleod)

(i) Horse artillery	—	6 troops
(ii) Foot artillery	—	8 companies
(iii) Light field batteries	—	2
(iv) Siege artillery	—	110 guns

This was the first time that the artillery was grouped into a division under its own commander; the total number of guns exceeded 200 in the division.

Post-1827 reorganisation : In 1845, the following reorganisation was ordered :

(a) European artillery to have 6 battalions of 4 companies each.

Total 24 companies.

(b) Native artillery to have 3 battalions of 6 companies each. Total 18 companies.

The above organisation remained without change till the Revolt of 1857.

2. Artillery of Madras Presidency

Ad hoc artillery : As earlier brought out, an ad hoc artillery of 12 guns was mounted at Armegaon in 1625, within six years of the British establishing their trade in India. Thereafter, as in the other two Presidencies, guns removed from ships manned by gun room crew were located at various forts and fortifications to guard their interests. In view of the threat from the French, Fort St. George was reinforced by a strong force from England which included 80 artillerymen from the King's troops as well as 70 men from the Company's artillery. These were further reinforced by 40 men from the Royal Artillery.

Beginning of regular artillery : Consequent to the orders issued by the Directors in 1748 to all three Presidencies, to raise regular artillery and do away with the ad hoc system of "gun room and its crew", the first company was raised in 1749. In 1752, orders were received to form the second company which gave one company each for the security of Fort St. George and Fort St. David.

The armament of the two companies was as under :

(a) 1 x 12 pounders

(b) 10 x 6 pounders

(c) 3 x 5 ¾ inch howitzers

The number and type of guns was not fixed for an artillery company during the early periods of the organisation of the army. Since the artillery had to operate under all conditions, sometimes in very small detachments of two or three guns, no effort was made to have uniformity of establishment. This enabled the commanders to select the best combination in terms of the type and number of guns required for specific operations.

Battle baptism of the Madras artillery : Guns and personnel from Madras were sent in 1756 to help Clive in his operations in Bengal and the latter acquitted themselves with great distinction in the Battle of Plassey. In 1756, during the siege of Fort St. George by the French, the artillery played a major part and also suffered heavy casualties. The Chief Engineer of the Fort gave the following account :

> To the credit of our Artillery, let it be remarked that the two 12 pounders from the north dismounted four 24 pounders opposed to them; and that of 32 pieces of cannon found on the enemy's batteries, 31 were disabled by our shot, which are many more than we had hurt by the enemy, notwithstanding our works were enfiladed, plunged into and taken in reverse.

The casualties in the artillery were as under :

	Strength	*Killed*	*Wounded*
Royal Artillery	148	15	27
Madras Artillery	70	24	30

The siege was lifted by Lally, the French general, in June 1759, leading behind 26 guns—18 and 24 pounders, most of which were disabled. It is not surprising therefore the Lally wrote that "on arrival at Poundicherry, we shall endeavour to learn some other trade; for the war requires too much patience.

In 1758, the British decided to take on the French who were entrenched in the fort of Masulipatam, their headquarters of Northern Circars in the south. After initial skirmishes at the Battle of Condore in December, where the French were defeated, the British arrived outside the fort on 6 March 1759. The fort was surrounded by swampy ground and protected on the north-west by an inlet of sea. Three separate batteries were erected by 26 March to take on the three main bastions on the fort. The three batteries had the following armament :

(a) *No. 1 battery*
 2 x 12 pounders

(b) *No. 2 battery*
 2 x 18 pounders
 2 x 24 pounders
 3 x mortars (8, 9 and 13 inches calibre)

(c) *No. 3 battery*
 2 x 18 pounders
 2 x 24 pounders

Normally, during breaching operations, the tactics were to move the guns forward by a series of parallels till they were within effective range. In this case because of the swampy ground, the guns had to remain in fixed positions. Since the British guns had longer range than the French ones mounted on forts, the latter moved some of their guns outside on a flank in a mobile role to neutralise the British artillery, but they were not very effective which was partly due to the nature of the ground which restricted mobility. The British guns continued to fire from 25 March to 4 April and made effective breaches, while all their batteries kept up covering fire upto the last moment of assault which made the French surrender with over 120 guns. The British achieved a major political advantage over the French and also gained over 1,600 square miles of territory ceded to them. At a tactical level, this was the first time that the British artillery was used in siege warfare, the forerunner of innumerable such battles in which the final outcome invariably depended upon the effectiveness of artillery fire for breaching, fire power cover for the assault and also for fighting inside the fort. It is surprising that the French gave in so quickly as they were exports in artillery, but from this action in defence of the fort and their earlier action during their siege of Fort St. George, it appears that they could not match the British artillery.

Expansion of artillery 1765-1784 : In February 1765, a third company was added to the establishment. The Court of Directors also permitted an officer of the rank of major—this was done not only to improve the career prospects of officers but also to have a senior officer for all three companies. The pay scales of the artillery and infantry personnel were revised in 1766 and the earlier advantage given to artillery was maintained.

	Artillery	*Infantry*
Captain	£ 200 per year	£ 182 per year
Lieutenant	£ 100 per year	£ 91 per year
Sergeant	6 pagodas per day	5 pagodas
Corporal	5 pagodas per day	3.14 pagodas
Private	4 pagodas per day	2.21 pagodas

Consequent to the expansion of the army, the Directors ordered in 1768 that the artillery should be formed into a battalion of five companies, the whole to be commanded by a lieutenant colonel who, surprisingly, was also to command a company. This was perhaps based more on financial grounds than on functional ones.

This anomaly was removed later in 1778 when certain improvements were made in rank structure and it was also laid down that the lieutenant colonel and major are not to command companies. Thus, for the first time, the artillery had a separate commander responsible to his Commander-in-chief for all artillery matters.

Inspection of artillery units : From the studies of the artillery of the Indian powers, the Moghuls, Marathas and Sikhs, there is no evidence that apart from Ranjit Singh (who regularly inspected his troops) any one else carried out any formal inspections and thereafter gave reports in writing to their higher authorities. A formal inspection carried out by a field commander, Brigadier General Joseph Smith, on the state and battle-worthiness of detachments of the 2nd and 3rd Company of artillery on 6 May 1771 at Trichnopoly is given in Appendix A. Apart from the normal aspects of inspection such as turnout, discipline and bearing, the units were put through firing practice of all types of guns held with them *i.e.* guns, mortars and howitzers and remarks made on their fitness for war.

Regular inspection of artillery units by the field commanders (unlike in the armies of Indians), where the local commanders were left on their own, was one of the major reasons for the higher proficiency of British artillery units. Since Ranjit Singh, drawing inspiration from the British, also carried out personal inspections, the Sikh artillery, notwithstanding certain technical weaknesses, was as efficient as that of the British.

Expansion 1784-1802 : Due to requirements of the Anglo-Mysore and Anglo-Maratha wars and also the increase in of the Company's territories in central India, there was an urgent need to expand the artillery arm. As we have seen, in Bengal, natives were inducted into the artillery in 1777, but in 1779 all the three battalions of golandaz were disbanded to be raised again in 1780 and further disbanded in 1785, native artillery men then being mixed with European artillery. If the British had strong reservations about having natives in this arm they were even more suspicious of Europeans unless they felt them to be totally trustworthy. For example, in 1757, when a large number of foreigners left the French service and deserted to the British, not a single person was sent to the artillery but they were formed into a separate infantry company. Again in 1761, after the capture of Pondicherry, when a large number of prisoners and deserters were held by the British, Colonel Cailland wrote a minute recommending that the whole lot be sent to the infantry.

In October 1784, orders were issued to raise the following units :

(a) *European artillery*
One battalion of 8 companies (previous 5 companies).

(b) *Native artillery*
One battalion of 10 companies (previous nil).

Raising of native artillery : Thus in Madras, a total of 18 companies were ordered to be raised. It is indeed surprising that native units were raised in 1784; at the same time in Bengal, they were under reduction and none was sanctioned for the Bombay army. More surprising is the fact that out of 18 companies, 10 were manned by natives—a clear turnaround from the policy of the Directors who did not want that natives should be associated with the artillery at all.

The new raisings seemed too good to last and in 1785 the following orders were issued :

(a) To disband all native artillery.

(b) To attach native gunners to each company of European artillery, *i.e.* 1 Subedar, 2 Jemadars, 6 Havildars, 6 Naiques, 1 Puckalie and 200 gunners.

The full text of the order has been given earlier in Section-1.

In view of reduction of 10 companies of native artillery, in 1786 orders were issued to raise two European battalions of five companies each, giving a total of 10 European companies. For these 10 companies, 30 companies of gun lascars, each having a total of 59, all ranks were attached which works out to a total of about 180 lascars for one European company having 80 ranks.

Since there were two lieutenant colonels, the seniormost officer was to command the whole of the artillery. This was found unsatisfactory, and later the establishment was revised to give the artillery one colonel, one lieutenant colonel and a brigade major on staff as provided to infantry and cavalry brigades, thus recognising the artillery arm at par with these two arms in protocol as an independent combat arm.

Expansion due to Anglo-Maratha wars : To meet the requirements of the Mysore War, in March 1799 a native company of artillery was raised but again disbanded in 1802 after the termination of the war. The reduction of this company was not an isolated case. Great reductions were made in overall army strength after the Battle of Seringapatam. However, the involvement of the British in the Anglo-Maratha wars obliged them to raise the force level again.

Since purely native units were not acceptable to meet the requirements of expansion, the following steps were taken :

(a) A draft of 200 selected men was sent in January 7 1800 from UK.

(b) Another draft of 300 men was sent from the European regiment in February 1800.

Each of the two battalions which had five companies was now authorised (in 1802) to have seven companies, thus giving a total of 14 companies. Even these were considered inadequate and in 1803, the Commander-in-Chief wrote to the government:

> That valuable corps from a want of recruits has become weak and inefficient; and should supply of recruits continue to be so inadequate to its demands, the army in a very short period of time will be destitute of artillery. I trust that your lordship will represent this circumstance, and its consequences to the Court of Directors. It must have hitherto escaped their notice; for I cannot suppose that the Honourable Court would otherwise allow a corps which has always done credit to their army and whose services are essential to its success to be reduced to a half of its proper establishment.

Reacting to this letter of the Commander-in-Chief in March 1803, the government ordered the raising of native artillery units as well as horse artillery. The lifting of an embargo on natives was not thus due to any change in higher policy but because events dictated it and because there was a shortage of reliable European manpower. The operative word here is 'reliable'. There was no shortage of Europeans who had deserted the European model armies of the Marathas but these were not acceptable, presumably on the principle that "once disloyal, always disloyal". It was perhaps considered better to have selected natives than to have Europeans whose antecedents were not known. This assumption is proved beyond doubt by the Directors who, while sending 133 men from the Swiss Regiment "Regiment de Manron" in 1808, for the artillery, wrote :

> In consideration of the long and faithful services of the Regiment de Menron under the British Government in India, and the deficient state of your artillery corps, we do not object to the transfer of a part of that regiment to the corps alluded to, notwithstanding our disinclination on general principles to any large proportion of foreigners being admitted into that corps.

The above direction is clear and leaves no doubt about the reservations of the Directors in having anyone in their artillery except the most trustworthy. While they had no objection to the Swiss regiment being part of their infantry, they were forced to have some of them as gunners because there was a shortage of Europeans to man that arm.

Re-raising of native and horse artillery : The year 1809 is landmark in the evolution of the British artillery in India not only because native artillery units were being re-raised but because after that, till 1858, they stayed with the armies and also expanded. Two companies were raised that year, the establishment being as under of each company :

Subedar	—	1
Jamadar	—	1
Havildars	—	6

Naiques	—	6	
Privates	—	80	
Drummer	—	1	
Fifer	—	1	
Bhisties	—	2	(watermen)

A European officer was to be detailed by the Commandant of artillery for immediate charge of each company of golandaz. It is interesting, indeed surprising, that no officer was authorised for the company, while during the same period a European company had as many as six officers as under :

Captain	—	1
Captain Lieutenant	—	1
Lieutenants	—	2
Fireworkers	—	2

The reason appears to be shortage of officers for the artillery, as the College at Addiscombe, which was training artillery officers for the Company in UK, was only opened in 1798, and the policy was not to have officers commissioned in this arm "other than those properly educated and qualified". The shortage was further aggravated due to the embargo on giving commission in the artillery from the ranks. It was also perhaps planned that native artillery units will not be employed on independent tasks and always placed in war alongside European artillery units in a "superimposed role". In fact there are not many cases where the native units were allowed to operate on their own. The odd exceptions were like the case of the capture of Karachi in 1840 where a golandaz company of Bombay artillery acted on its own.

In 1803, along with the raising of these two native companies, a horse artillery brigade was raised which had one European and one native troop; the native troop was disbanded in 1810. To balance the raising of two native companies and native horse artillery, the same year the directors sent 442 recruits from England.

Battle baptism of mixed artillery : The native gunners had already proved their worth as early as 1778 in Bengal when a golandaz company was sent from Allahabad to reinforce the government of Bombay. That they could be as efficient as British gunners is proved by the account of the Battle of Travancore as narrated by the eminent historian W.J. Wilson.

> In December 1809, the British sent a force of artillery and infantry into Travancore due to their difference with the Rajah and reports of an alleged plot to murder the Resident. The artillery element consisted of 45 Europeans and 82 natives manning 4 x 6 pounders and 2 x 5.5 inch howitzers.
>
> On 19 January 1809, Cochin, defended by the British, was attacked by a very strong force of Travancore troops. The attack although repulsed made the Force Commander Major W. Hemett send a report to his superiors, the last para of which read 'on the other side of the river, close to the mouth, they have erected a battery of two guns which prevents vessels from coming in and going out and which played upon us with some effect on our charging the enemy on the south side. I trust that you will immediately dispatch the armed cruiser to keep the mouth of the river open.'
>
> On 19 February, the British decided to attack the position held by Travancore forces at Killianoor with about 5,000 men and protected by a strong gun position with a deep nullah in front. The guns of the Rajah were extremely effective as Colonel Chalmers of the British Forces reported heavy fire which adversely affected the advance of British.
>
> Chalmers remarked on 23 February that the troops had to advance against the batteries under a 'heavy fire of musketry, round and grape'. The British therefore decided to move their own artillery forward to silence the guns of the enemy. Capt. Foote of H.M.S. 'Piedmontaise' volunteered to his service on shore and landed a detachment of seamen. Half of them went with Lieutenant Colonel Picton under Lieutenant Turner and the other half under Capt. Foote accompanied Lieutenant Colonel Stuart. They were employed in bringing up the artillery guns in front of enemy's batteries which they did with 'alacrity and courage'. Thereafter the assault 'was covered by a well

directed fire of artillery until the head of the column had nearly reached the batteries'. The casualties in this brigade were much less than they would have been otherwise.

The war between the British and the Rajah lasted till 2 March when the latter surrendered. The above battles were classic artillery engagements from both sides and with credit to both the Rajah and the British. First, we have one of the few examples of the artillery of Indian powers stalling the British offensive by exploiting their artillery firepower. Second, the artillery of the British (which eventually helped to turn the balance of battle in their favour) was manned not by a pure European outfit but a mixed crew of Indian and European gunners, which tends to dispel the notion held by British historians that the mixed artillery experiment was ill judged. The strength of the Indian artillerymen was predominant in this action.

The lesson learnt in 1808 during this battle, that a mixed crew was not a liability, came too late, as such units had already been disbanded in 1802. In any case, by 1808, the British had raised native artillery in their armies which came to stay till the Revolt of 1857. This battle in which the British artillery had double the number of Indian gunners to Europeans leaves no doubt about the professional competence and discipline of Indian gunners.

Reorganisation 1810-1857 : To place artillery on the same footing as infantry and cavalry, the rank of Subedar Major was introduced in 1819. The Governor General was "pleased to accord the same distinction to the Corps of Artillery."

1818 was an important year as the following orders were issued for reorganisation :

(a) *Native artillery* : Expanded into a battalion of 10 companies with 10 companies of lascars attached. Men were drawn from native artillerymen earlier attached to European companies and volunteers from native infantry. Commanded by a Colonel and with a Lieutenant Colonel as No. 2.

(b) *Horse artillery brigade* : Organised into 6 gun troops

and one rocket troop, out of which two gun troops were native troops. Men were drawn from Body Guard and cavalry. No private above 30 years of age and under 5 feet 5 inches in Bengal.

(c) *European artillery* : Expanded to 2 battalions of 7 companies each (total 14 companies) with 7 companies of lascars attached to each battalion. Rank structure at senior level was revised to give one colonel or lieutenant colonel commandant and one more lieutenant colonel.

In 1820, however the total strength of the native battalion was reduced but the number of companies remained the same as 10.

The absence of commissioned officers in native artillery companies as compared with European companies has been commented upon earlier. In early 1820, the Commander-in-Chief impressed upon the government the necessity of increasing the number of European Officers, especially in the golandaz battalion, but this was opposed by Sir Thomas Munro on the following grounds :

> In support of the expediency of the proposed augmentation of European Officers with the Golandaz Corps, it is observed that such a corps being composed of natives is as much, if not considerably more, dependent upon its European Officers than any other. This is a principle which has never yet been admitted with regard to our other native troops and to the justness of which I cannot assent. I am so far from thinking that the efficiency of native troops is increased in proportion to the increased number of European Officers that I think that the number of officers may be too great, and that when this is the case it injures the discipline of the corps and lessens the respect of the natives for their European Officers. Native troops are quite orderly and easily managed. The Native Officers are well acquainted with all their duties and expert in their execution. They conduct almost all the interior details, and leave but little for the European Officers to do. They are however, apt to grow indolent, and careless when left to

themselves, and European Officers are therefore absolutely necessary to direct them, but not many. One to a company is quite enough for every useful purpose.

This observation of Sir Thomas Munro's does not seem to have any logic. One officer to a company in infantry was acceptable; in fact both native and European infantry companies had establishments of one officer each. But to say that one officer is enough for a native artillery company whereas in 1820 a European artillery company had five officers does not stand to reason. As for the artillery arm the Directors insisted on officers being "properly qualified".

However, later the policy was changed and native artillery units were given more officers but still less than in European units as the following authorisation in 1825 indicates :

(a) European battalion of four companies
— 25 officers

(b) Native battalion of ten companies
— 25 officers. It had however 30 native officers (subedars and jamadars) for which British companies had no equivalent of officer grade.

It is of particular interest to point out that as regards the formal establishment on paper, a native company as such was not authorised any officer. Officers were held at battalion level and the Commandant distributed officers to companies on a 'as required' basis, as the following establishment of a native battalion of Bengal in 1845 with six companies shows :

(a) Headquarters		
Colonel	—	1
Lieutanant Colonel	—	1
Major	—	1
Captains	—	5
First Lieutenants	—	10
Second Lieutenants	—	15
(b) Company		
Subedar	—	1
Jemadars	—	2
Havildars	—	6

Naiks	—	6
Privates	—	88

In 1824, some reorganisation was carried out as under :

(a) The horse artillery brigade was expanded to one European and one native brigade, each having four troops.

(b) The European artillery was reorganised into three battalions of four companies each

(c) The native artillery remained with 10 companies but certain changes were made in establishment.

In strength the native artillery was almost at par with the European artillery. The strength was as under :

	European	*Native*
(a) Foot artillery companies	12	10
(b) Horse artillery troop	4	4
(c) Rocket troop	1	—

Again it seemed too good to last. In fact, the reorganisation of 1824 seems quite surprising. The British may have had to be forced to raise native artillery units but to raise their strength to this level against all their philosophy and directions in keeping control of the artillery arm could have been dangerous. However, all the new raisings were brought to a more rational level from their point of view, and the following reductions were ordered :

(a) 1831

(i) Reduction of number of companies from 10 to 6 in the golandaz battalion.

(ii) Reduction of the number of troops in native horse artillery brigade from 4 to 2.

(b) 1845

Disbandment of native horse artillery brigade. The 2 troops held with this Brigade placed under the command of European horse artillery brigade.

Final organisation : In May 1845, the Court of Directors fixed the organisation of the Madras Artillery as under :

	European	*Native*
(a) Foot artillery companies	16 (4 battalion)	6 (1 battalion)
(b) Horse artillery troops	4	2

The above organisation remained unchanged till the Revolt of 1857.

Light field batteries: As in the case of the Bengal Artillery, orders were issued to convert foot artillery companies drawn by bullocks into horse drawn batteries to achieve greater mobility. The first to be converted were the batteries of the Hyderabad force. The establishment was fixed as under :

(a) 4 x 9 pounder guns
(b) 2 x 24 pounder howitzers
(c) 92 horses
(d) 7 ammunition wagons

3. The Artillery of Bombay Presidency

Although Bombay was the first possession of the British Crown in India and, during the early stages of the arrival of British in India, their most important and strongest place because of its geographical and political circumstances, its army mostly acted as a reinforcing army for operations by the Bengal and Madras armies. In fact at one time, Lord William Bentinck proposed that the Bombay army be abolished altogether as it was serving no useful service and was uneconomical. This was not accepted by his successor, Lord Metcalf, and no reduction was ordered by the Court although certain departments were asked to reduce their establishments.

The beginnings : From 1668 to 1748, Bombay, Surat and other possessions were protected by an ad hoc artillery, *i.e.* guns removed from armed ships and manned by sailors, the whole system being called "gun room crew".

In 1748 when the Directors in England issued orders for raising of regular artillery companies in all three armies, the first ever company was raised in 1748 in Bombay, the forerunner of other companies in Madras and Bengal. This company was formed by getting men from the European infantry units and the gun room crew. It is of interest to note that the first

Commander of the Bombay Forces in 1748 was Major Goodyear, an artillery officer who was sent from England and belonged to the Royal Artillery.

In 1753, the Directors showed their concern for the artillery arm of the Company and wrote that they were fully satisfied: "How great a share of our dependence must in case of troubles be on artillery and upon the skill of the people appropriated to its service." By 1755, three companies were raised. In the same year three companies of the Royal Artillery arrived in Bombay. The following figures of the strength of the garrison in Bombay show the importance given to the artillery arm :

Royal Artillery	—	227
Company's artillery	—	285
European infantry	—	849
Native sepoys	—	2412
Total	—	3773

Thus, out of a strength of 1361 Europeans, 512 belonged to the artillery and there were a total of 512 artillerymen for 3,261 infantry soldiers or six artillery companies.

During the Battle of Plassey in 1757, Bombay provided gunners to man the artillery of Clive. In fact, from 1748 to 1768, the artillery of Bombay took a major part in operations mostly outside the presidency, like Chandernagore (1757), Pondicherry (1760), Buxar (1764) Madura (1764), apart from fighting in its own presidency against local powers. Till 1759, officers of the artillery were borne on the list of European Regiment (infantry) but, in 1759 the Corps became distinct.

Growth from 1768 to 1785 : The fourth company of the Company's artillery was raised in 1768. By 1785, when a major reorganisation was ordered in all three armies to achieve a degree of standardisation, the strength of the three arms was as under :

(a) *Artillery*

- *(i)* European — 1 battalion (4 companies)
- *(ii)* Native — Nil

(b) *Cavalry* — Nil

(c) *Infantry*

(i) European — 2 battalions

(ii) Native — 12 battalions

Thus, till 1785 no native artillery was raised, whereas in the Bengal and Madras armies such units were raised in 1777 and 1784 respectively, although they were disbanded later. In fact in the Bombay army, the native artillery was not raised at all till as late as 1826. A European artillery regiment with four companies was the standard in all their armies in 1785. It is interesting to note that Captain Thomas Keating was ordered to take over command of the whole of the artillery in 1764 with the rank of lieutenant colonel. He was from Engineers but could not hold that rank in that arm. This was a special case as in the other two armies this higher rank was sanctioned for artillery only in 1785. A large number of topasses were being enrolled in the infantry arm. As in 1769, 500 topasses were enlisted, but due to a ban on Roman Catholics being accepted in the artillery, none was accepted for this arm.

Hostilities against Hyder Ali by the British started in 1768 and units and detachments from the Bombay artillery along with the infantry took part in all subsequent battles along with the artillery of Bengal and Madras.

Growth from 1785 to 1857 : Due to requirements of wars with Tipu Sultan in the south, the Anglo-Maratha wars and later the Anglo-Sikh wars, the artillery arm of the Bombay army was expanded but not at the same speed and scale as in the other two armies. Over the period, both native and horse artillery units were also raised. By 1857, the strength was as under :

(a) Foot artillery (European) — 12 companies

(b) Foot artillery (Native) — 12 companies

(c) Horse artillery (European) — 4 troops

(d) Horse artillery (Native) — Nil

Two salient features stand out from the above growth. First, the strength of the native foot artillery is at par with that manned by Europeans, a parity which was against the policy of the Directors and neither attempted nor achieved in Bengal or Madras. Secondly, unlike in these two armies, the horse artillery was European-manned only and no native units were raised.

The explanation for the first is that the Bengal army was being seriously affected adversely in discipline, and the morale of units had been shaken due to pandering to the high castes who formed the bulk of that army. The Bengal army, unlike the Madras and Bombay armies, was always difficult to handle because of high caste men. On 15 June 1850 , Sir Charles Napier, the Commander-in-Chief, wrote to the Duke of Wellington on the problem of caste : Instead of being discouraged it has been encouraged in the Bengal army. In the Bombay army, it is discouraged and that army is in better order than the Bengal army.

In the Madras army, because of the large expansion, fresh recruits of the right type were difficult to come by. In view of all these factors, the directors allowed expansion of the native artillery in Bombay to near parity with Europeans. They did, however, balance it to some extent by not having any native horse artillery.

The faith in the loyalty of the Bombay army appears to have been fully justified by subsequent events of the Revolt of 1857. Out of 12 native companies only two, the 3rd and 5th company of the 4th battalion, mutinied in Sind. Both were newly raised in 1843. In fact, in the case of the 3rd Company only a few men had mutinied.

European foot artillery : By 1785, a battalion of four companies had been raised. In 1782 three companies were sent to the south along with other reinforcements to deal with the war against Tipu Sultan. In April 1783, part of this force was attacked by Tipu at Bednur, causing heavy losses to the artillery and infantry, Forbes says : "Thus perished the flower of the Bombay Army". In 1792, a large Bombay force with four companies of artillery was sent in February to join Cornwallis at Seringapatam; it took part in action which led to a treaty.

In 1796, three companies took part under Wellesley for operations against Tipu and Seringapatam and in September 1803, two companies fought at the famous Battle of Assaye. In 1820, two battalions of five companies each were formed and by 1846, the total strength was four battalions of three companies each. In fact, in all, upto 1846, a total 14 companies was raised, but in 1820 two companies were reduced in order to help in the raising of horse artillery.

European horse artillery: The first troop was raised in 1811. Its great services in the Anglo-Maratha War in 1817 led to the formation of second troop in 1820 and two more were added in 1824. All of them fought with great distinction in Sind, Afghanistan, Central India, Punjab and in the Revolt of 1857.

Native foot artillery: The first company was raised in 1826 and by 1846, a total of 12 companies formed in four battalions were raised. The units took part in almost all actions of the British and were never left behind. They fought in Afghanistan, Multan, Punjab, Aden, Persia and the Revolt of 1857. During the actual battles they were either on their own or grouped with other units of horse artillery or European foot artillery and there is no record of their ever being considered less than their European counterparts in bravery or professionalism as the following events prove :

(a) In 1839, a Bombay force of infantry, 4th Company, 1st Battalion European artillery and 6th Company of native artillery seized the fort and harbour of Aden to ensure safe passage of shipping.

(b) In February 1840, a Bombay force of four Infantry Battalions and 1st Company of golandaz battalion was sent to capture Karachi. No European artillery was grouped with this force, although the infantry element had one European battalion.

(c) In May 1840, a Bombay Force was sent to Afghanistan to assist the forces of the Bengal Army. En route they found Ghazni very strongly held and it was decided to storm it. The artillery element—the 3rd and 4th troops of

horse artillery, 2nd company of 2nd European artillery and 1st Company of golandaz—"swept the ramparts at a range of 250 yards and rendered great service." The resistance was overcome without much difficulty.

(d) In 1856, a Bombay force was sent to Persia and met the Persian army at Khoosab. The artillery consisted of the following :

(a) 3rd and 4th troops horse artillery

(b) 2 companies, 1st European artillery

(c) 1 company, 2nd European artillery

(d) 4th company, 4th Native artillery

The battle led to the defeat of the Persian army. According to the eminent historian of the Bombay army, Sir Patrick Cadell, the battle was virtually fought by the cavalry and artillery.

Conclusion : The artillery units of the Bombay army, whether horsed, European-manned or native-manned, played a very important part in the conquest of India by the British and their subsequent retention of power. Although these units were mainly employed outside the presidency, their contribution in the success of British campaigns was significant, particularly in the reliability and loyalty of the troops to their employers. The role played by the native artillery when functioning independently or jointly with the European artillery showed without doubt that they were as good as the latter. The grouping of the Bombay force dispatched for the capture of Karachi included a European battalion which was totally dependent upon the native artillery, and confirms that the British had developed full faith in the proficiency of Indian gunners. The latter also proved their worth when operating jointly with British horse and foot artillery.

It is ironic thus that the display of such efficiency on the part of Indian gunners made the British more resolute after the Revolt of 1857 not to allow "such dangerous weapons" in the hand of Indians.

Appendix 'A'

Report on the Inspection of Datachment of 2nd and 3rd Company of Artillery Battalion Reviewed at Trichnopoly on 6 May 1771 By Brigadier General Joseph Smith

Officers	—	Properly armed. Salute well and in good time. Appear to be good at gun and mortar practice. Dressed clean but not uniform, part being in regimental and part in frocks.
Men	—	Of good size, well limbed, clean and well dressed.
Exercise	—	At the field pieces.
Firing	—	From six 6 pounders. A hundred round very briskly but not in very exact time, many tubes missing fire. From two 6 pounders with shot at the target, three rounds each. From a 4½ inch mortar, 5½ inch mortar, two 4½ inch and 5½ inch howitzers three rounds of live shell each, distance 650 yards. Shells from mortars burst very properly—part of the howitzer shells went dead.
Small arms	—	Clean and in good order.
Accoutrements	—	Good
Clothing	—	Good, clean and well fitted on.
Complaints	—	None

This detachment in good order and fit for service.

Signed

Trichnopoly — Joseph Smith

6 May 1977. — Brigadier General

EQUIPMENT AND MOBILITY

Although some sort of coordination between the three armies of the presidencies was attempted in 1796, distance and other political factors, ensured that they developed their own identity and characteristics. The organisation and equipment of the artillery of three armies thus varied to quite an extent. This study covers a period of 110 years, *i.e.* 1748 to 1857 during which major changes tool place as necessitated by military requirements.

1. Artillery Weapons

Guns and carriages: The so-called modern gun, which is breech loading with rifled barrels, was used only from 1855, when the Armstrong gun was 'invented' by William George Armstrong. All guns prior to these were muzzle loading and usually threw solid iron round shells and grapeshot. The new guns which threw elongated shell was adopted only in 1859.

The type of guns used were either made of iron or of brass. Brass guns were manufactured at Cossipore and supplied to all presidencies. However, all iron pieces were obtained from England. Even the shot and shells for iron guns were sent from England. Gun carriages were all made of teak and manufactured in each presidency under the supervision of an officer, generally from the artillery.

To facilitate commonality, in 1800, the Governor General gave his approval for constructing 6 pounder gun carriages for all three presidencies. The weight of the carriage of a 6 pounder field gun with limber and ammunition boxes was about one ton. The transportations of guns with their requirements of ammunition and other accessories was therefore a major problem, particularly in the case of heavy guns. For example, in 1770, a number of 18 and 24 pounder guns were received from England but were pronounced too heavy (the former weighed 40 to 41 cwt and latter from 49 to 51 cwt).

Types of weapons : Artillery weapons were of the following types :

(a) Light guns *i.e.* 3, 6, 9 and 12 pounders with a flat trajectory.

(b) Medium guns, *i.e.* 18 pounder with a flat trajectory.

(c) Heavy guns, *i.e.* 24 and 32 pounders with a flat trajectory.

(d) Howitzers of various calibres having shorter barrels and curved trajectory. These were very useful to fire into forts during siege warfare and also during field operations over their own troops and behind the enemy troops and defences.

(e) Mortars of various calibres performing the same role

as howitzers but with an even steeper trajectory. They were lighter and more mobile than guns.

(f) Carronades of various calibres generally employed in static garrisons and forts. These were short iron guns with no trunnions and were introduced in 1779.

(g) Rockets were introduced in 1815 but later discontinued in 1828 as they were found to be of little use in war.

Types of artillery : Based on role and type of guns held, the artillery was classified as under :

(a) *Infantry battalion guns :* These were three or six pounders held by infantry battalions on a scale of two per unit, and were manned by personnel of the battalions. Later, in the case of native units, they were manned by Europeans from the artillery units.

(b) *Cavalry regiment guns :* These were six pounders issued to cavalry regiments and manned by them. Known also as galloper guns, these were withdrawn on formation of horse artillery.

(c) *Foot artillery* : This was the basic artillery of the British having 6, 9, 12 and 18 pounder guns as well as light howitzers and mortars. These were drawn by bullocks and accompanied by field formations, except for the cavalry units. They could be handled with rapidity during actual fighting.

(d) *Light field artillery* : This was basically foot artillery but drawn by horses to give better mobility. (See Section 2)

(e) *Heavy field artillery* (See Section 2)

(f) *Heavy artillery* : This formed part of the siege and reserve artillery and was brought into action to dale with forts, fortifications and the enemy's artillery. It had 24 and 32 pounder guns, heavy howitzers and heavy mortars. A heavy gun could fire as many as 400 to 500 rounds in 24 hours or upto 60 per hour, allowing for in-between cooling and maintenance, as against four rounds per hour fired by Moghul guns. Thus a battery of six guns could fire upto 300 rounds at a specific point on the wall of a fort giving no respite to defenders to carry out any repair to the breech. It is not surprising, therefore, that quite often the defenders surrendered as soon as the guns opened fire or were brought into action.

(g) *Siege artillery* : This had heavy guns brought specifically into action for siege warfare. Sometimes this term is mixed up with 'siege train' which, in fact, includes not only siege artillery but also other components such as engineers, working parties and materials for siege.

(h) *Artillery park* : This term refers to reserve artillery which was available immediately to a commander over and above the integral artillery grouped with formations. This was placed under a separate artillery commander and the whole or part of it was brought into action to meet specific tactical requirements.

(i) *Horse artillery* : Mainly armed with 6 and 12 pounder guns and light howitzers, it worked closely with the cavalry, making the combination very formidable. Horse artillery was also used during normal operations with the infantry, both for attack and defence because of its very high mobility, as well as for independent actions. In protocol it was the seniormost arm of the army.

(j) *Post artillery* : This refers to guns fixed on forts and in garrisons.

(k) *Coast artillery* : Initially, all artillery was deployed near the sea, due to the location of British trading interests and fortifications. Such artillery was sometimes referred to as coast artillery. Later, when the British moved inland, it lost its importance.

(l) *Field train* : This term was used during initial formation of a regular artillery to denote a battery of light guns.

(m) *Mountain train/artillery* : These units were raised for operations in Afghanistan. They had light guns which could be broken up and carried on mules and were easy to handle (See Section 2).

(n) *Elephant artillery* : Heavy guns drawn by elephants instead of bullocks (See Section 2).

(o) *Camel artillery* : Light and medium guns drawn by camels (See Section 2).

2. Specialised Artillery

It is necessary to look at the special types of artillery units which were raised later to meet the specific needs of different operations. These included :

(a) Field batteries; *(b)* Heavy field batteries; *(c)* Elephant batteries; *(d)* Camel batteries; *(e)* Mountain batteries.

Field batteries : Because of the performance of horse artillery in battle, it was decided in the Bengal artillery to replace bullocks with horses in foot artillery units. An experimental field battery was ordered in 1817 which was equipped with 12 pounders. In 1818 ordered were issued to raise 17 such batteries equipped with eight guns : *(a)* 2 x 12 pounders; *(b)* 4 x 6 pounders; *(c)* 2 x 5½ inch howitzers. Each gun was to be drawn by six horses with the same number of wagons which made a total of 96 horses.

The policy of the Directors at home was to gradually replace horses with bullocks, but due to various reasons progress was quite slow, although the Directors reiterated the policy in 1834. The progress of raising and changes in the organisation were as under :

(a) 1817: Experimental field battery raised; *(b) 1818*: Three batteries with eight guns of mixed calibre raised : *(c) 1820* : One more battery raised; *(d) 1826* : One more battery raised at Dum Dum; *(e) 1826* : Orders received to have only 12 batteries instead of 17 as originally ordered in 1818; *(f) 1828* : The establishment of guns reduced from eight to six.

The target of 12 companies was never achieved. In 1845, just before the Sikh Wars, there was only four such batteries. Some of the batteries in between were converted into camel and elephant batteries. Light field batteries were found to be extremely useful in the British operation in Afghanistan from 1838 to 1842 and in the Anglo-Sikh wars.

Heavy field batteries : In July 1848, three such batteries to be drawn by elephants were raised in the Bengal artillery. Each battery was equipped with three guns (one 24 pounder and two 18 pounders). It was felt that elephants may not be reliable under all conditions, and bullocks were provided as standby. It was planned to provide one battery per division but this could not be carried out due to the advent of Anglo-Sikh wars. During the Revolt of 1857, ad hoc heavy field batteries with a minimum of two guns and some mortars were ordered to be taken with each column to reduce forts and help clear opposition.

Camel batteries : In 1835, one of the light field batteries was converted into a camel drawn battery. They were found to be sufficiently manageable and steady under fire. They walked four miles in an hour and trotted seven miles. One such battery marched from Nasirabad to Multan in 1830, sometimes travelling more than 30 miles in a day. Camels could drag even 18 pounder guns over sandy terrain. However, over wet and slippery places the camels were apt to sprain or dislocate the shoulder and hip joints. The camel battery was converted to a light field battery in 1852.

Mountain batteries : In 1814, because of the Nepal wars, Lord Hastings asked the Bengal artillery for some howitzers for hill service. Twelve pounder guns which could be broken up and separate parts carried coolies on bamboo poles were successfully tried. However, this was only an experiment and elephants were used instead, as they could go up very difficult ground.

In 1844, orders were issued to examine the possibility of raising units for service in the Frontier and Afghanistan. These were mountain batteries armed with four 12 pounder howitzers and four three pounder guns. These were native units which had the following establishment :

Subedar 1, Jemadar 2, Staff sergeants 2, (Europeans), Havildars 6, Naicks 6, Privates 88, Buglers 2, Sirdar Syce 36, Syce 132, Farriers 2, Grass cutters 120, Mules 168.

The first battery was raised in 1854 and one more was raised in 1857. Much later, after the Revolt of 1857, a number of mountain batteries were raised.

3. Number of Guns

The number of guns in an artillery company or a troop was not fixed for some considerable time during the early stages of the formation of the Company's artillery although later efforts were made to standardise it. The British army was reorganised after 1796 and efforts were made to have some uniformity in units and formations. The army was compelled by circumstances to operate on an "as required basis" and as such the number of guns accompanying a formation varied a fair amount. Some example of variations are as under :

(a) In 1781, the guns allotted to the reorganised army of Madras were as under :

  (i) No. 1 Brigade : 9 x 12 pounders; 5 x howitzers.

  (ii) No. 2 & 3 Brigades : 1 x 18 pounder; 1 x howitzer; 10 x 6 pounders.

  (iii) No. 4 & 5 Brigades; 10 x 6 pounders; 1 x howitzer.

(b) At the Battle of Plassey, Clive had eight guns and one howitzer.

(c) When No. 2 Company of the Bengal artillery was raised on 19 September 1758, it had an admix of 6 pounders (6), howitzers (1), 24 pounders (4), 18 pounders (4), 8 inch mortar (1) and 5½ inch mortars (1).

(d) In the Bengal horse artillery, a troop had 5 x 6 pounders and one howitzer whereas the other two presidencies had 4 x 6 pounders and two howitzers.

4. Mobility

Since the British, unlike Indian powers, considered the artillery essential for any operation, they ensured that guns were given the maximum mobility both during the approach to the battle area as well as during the actual fighting despite the problems of underdeveloped roads and the unsuitability of draught cattle for the guns as the former were found to be generally very weak. Prior to the first major battle fought by the British at Plassey, when reinforcements in the way of 12 guns and one howitzer arrived on 28 December 1756 from Madras at Mylapore, they had to be moved to Calcutta. Due to the poor condition of the roads and the absence of draught animals, the guns were dragged all the way by men over deep creeks and morasses. Clive, who fought the battle next day at Budge Bridge, writes that the "enemy was much alarmed at the quickness of our firing and startled at the appearance of our cannon which they could not imagine were transported over the ground we had passed at the night of 28/29 December." To give greater mobility to the guns, particularly in the thick of battle where the guns had to be manoeuvered to change formations and positions to meet tactical needs, each artillery unit was given a large number of lascars; one lascar company to one artillery company being normal. In quite a few cases many more lascars were attached. The following list indicates the requirement of horses for the carriage of guns and accessories and planned mobility :

(a) For horse artillery, the number of horses was as under :

(i) 6 pounder gun	—	6
(ii) Light howitzers	—	6
(iii) Tumbrils	—	24
(iv) Forge wagon	—	2
(v) Store cart	—	2

(b) For heavier guns the number of horses was as under :

(i) 18 pounder	—	8
(ii) 24 pounder	—	10
(iii) 10 inch howitzer	—	8
(iv) 10 inch mortar	—	6

(c) Horses required to transport 1000 rounds of ammunition were as under :

(i) 18 pounder	—	43
(ii) 24 pounder	—	57
(iii) 10 inch howiter	—	188
(iv) 10 inch mortar	—	188

One heavy gun could fire 400 to 500 rounds in 24 hours. As such, carriage of ammunition posed a logistical problem when a large number of guns were employed. For example, in six days, from 6 to 11 December 1807, at siege of Ganaori, which was considered a small operation, the following ammunition was expended :

(a)	18 pounder	—	2310
(b)	8 inch howitzer	—	79
(c)	5½ inch mortar	—	174

Again at the siege of Kamonah on 18 November 1807 alone the following ammunition was expended:

(a)	18 pounder	—	580
(b)	12 pounder	—	484
(c)	8 inch howitzer	—	269
(d)	5½ inch howitzer	—	339
(e)	5½ inch mortar	—	264

The average rate of movement of guns drawn by horses and cattle was :

(a) Horse drawn

(i)	30 minutes	—	2 miles
(ii)	1 hour	—	4 miles
(iii)	4 hours	—	8 miles
(iv)	10 hours	—	16 miles

(b) Cattle drawn

15 miles a day (the same as for infantry).

The above was only a planning guide and varied in the different presidencies. In the Bengal horse artillery, every horse pulling guns and wagons had a rider, whereas in the other two presidencies horses of draught were not ridden. For this reason, a troop of guns in Bengal had 178 horses whereas in the other two armies, it was authorised 230 horses.

Whenever forced or rapid moves were required the above guidelines were exceeded by a wide margin as the following examples indicate :

(a) On 14 July 1799, a force of two cavalry regiments, 400 infantry and light guns of Bengal Artillery under Colonel Dalrympla marched 40 miles in 24 hours to deal with Dhoondiah Waugh who had escaped with his force

after the Battle of Seringapatam and asserted his right to the sovereignty. The latter was defeated in battle.

(b) In September 1799, Colonel Sentleger with a force of 4 guns, cavalry and infantry was sent to capture Soonda. He was complemented by his commander for "having brought his troops and guns though jungles, over swamps and by the worst roads that I have seen in India.

(c) On 20 Feb. 1818, Smith with a force of horse artillery and cavalry came up with the Peshwa mounted forces at Ashti and completely scattered them. The Bombay Horse Artillery had marched 2250 miles in 7 months.

(d) In February 1760, Shah Alam, the Moghul Emperor, attacked Patna. The British sent a force of artillery and infantry under Capt. Knox, an artillery officer, to proceed to Patna by forced march by a byepass route through jungles during April, the hottest part of the year. The force marched 300 miles in 13 days with guns over unmade road with the help of troops to assist the slow-moving draught cattle.

5. Draught Cattle

Although the use of horses draught for guns was introduced much later in the period of this study, the British artillery was mainly dependent on bullocks for draught right uptil the Revolt of 1857. This posed a major problem, particularly during operation in the south as the availability of suitable animals was severely limited. In May 1791, the British army under Lord Cornwallis made contract with Tipu Sultan at Seringapatam. Several of the draught cattle had died, supplies had failed and bad weather conditions had combined with non-arrival of the Maratha army (which was to cooperate with the British). They thus decided to retire. Because of the lack of animals, guns had to be abandoned and burst. This was the biggest disaster in the annals of British artillery in India.

The animals found in the south were of inferior quality. Whereas ten were required pull a tumbril here, of those bred in the north-west of Bengal only six were adequate. The quality of animals from Mysore was very good and after the subjugation of Mysore in 1799, the establishment of draught cattle belonging to Tipu was taken over to be maintained as a breeding steed.

The problem of draught cattle, however, remained. In 1825 it was belatedly decided in the Madras Army to put an end to the ad hoc system of engaging and dismissing cattle and their drivers on an "as required" basis. On 28 December an order for the proper regulation of drivers and drought bullock was issued. Given below are some extracts :

The Honourable Governor in Council having resolved that 8 companies, or karkhanahs of drivers and draught bullocks, consisting of 1 darogah, 4 chowdries, 80 drivers, and 160 draught bullocks each, shall be raised for the service of the European Foot Artillery under this Presidency, had been pleased to publish the following regulations for general information :

"The drivers and cattle are to be under the general control of the senior officer of artillery wherever they may be stationed; but in special charge of the officers commanding the companies of foot artillery to which they may be attached".

The pay and batta of the artillery drivers are fixed as follows :

	Monthly pay			*Daily batta*		
	Rs.	A.	P.	A.	P.	C.
1 Darogah	17	0	0	2	5	87
1 Chowdry	12	0	0	1	10	40
1 Driver	6	8	0	1	2	93

Batta to be allowed in the field, at field stations, or when marching.

The drivers to be subject to the rules of military discipline and the articles of war, and are not to be discharged from the service but under authority from headquarters.

The drivers to be allowed medical and to benefit by the regulations for the issue of grain, or compensation money, and family certificates, the same as the regular troops. Those who may be disabled in the execution of their duty, or wounded in action to be eligible to the pension list, and the families of drivers killed in action will be entitled to pensions, the same as the heirs of sepoys.

The companies or karkhanahs of cattle, consisting in the first instance of bullocks of all serviceable ages from six upwards, to be formed and delivered to the artillery by the Commissariat, and to be annually recruited by bullocks not younger than six years of age, from the breeding establishment in Mysore, on the requisition of headquarters, though the Quarter Master General of the Army.

No standard height is as yet fixed for the bullocks; and the present allotment to all descriptions of ordnance, and ordnance carriages, shall continue in force until further orders.

Each draught bullock is allowed 2 seers of gram, and 14 lb of dry forage in the field or marching with guns or carriages; and half a seer of common salt per month.

In March 1826 the uniform of artillery drivers was ordered to be blue, faced with red.

Battle Baptism : The drivers of the newly formed bullock companies gave an excellent account of themselves during battle. Wilson had paid glowing tributes to their service. He wrote :

> The European troops and batteries were frequently driven by Madras natives who uniformly behaved in the most gallant manner. For instance, at Lucknow in December 1857 where the guns of the E. Troop were recorded by Lord Clyde to have been fought with great ability. Major (now Major-General) Chamier wrote of them thus :
>
> "I served subsequently during the campaign with Major Cotter's Battery the drivers of which were Madras Natives. We were engaged in several actions under General Sir T. H. Franks on our march from Banares to Lucknow; also during the siege of Lucknow under Lord Clyde; and afterwards in the pursuit of Koor Singh, and in several engagements under Sir Edward Lugard at, and in the vicinity of Azimghur, and the Judgespore jungles. The conduct of all Battery Drivers was soldierlike and brave,

> and I never witnessed a single instance to the contrary. They drove fearlessly and well, and their conduct was favourably noticed in my presence by Colonel Maberly, R. A., who commanded the Artillery with General Frank's force".

The problem of draught cattle for guns was mainly in the Madras army. In the Bengal and Bombay armies, particularly in Bengal, the quality and availability was much better and no major problems were faced in this regard. Even before the formation of Karkhanah companies in the Madras army in 1810, 26 companies of ordnance drivers, each of 5 sirdars and 105 drivers, were raised in the Bengal army.

ARTILLERY IN SIEGE WARFARE

A siege by Indian powers mainly depended upon strict investment and starving out the garrison, since the lack of effective artillery meant the walls could not be breached. Although the Moghuls had heavy guns, because of their limited rate of fire and the absence of a proper technique (*i.e.* system of parallels), the use of howitzers and mortars to fire into the fort and the concentration of fire by heavy guns under the cover of rest of light artillery, it was rare that their artillery could breach the walls or gates of a fort.

Lakes in his *Sieges of Madras Army* makes telling remarks on the technique or lack of technique of the Moghul Army on their concept of carrying out a siege and the use of guns :

> When one of their armies sits down before a place, the object appears rather to be to harass the besieged and weary them out by a strict blockade, than to effect an entrance by breaching the walls; for although guns are used, they are placed at such a distance from the town, out of musket shot, and not always in battery, that their effect is uncertain, and even this desultory fire is only kept up at intervals during the day; for at night, to guard against the consequences of a sally; the guns are always withdrawn to the camp; and this ridiculous process is continued till the besieged are tired out and a compromise is entered into.

1. Technique

The artillery played a dominating role in siege operations and a special technique was adopted to capture the forts. Basically the tactics were as under :

(a) The fortress was invested by a force superior in number to those besieged and the troops deployed all round so as to cut off all supplies and reinforcements.

(b) Surprise was maintained till the final attack to keep the enemy guessing on the point of final attack.

(c) A "Base of operation" where all supplies were stored and "Line of operations" from it to the army was established.

(d) The Artillery Commander, with the advice of the Engineer, put up a plan of attack to the Force Commander which was then given the final shape, with particular reference to the number and places of breaches to be made by artillery, the details of assault columns and the plan for approach to the walls both artillery and infantry by the "techniques of parallels" or by successive battery positions firing to find weak spots.

Role of artillery : The role of artillery followed a particular sequence :

(a) First the guns mounted on forts were silenced and defenders on ramparts were kept under fire.

(b) Then the garrison was harassed by firing mortars and howitzers into the fort, causing casualties to personnel and damage to defences in an attempt to break their morale and will to fight.

(c) After this, the artillery was deployed for breach outside the range of fortress guns in specially protected trenches and the fire of the enemy was kept suppressed. This was normally about 600 yards from the walls of the fort. Along with gun batteries so deployed, the infantry elements also moved in these trenches or those separately built for them close by.

(d) The guns and infantry were then progressively moved forward by making a second "parallel" trench and approaching the "zigzags" joining it. The guns were finally placed at a parallel from where they would start breaching operations. Normally the last artillery parallel was about 300 yards from the walls but the actual distance was decided by the type of guns available and the strength of the walls to be breached. The guns had to be brought so close, as in those days, they had low muzzle velocity and at longer distance the remaining velocity of the shots would make them ineffective against walls. Secondly, it was essential to bring very accurate fire on the preselected point and guns at longer range would not be effective for breaching. From the last gun parallel, forward trenches for infantry were prepared from where the assault would be launched.

(e) During the actual assault through the breach, a number of artillery parties invariably accompanied to operate captured guns of the enemy, spike them or capture them. Sometimes guns with crew were taken inside during assault to help overcome resistance within the fort

A sketch showing the system of attack by parallels is given below :

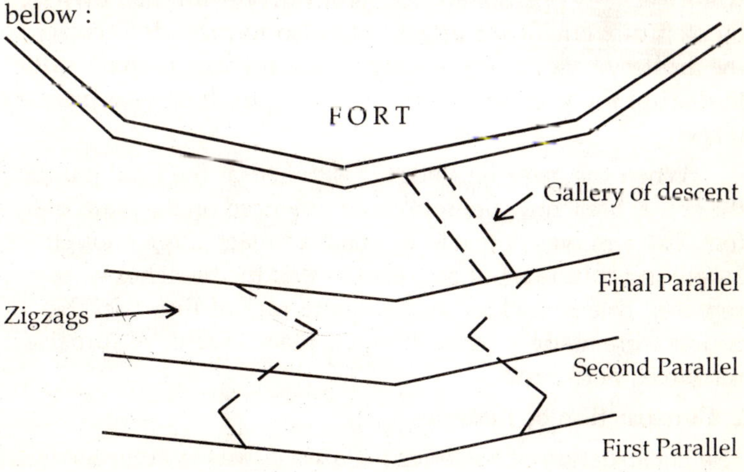

(*a*) First parallel about 600 yards from the fort for first gun position.

(*b*) Second parallel about 450 yards away for second gun position.

(*c*) Third parallel about 300 yards away for final gun position.

(*d*) Zigzag trenches for communication.

(*e*) Galleries for movement of infantry for final assault.

Obviously, the first phase of operations was to deploy the guns in the first parallel as soon as possible; without this deployment, the fire of enemy artillery and garrison could not be suppressed, short of firing into the fort itself by mortars and howitzers. The size of artillery frontage depended upon the frontage presented by the fortress. The guns had to fire at right angles to this frontage. Normally one battery was required to cover every face of the work that could interfere with the approach. The number of guns required for the fortress mainly depended upon the construction of the fort, and not the number of guns on the ramparts of the fort.

The batteries in the first parallel having formed the base remained there to provide fire cover to the batteries being constructed at the second forward parallel. The infantry element was invariably positioned alongside not only for their own step by step movement for attack, but also to provide security to the artillery bases as the enemy would invariably make sallies to disrupt the preparations for attack, guns being his primary target.

When the guns had been positioned at the final parallel, the actual breaching operations commenced on the walls of the fort. The aim was not only to make a breach large enough for assaulting columns but also ensure that the breaches were not repaired due to lack of an adequate rate of fire. Breaches of course were made at more than one place to achieve surprise if resources permitted.

2. Construction of Batteries

The construction of batteries for a siege was a complex task.

The following example provides a description of the nature of the task: in December 1807, a small fort at Ganaori had to be attacked. The batteries were finally erected at 336 years. The guns available were as under :

(a) 6 x 18 pounders, 2 x 12 pounders, 2 x 8 inch howitzers, 2 x 5½ inch mortars, 1 x 5½ inch howitzer.

The shape of battery was as under :

(a) *Deployment*

(i) 6 x 18 pounders in centre

(ii) Mortars on left flank

(iii) 12 pounders and howitzer on right flank

(b) Length — 153 feet

(c) Height of parapet — 7½ feet

(d) Length of merlon inside — 15 feet

(e) Inner face: Composed of gabions 3 feet 8 inches high, 3 feet in diametre filled with earth well rammed. Outside layers of sand bags 3 feet thick; space between gabions and sand bags well rammed feet in breadth. Total thickness of parapet 12 feet.

(f) Fascines of length 9, 6, 5 & 4 feet long. Length of fascines in each row :

(i) First row — 6 & 9 feet

(ii) Second and third row — 5 & 9 feet

(iii) Fourth to sixth row — 4 & 9 feet

(iv) Seventh and eighth row — 6 & 6 feet

(v) Ninth row — 5 feet

(g) Embrasures: Covered with bamboos laid over and fastened down with hooked of crooked pins. Wood frontlets 4 inch thick were used in front of breech of guns as protection for gun crew. They were found covered with match lock shot of enemy and saved many lives.

(h) Flank batteries were sunk 3 feet below the level of soil;

they were 7½ feet high. Thickness of merlon 12 feet made up of 3 feet of gabion, and 9 feet of fascines. Sides of embrasures were covered with buffalo hides to prevent them from catching fire. They were kept constantly wet.

(i) Battery magazines were sunk 6 feet, the roofs being supported by strong beams and planks and covered with tarpaulins and earth laid over these. The entrance from battery was about 8 feet in length and turned off at right angles to the magazine. Only one day's ammunition was kept which was replenished every night.

The daily expenditure of ammunition makes for interesting reading.

	18 pounders		*8 inch*	*5½ inch*
	Shot	*Case*	*howitzers*	*mortar*
6 December	364	30	—	—
7 December	470	—	—	—
8 December	333	11	—	35
9 December	386	12	27	63
10 December	330	—	26	28
11 December	362	12	26	48
Total	2245	65	79	174

The sequence of operations was simple. The breaching battery opened up on the 6th, the other two on the 9th and 10th and on the 11th the besiegers abandoned the fort in the evening. The operation to capture Ganaori was rather simple in that only one battery position was prepared and the number of guns involved was not many. When heavy guns were deployed the preparation of successive battery positions and the supply of ammunition posed a complex problem.

Alternative tactics : Another siege operation carried out against the fort of Deeg in December 1804 gives an idea about the number of gun positions required to achieve surprise as well as to give covering fire. In this case the system of parallels was not resorted to, but guns were fired from successive positions around the fort to find weak spots.

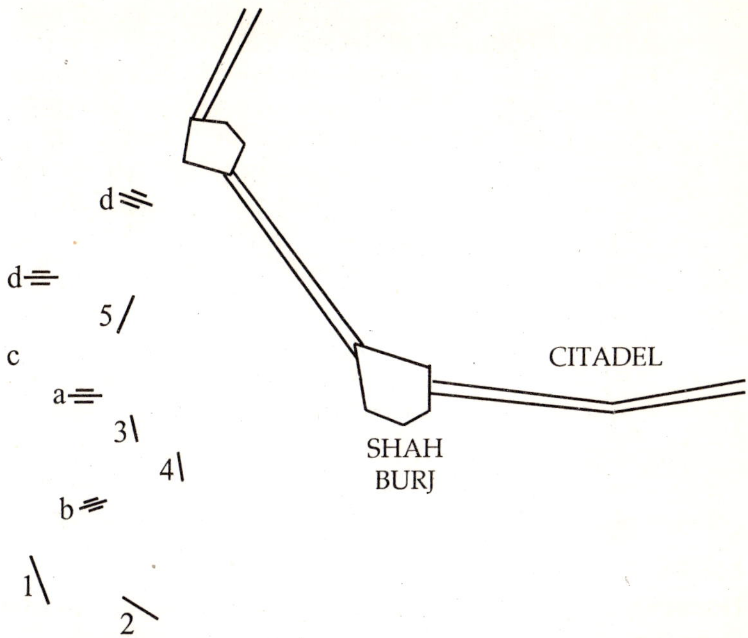

The ramparts varied from 25 to 36 feet in height and carried 31 guns of various calibers from 74 to 4 pounders. Outside the fort, the garrison had 21 guns and howitzers. Citadel mounted 28 guns from 60 to one pounders and 20 zamburaks or one pounder swivels.

The sequence of artillery deployment and action was :

(a) Force with 6 x 6 pounders and 4 x 12 pounders moved to a grove on 125 December and established themselves about 800 yards from Shah Burj. A parallel was constructed (No. 1) for mortar battery and for 2 x 6 pounders on the right (No. 2).

(b) On the night of 14 December, a breaching battery of 6 x 18 pounders was set up at a new parallel (No. 3) along with 4 x 5½ inch mortars (No. 4) on its right.

(c) 2 x 2 pounders were placed *(a)* & *(b)* adjacent to No. 3 & 4 parallels to provide covering fire.

(d) On 20 December, a new position was prepared (No. 5)

for 3 x 18 pounders as the fire of 6 x 12 pounders was not very effective due to fire of guns of defenders and interference from their sallying parties. These three guns opened fire on the walls under the covering fire of several 12 x 6 pounder guns placed at *(c)* & *(d)*. The fire was effective and a practical breach was made and on 23 December an assault was carried out. One officer with a party of artillerymen went with the assault to spike and secure the guns. Later, an officer with 2 x 12 pounder guns was sent in to blow the gates of citadel, but before the guns could be brought into action, truce was declared and the garrison evacuated the place.

The siege of Deeg was carried out not by a system of parallels moving forward but by preparing gun positions at different places to find weak spots and then effecting a breach.

3. Artillery during Assault

The artillery parties invariably accompanied the leading assaulting columns. For example, in 1764 the British ordered a siege against Mohomed Yusuf in the south. After breaches were made by the artillery, the orders issued for attack by their Commander, Major Charles Campbell, included the following :

(a) *Right flank.* A party of a non-commissioned officer and 6 artillerymen to move with their haversacks, few charges of grapeshot fixt for 3 & 6 pounds, tubes, sponges and rammers, lightened match in a pot and portfires ready.

(b) *Right flank.* A party of a non-commissioned officer and 6 artillerymen with 3 pounder grape fixt and all necessaries to follow the troopers to use the gun of the enemies which is supposed to be there.

The role of these artillery parties was to secure the enemy's guns in the fort, and use them during the fire fight or to blow them up so that they could not be used again. Quite often, actual guns were taken inside the fort during assault to help the assault columns. An example of an assault where guns accompanied the columns and helped in overcoming resistance inside was the capture of Aligarh fort in September 1803. The main entrance to the fort, a massive gate, was blown open by the fire of 12 pounder guns. Thereafter, the storming party was accompanied by guns and succeeded in opening two more gates inside the fort by firing at point blank range. The last gate was however too strong but again its wicket gate was blown open by the gun and the assault went through. The guns throughout were manhandled inside the fort and required exceptional courage as unlike the accompanying infantry soldiers who could defend themselves, the gunners had to move and work their guns. In this assault the casualties of the officer and gun crew were 2 gunners and 4 lascars killed and 1 officer, 7 gunners and 1 lascar wounded.

The action of artillerymen who suffered very heavy casualties was commended by the Governor General. The Duke of Wellington declared the capture of Aligarh as "One of the most extraordinary feats".

4. Impact of British Guns in Siege warfare

In almost all cases, with a few notable exceptions, British guns managed to force the defenders to surrender or made effective breaches for the assault to go in, as is shown by the following examples :

(a) After the Battle of Sabraon in February 1846, the Kiladar (Fort Commander) of Kot Kangra refused to surrender. A force with a siege train was sent in. The Kiladar held on but when the guns reached there after having to be dragged there with great difficulty, the Kiladar gave up without fighting.

(b) In 1838, the British Government assumed administrative control of the territories of Jhansi. The mother of the late Raja decided to give fight from the fort but as soon as the British artillery arrived and prepared to open fire the Rani and her followers evacuated the place on 5 January 1839.

(c) In 1803, the Raja of Kalpi put up a strong opposition to

the British move in Bundelkhand from the fort, but no sooner had the British opened up with only three guns (2 x 18 pounders and 1 x howitzer), than the Raja capitulated.

(d) When the British Grand Army (under General Lake) reached Agra in October 1803 they faced the great fort which carries the inscription : "The ruby encircled fort built up to heaven." After severe fighting, the British secured the outskirts of the fort. To capture the fort, which had a large number of guns from 1500 pounders to one pounders, the British completed the deployment of their guns by 17 October as under :

(aa) 8 x 18 pounders and 4 howitzers were erected within 350 yards.

(bb) One Enfilading Battery of 4 x 12 pounders was erected on the right flank.

(cc) One Enfilading Battery of 4 x 12 pounders was erected on left flank.

(e) On 16 December 1803 a treaty was concluded with Ambaje Rao, a chief under Sindhia, who held the fort of Gwalior. When the British forces arrived at the fort to take possession the Kiladar refused to surrender. The force commander asked for the battering train and on its arrival opened up with their guns and a breach was made on 4 February 1804. The garrison thereafter surrendered without having to be stormed.

As soon as the guns opened up, the garrison capitulated and marched out on the morning of the next day. It is indeed surprising that the fort surrendered so easily as the number of guns held in the fort were 162 including the 1500 pounder "Great Gun of Agra".

Not all forts of the Indian powers surrendered so easily. The British laid siege to the fort of Bharatpore in January 1805. The artillery available was as under :

(a) 6 x 18 pounders

(b) 7 x 12 pounders

(c) 48 x 6 pounders

(d) 8 x 5½ inch howitzers

(e) 2 x 4½ inch howitzers

(f) 4 x 8 inch mortars

(g) 4 x 5½ inch mortars

The guns were fired from 2 to 9 January but the British managed to make only two unsatisfactory breaches and that too at the wrongly selected place. The actual assault which was launched in a hurry cost the British 446 killed and 2479 wounded, which included 16 officers (killed) and 93 (wounded). The failure has been attributed to various reasons such as lack of intelligence, inadequate reconnaissance and want of judgement. Cardew adds that "Lake undertook the siege with totally inadequate means with respect of siege equipment and the number of artillerymen and pioneers at his disposal." This view is not borne out by facts. The British had an adequate number of guns available. The lack of planning and the unsatisfactory nature of breaches seems to have come about because of complacency on the part of British as they had got used to forts surrendering the moment their guns appeared or when just a few rounds had been fired. Combined with this, there is no doubt that the defenders put up a very fine defence. The brother of the Raja was killed by a shot from a British gun when he was visiting the soldiers who were manning the breach. Even during the second siege of Bharatpore in 1825-1826 when a whole artillery division with a siege train of 110 guns, 6 troops horse artillery, 2 light field batteries and 8 companies of foot artillery, the guns could not make a real impression on the fortifications and mining had to be resorted to. Again in 1792, the British were unsuccessful in capturing Seringapatam Fort held by Tipu who put up a brave defence.

An interesting incident relating to siege warfare occurred in June 1767, when the British attacked the fort of Washinellor in the south held by Polygers. The British commander, Colonel Campbell, reported after the artillery opened up :

On the 19th, the gun battery was opened at daybreak and

began to knock off the defences of the towers flanking the curtain I intended to breach, which being built of sun dried bricks cemented with clay, the shot penetrated but did no great damage.... That evening although upwards of 500 shot had been thrown in, I did not judge the breach practicable.... The contempt of death they have acquired is inconceivable. While the 4 guns played upon the breach, they were repairing it very calmly with palmyras and heaps of straw, nor did the survivors seem in the least concerned at the fate of their companions, some of whom every discharge from the battery tore to pieces.

5. Conclusion

The British in India were pioneers in the employment of artillery for siege warfare despite the fact that the Moghuls not only had guns prior to 1748 but also had much heavier guns. However, the latter depended upo starving garrisons or on the treachery of defenders in letting the attackers in. Sieges were long-drawn out affairs and sometimes lasted more than one year. It now appears surprising that Indian defenders of forts gave up so easily whenever British guns appeared on the scene. Part of this reaction was purely psychological (*i.e.* fear of the artillery) but psychology cannot be lasting unless the artillery was really effective. Cases of forts surrendering due to fear of British artillery lasted throughout the period of this study (1748 to 1857) with only a few exceptions.

The role of the British artillery in overcoming opposing powers by cracking open the main bastions of their military power (which invariably centred on their forts), was crucial to the conquest of India by the British.

HORSE AND ROCKET ARTILLERY

Background : During the early period of their expansion, the British depended mainly on their infantry and European manned artillery to fight their battles against Indian powers; the latter, in turn, were mainly dependent upon their cavalry with infantry and artillery relegated to supporting arms. During the Anglo-Mysore wars, although the British were victorious, the absence of cavalry was flet. To make their army more balanced, during the post-reorganisation of their armies in 1796, this arm was gradually expanded and regiments with six troops each were raised in all three presidencies.

The British had noted that the artillery of Indian powers suffered from a serious drawback, in that their drought cattle pulling the guns could not keep pace with the movements of cavalry during advance and retreat and therefore had to be left behind. The three arms of those days had their own built-in characteristics. The infantry had some mobility, very limited fire power and high shock action during the final charge. The cavalry had high mobility, very high shock action but very limited fire power. The artillery had some mobility, very high fire power and high shock action.

The limited fire power of the infantry was made up by the presence of the artillery, and both had about the same mobility except in certain types of terrain where guns could not be employed. To make up for the lack of fire power of the cavalry, it was imperative to have an artillery which had some mobility with it. The British therefore decided to raise horse artillery units which, in due course, occupied the pride of place in their armies as "Right of the Line" or the seniormost arm of the British army, a protocol which is observed even now.

By virtue of its mobility, fire power and shock action, the horse artillery was to play a crucial role in the operations of the armies of the East India Company. The above does not only apply to the British horse artillery. Speaking of the native horse artillery, Cardew wrote that "the irregular cavalry in the period before the Revolt seems on the whole to have shared with the horse artillery the distinction of being the most efficient service of the native arm." This was praise indeed, given that the British had an inbuilt prejudice against natives manning their artillery and also because the native horse artillery formed only a small part of the British army which had a very large native element in their cavalry and infantry

1. Experimental Horse Artillery

On 19 June 1797, the Governor General ordered on the authority of the Court that an experimental horse artillery be organised with a view to ascertaining how far such an establishment could be useful for service with the army in India.

The experimental horse artillery was still being raised when it was ordered to proceed on an expedition to Egypt along with other units of the Royal Artillery and the artillery of the Company. The horse artillery had a portion of the bodyguard attached to it under the command of Capt. Brown of the Bengal Artillery. It consisted of the following :

(a)	*Horse artillery (under raising)*		
	Officer	—	1
	Conductor	—	1
	Sergeants	—	3
	Corporals	—	3
	Gunners	—	6
	Matrosses	—	14
	Farrier	—	1
(b)	*Golandaz*		
	Havildars	—	2
	Naiks	—	2
	Privates	—	20
(c)	*Others*		
	Lascars	—	43
	Sycye	—	9
	Grass cutters	—	9
	Horses	—	9
(d)	*Bodyguard*		
	Jemadar	—	1
	Havildars	—	2
	Naicks	—	2
	Troopers	—	22
	Lascars	—	12
	Sycre	—	27
	Grass cutters	—	27

The horse artillery also had the establishment of quartermasters and artificers. The establishment itself is interesting in that it had a mix of European and native gunners.

It is obvious that the golandaz in this case were provided to man the guns also, as lascars have been provided separately.

The expeditionary force however saw no action and returned to India in August 1802. Much valuable experience was gained however. The horse artillery troop lost all their horses for want of water and guns had to be carried on camels for some time. After its return the horse artillery was refitted and joined the army in 1804 under General Lake.

2. Guns With Cavalry Units

Well before the advent of the horse artillery, the need was felt for cavalry units to have some guns functioning with them all along to compensate for the lack of fire power. It was therefore ordered on 16 April 1786 :

> "When the battalions of European and Native infantry or regiments of cavalry are commanded to take the field for service, they are to be equipped with two field pieces each; two tindals and twenty-eight lascars are also to be attached for working the Artillery and one European non-commissioned officer and eight privates for pointing the guns and taking care of the ammunition and stores."

The guns attached to units were all 6 pounders.

In 1819, however, the above system was cancelled and the following orders issued on 8 May :

> The Governor in Council is pleased to direct that the galloper guns shall no longer be considered to form a component part of a regiment of dragoons or cavalry, and that the guns and establishments attached to them be accordingly discontinued from the date of this order.

The reasons given for the change were :

> The introduction of galloper guns as a component part of regiments of cavalry was an experimental measure, intended as a substitute for horse artillery. For several years, these guns, when in action, were placed along the line in the intervals between the several corps, but this system was discontinued, and the cavalry guns were placed in battery, sometimes alone, and sometimes with the artillery guns. In March 1815, it was directed that

> whenever cavalry guns were brigaded, or brought to act together in battery, the command of them should be given to an artillery officer. This arrangement, although a considerable improvement, was still far from satisfactory, for when the gallopers came to be placed in battery with the horse artillery, their inferiority was always conspicuous, and their want of proper organisation rendered the union incomplete and inconvenient. The artillery officer in command had no knowledge of the men, and there was much difficulty in assimilating the various systems of discipline, and practice which obtained amongst the several regiments. For these reasons, the Commander-in-Chief, when revising the organisation of the cavalry and artillery in 1818, recommended the abolition of the establishment of artillery attached to regiments of dragoons, and native cavalry, and a corresponding increase to the establishment of the horse artillery.

With the establishment of a regular horse artillery and the need to ensure that cavalry units were not left without artillery fire power, fresh orders were issued on 13 January for attaching regular horse artillery to cavalry units :

> The plan adopted by Government for attaching flying artillery to the cavalry corps having been communicated to the heads of regiments respectively, the Commander-in-Chief is now pleased to direct that the detail of European artillery and gun lascars to be attached to each regiment be sent to the several corps from the 1st and 2nd battalions of artillery agreeably to the following arrangements, *viz.*, 1 Lieutenant—Fireworker, 1 Serjeant, 1 Corporal, 1 Syrang, 2 Second Tindals and 20 Lascars for each regiment of European dragoons, and 1 Serjeant, 1 Gunner, 1 First Tindal, and 18 Lascars for each regiment of native cavalry.

The Commandants of the battalions of artillery were directed to select the most active and intelligent non-commissioned officers and men for this duty.

3. Baptism of Horse Artillery

Lieutenant General Lake took over as Commander-in-Chief in

1801 and he paid special attention to combining the movement of cavalry and horse artillery. He was also very particular that cavalry regiments must have their own galloper guns for immediate artillery support. In 1803, when the main army under him moved out for operations against the Mahrattas its three cavalry units, 27 Light Dragoons, 2 native Cavalry and 3 native Cavalry had six guns with them. The same guns distinguished themselves during the action at Laswarse in November 1803 against the Mahrattas.

On its return from Egypt the experimental horse artillery and refit joined as a horse artillery troop under Lake. The first real combined action of the horse artillery and cavalry took place in November 1804, when after the defeat at Deeg, Holkar was being pursued by Lake. The former, while camping for the night at a village short of Mainpuri, was attacked by horse artillery and cavalry only on first light which made him flee from Mainpuri leaving more than 3,000 dead, the British losses being two killed and 20 wounded. Even allowing for exaggeration, the casualties must have been quite high as the attack combined all the main principles of attack such as surprise, fire power and shock action. In his despatches, Lake wrote to the Governor General : "I have great satisfaction in reporting to your lordship the very meritorious conduct of corps of horse artillery who by the rapidity of their movements were able to do great execution."

In due course the horse artillery became the most potent arm of the British whether manned by Europeans or Indians and whether operating on their own or in combination with cavalry or infantry. The following examples highlight this :

(a) *Sobraon—10 February 1846.* Sir Herbert Edwards, who was first-hand witness to an attack by a Brigade on the left, describes it as "beyond comparison, the finest attack of the campaign." The artillery galloped up and delivered their fire within 300 yards of the enemy's batteries and the infantry charged with bayonets and carried the outworks without firing a single shot.

(b) *Chillianwala—13 January 1849.* In this crisis, when

everything seemed to frown on the Bengal Army, the behaviour of the Bengal Horse Artillery was superb... Never did it render more valuable, more efficacious service to its country, never did it tend more to save a rash and headstrong general from the defeat he deserved than on that memorable 13th January. According to Cardew, the action of the horse artillery was the salvation of the whole Division.

4. Raising of Regular Horse Artillery

Based on the great success of the experimental horse artillery of Bengal during operations, orders were issued in April 1805 for the Madras army to raise a unit to be composed of drafts of selected men from the artillery and native cavalry. By a General Order of 6 January 1806, it was ordered that the unit was to be designated as "The Squadron of Horse Artillery" and was to be composed of both Europeans and Natives, the respective nomenclature being given as "First Half Squadron" and "Second Half Squadron".

The establishment of personnel and equipment authorised was as under :

(a) *Personnel—First Half Squadron*

Captain	—	1
Lieutenants	—	2
Lieutenant Fireworkers	—	2
Assistant Surgeon	—	1
Sergeants	—	5
Gunners	—	10
Matrosses	—	82
Native Trumpter	—	1
Native Farriers	—	2

(b) *Personnel—Second Half Squadron*

Lieutenant	—	1
Second Lieutenant	—	1
Subedar	—	1
Jemadar	—	1
Havildars	—	4

Naickes	—	4
Privates	—	70
Trumpter	—	1
Farrier	—	1
Recruit boys	—	2
Horse keepers	—	32
Horses	—	83
Grass cutters	—	84

(c) *Non-effective staff*

Adjutant and Quartermaster	—	1
Sergeant Major	—	1
Quatermaster Sergeant	—	1
Riding Master	—	1
Rough Riders	—	2
Drill Corporal	—	1
European Farriers	—	2

(d) *Ordnance and Animals Equipment*

	Horses In draught	*To carry men*
2 x 12 Pounders	12	6
4 x 6 Pounders	24	12
2 x 5.5 Inch Howitzers	12	6
2 x Tumbrils (17)	48	24
1 x Forge Cart	2	—
1 x Store Cart	2	—
1 x Spare Carriage	4	—
Horses for riders	—	57
Spare horses	18	—
Total	122	105

Operations of horse artillery : The raising of the horse artillery in Madras came none too soon. A force under Lieutenant Colonel Doveton consisting of one troop of horse artillery, two regiments of cavalry and three infantry battalions was sent to Candrish in 1808 (Khandesh) to deal with a confederacy formed by three dependents of Holdar, Mohiput Rao Holdar, Wahid Ali Khan Bungush and Daudin Khan who wanted to take advantage of the confusion following Holdar's disability. The force marched 100 miles in 48 hours which would not have been possible if it had had foot artillery pulled by bullocks as against horse artillery which could keep pace with the movements and manoeuvres of the cavalry. The force inflicted a defeat on the confederacy after contact and battle.

In 1808, an expeditionary force was ordered to be assembled for the purpose of taking possession of the island of Karrack in the Persian Gulf. Apart from other troops, Madras sent elements from the newly raised troop of the native horse artillery as part of the contingent. They did proceed overseas but the actual operation did not take place and they returned to Madras in September 1812. An interesting aspect of the reputation earned by the native horse artillery was that on the recommendation of the successive British Ministers in Persia and by the Commander-in-Chief, Subedar Shaik Moideen Bahadur of this troop was presented with the gold medal of the "Lion and Sun" by the Prince Royal, Abbas Mirza, and the British government gave a pension of 110 and 50 pagodas a month to his family on his death. He was also presented with a horse and a palanquin and grant of land. This was very generous pension as a Subedar of native artillery was otherwise authorised a pension of 8 pagodas per month.

Redesignation : In 1809, the Squadron of Horse Artillery of two troops was redesignated "The Corps of Horse Artillery" with three troops; two Europeans and one native. Its organisation was revised suitably to man the following armament :

	Old establishment	*New establishment*
6 pounders	4	10
12 pounders	2	2
5.5 inch howitzer	2	2
Total	8	14

Disbandment of native portion : In 1810, however, the native portion was disbanded because of changes in policy. While disbanding the troop, the Government was generous in that, non-commissioned officers were promoted as Jemadars in native cavalry units and privates were sent as havildars in the cavalry. Unfit privates were sent on the pension of a Naick of cavalry.

Reorganisation : While reorganising the horse artillery into two European troops, each troop was given eight six pounder guns; 5.5 inch howitzers and 12 pounder guns being discarded. This was perhaps done for sake of uniformity and ease of administration maintenance, training and carriage of ammunition.

4. Expansion of Horse Artillery

The first major formation of horse artillery in Bengal was in 1811, when a troop of native artillery was formed for service in Java but was reduced on its return. Again in 1817, three troops of the horse artillery were formed by withdrawing galloper guns from the cavalry units.

The next major expansion took place in 1818 when it was ordered that the Madras army should raise a horse artillery brigade, which was to consist of seven troops as under :

(a) 4 European troops, *(b)* 2 Native troops, *(c)* 1 European rocket troop.

Each gun troop was to have 8 six pounder guns. Although the Commander-in-Chief recommended that one of the gun troops be armed with 9 pounder guns, this was not accepted as it would have been more expensive and also because nine pounder guns had still not been introduced in India.

The men for the native troops were found from among volunteers in the bodyguard, cavalry and recruiting depots. The pay of the horse artillery was the highest in the army. It exceeded that of the native cavalry by the following amount, in rupees :

(a) Subedar 10, *(b)* Jemadar 8, *(c)* Havildar 4, *(d)* Naick 3, *(e)* Private 2.

The native horse artillery thus came to be the most favoured corps of the native army of the company

The establishment of a native troop was fixed as under :

	New	Old (1803)
Captain	1	—
Lieutenants	3	1
Second Lieutenant	—	1
Subedar	1	1
Jemadar	2	1
Havildars	4	4
Sergeants	4	—
Naicks	4	4
Corporals	4	—
Privates	132	70
Horses	216	83

Thus the number of officers and men was more in 1818. This is partly explained by the number of guns now authorised : 8 as against 4 earlier. There were also European sergeants and corporals. This was not because of the lack of expertise of native artillerymen; by that time they were well versed in their duties but they were put there perhaps to "keep an eye" on the natives generally. However on 8 June 1821, the Government reduced 12 European non-commissioned officers from the native troops and instead increased the strength by 12 havildars.

Reorganisation of 1825 : 1825 was a major landmark in the history of horse artillery which was reorganised as follows :

(a) *Bengal :* In 1825, three brigades of horse artillery were raised; each brigade was to have one native troop. Thus Bengal had 12 troops of which 3 were natives.

(b) *Bombay :* The first troop was formed in 1811 by drafts from foot artillery and infantry. By 1824, the Bombay Army had four troops of Europeans. No native horse units were raised.

(c) *Madras :* In 1824, two brigades of horse artillery were raised, each with four troops. Out of these one brigade was European and one native. Thus Madras had 8 troops of which 4 were native. Each gun troop was authorised 8 six pounder guns.

5. Reduction of Native Portion

By the end of 1825, along with expansion of other native foot artillery units, the presence of natives in the horse artillery was quite strong. In Bengal and Madras, out of 17 troops, 7 were manned by natives. Given the overall policy of the British about manning their artillery by natives, this seemed too good to last and, sure enough, orders were issued for the Madras Army to the following effect :

(a) *1831 :* Native horse artillery brigade reduced to having two troops instead of four.

(b) *1845 :* Native horse artillery brigade disbanded. Its troops attached to the European brigade.

The native portion of the Bengal horse artillery was not touched. Thus on the eve of Revolt, horse artillery had the following composition :

	European troops	*Native troops*
(a) Bengal	6	3
(b) Madras	4	2
(c) Bomaby	4	—
Total	17	5

Despite this reduction the native horse artillery acquitted itself well. A very fine example of its sense of purpose is narrated by Carnac when a native troop of the Bengal horse artillery was ordered to move to Bamian in Afghanistan in September 1839, across the Hindukush. He refers to the 4th troop of 3rd Horse artillery brigade of the Bengal Army :

> Bamian lies north west of Kabul about 12 miles distance but separated by the valley of Bamian having a broad belt of stupendous mountains, the highest range of which exceeds in altitude 12,000 feet. The troop entered the mountainous road near the village of Urghundi and while toiling up the steep ascent, which was rendered more difficult by huge stones and fragments of rocks, there the troop was met by Major Thomson of Engineers who had just returned from Bamian and he emphasised the

impossibility of troop moving over the terrain but the troop moved on. Instructions were also received from HQ at Kabul to return their guns with ammunition etc. to Kabul and wait for elephants to be sent as it was planned to dismantle the guns and mount them on elephants. The troop with all six guns however proceeded after getting permission from HQ and at number of places the guns and ammunition and accessories were pulled by hand as it was not possible to pull them by horses. Troop was assisted by infantry soldiers and some 200 local Hazarihs. The ascent was occasionally so steep (angle of 45 degrees) that the men working at drag ropes could not keep their footing. The ascent was however accomplished. Thereafter the descent was even more difficult as one false step implied immediate destruction. On 6 October the troop entered the village of Bamian.

The march to Bamian has been described in much greater detail by Carnac. It has been said to be "perhaps the most extraordinary march ever performed by artillery; extraordinary both from the obstacles overcome and the circumstances of the men of this troop being natives of Hindustan."

6. Rocket Artillery

During 1815, orders were issued to form a rocket artillery in the Bengal and Madras presidencies on an experimental basis. A rocket troop each was formed. Its establishment was :

Captain	—	1
Lieutenants	—	2
Lieutenant Fireworker	—	1
Non Commissioned Officers	—	10
Troopers	—	80
Sirdars	—	5
Sowars	—	60
Camels	—	70
Horses	—	26
Carts	—	4

The troop had 960 rockets on establishment. These were

distributed to field and horse artillery batteries as required by the situation. It was however felt that the advantage of such an organisation was not commensurate with its expense and both the troops were disbanded, and in 1921 the troop in the Madras Army was disbanded as well, both being converted into horse artillery troops.

On 20 November 1821, the rocket troop in the Madras Army was converted into a reserve troop of the Horse Artillery Brigade with the following establishment :

1 Captain	2 Rough riders
5 1st lieutenants	2 Farriers
1 Troop quarter master	2 Trumpeters
1 Troop serjeant major	4 Corporals
1 Troop quarter master sergeant	8 Bombardiers
4 Serjeants	56 Gunners
1 Drill Corporal	14 Officers' horses
4 guns, and 2 ammunition wagons were authorised.	110 Regimental horses

This change was made at the recommendation of Major-General Sir Thomas Munro, then Governor of Madras, who recorded a minute on the subject from which the following are extracts :

> The Rocket troop has been found from experience to be of little or no use on service, as the rockets are more dangerous to our own troops than to those of the enemy, as well from their uncertain flight, as from their being liable to explode the moment they are let off. As the defect of the rocket seems to be owing to the decomposition of its powder by the heat of the climate, and as no means have been found to remedy it, I have long thought that the maintenance of the Rocket troop was an idle waste of the public money. I have lately communicated on this subject with His Excellency the Commander-in-Chief who has suggested that the Rocket troop should be commuted into a reserve troop of Horse Artillery.
>
> It will be a depot to the other troops, and may, by the

addition of men and horses, be, at any time in a few weeks, converted into a third European troop of Horse Artillery. As such a troop will be very useful, and as the Rocket troop is of no use whatever, I recommend that the proposed commutation be authorised by the Board."

The only recorded instance of rocket artillery being used during operations was in February 1817 when a troop from Bengal artillery was employed against Daya Ram, the Taluqdar of Hathras in the district of Aligarh. The fort was invested on 12 February and taken on 2 March.

On 22 February, the rocket troop opened up at 10.30 a.m. with 32 pound rockets from their frames. Of the 138 discharged that day, about one fourth took effect in the Katra, setting it on fire. The very wildness of their flight was an additional source of terror. Thereafter, rockets were fired on 23rd, 26th, 27th and 1st/2nd March.

This was not the end of the experiment. Again in 1823, Captain H. Nicholson arrived in Madras from Bengal to demonstrate and explain the new rocket system of Sir W. Congreve after whom the famous rocket is named. A small rocket establishment under Capt. P. Montgomerie of the artillery was sanctioned and raised in May 1823. There is no record of Congreve rockets being used.

As the horse artillery and cavalry expanded during the post-1796 reorganisation period, it became necessary for the Company to have their own organisation to meet the requirement of horses as it was difficult to procure them in the required size and strength from the open market, particularly for horse artillery. A stud department was therefore opened at very heavy expense. In Madras, there was no stud department and all horses were purchased by the Commissary for the army. The horse artillery was first allowed to make the choice and the cavalry was next in line. In Bombay, a stud department was established in 1830.

Even then, the stud departments could not cope with the demand due to expansion and also the requirement of additional horses for light field batteries which were raised for service in Punjab and in which light guns of foot artillery were pulled by horses instead of cattle. Additional requirements were therefore met by purchases from local dealers and agents.

THE OFFICERS

Efficient manning of the armies of the East India Company by officers was a major problem, particularly because of the requirements of Napoleonic wars and the policy of not having natives as commissioned officers. This was the case for all three combat arms, but in the case of the artillery it was more acute, as its officers were put through more severe initial selection and subsequent training peculiar to that arm. Also, the selected officers had to be totally dependable and reliable. There was a restriction on giving commissions in the artillery from the ranks.

1. Selection of Officers

Before 1786, young men from England were directly commissioned. This explains the posting of a civilian, Mr. Benjamin Robins, in December 1750 and later of Lieutenant Colonel Fredrick Scott, an infantry officer, as Captain of artillery. In 1786, however, some cadets were sent for training to the Royal Military College, Woolwich, but vacancies allotted to the Company were not adequate and a separate Academy at Addiscombe was opened in 1798. Initially, training was given only to cadets of the artillery and engineers but in 1816 cadets for infantry were added. Between 1809 and 1861, this Academy trained about 3,600 officers.

Interestingly, officers of the cavalry had neither any formal selection nor training. Commissions were given to friends and relatives of the Directors and on joining the regiment they under-went a very light test in drill and riding. Thereafter, an officer learnt his profession in the unit itself. With such training he was later eligible to command brigades and divisions.

Indeed, the problems later faced by artillery officers for higher command were partly due to the fact that officers of the cavalry were generally close to the Directors at home and they feared competition from highly trained and professional artillery officers. Thus they tried to persuade the Directors to embargo the careers of artillery officers.

Cadets for Addiscombe were between the ages of 15 and 22. For the Academy at Woolwich, this age was between 15 and 17. The training lasted two years and cadets were selected after an entrance examination. Purchase of commission, as in the Crown's service, was never legalised or regulated in the Company. To avoid unpleasantness and supersession, officers who had purchased their commissions in England were generally allowed to remain behind, as otherwise an officer who had purchased commission as a lieutenant colonel would, on proceeding to India, become senior to a lieutenant colonel with many years service, because officers of the Crown were considered senior to officers of the Company.

After the Addiscombe Academy was opened (initially only for artillery and engineer officers), the Directors issued instructions in which they made it clear that appointments (to the commission in artillery) of persons other than those "properly educated and qualified" were inconsistent with their views. Not only did they lay down this stipulation but they also ordered in 1810 that commissions in artillery which had been granted to men in the inferior rank be cancelled.

It was a normal practice in the army to give commissioned rank to personnel from other ranks who had shown exceptional bravery or rendered such service during operations. For example, in April 1796 during the siege of Rachore, Conductor Lindsay led a force of 42 artillerymen followed by infantry, and assaulted and secured the fort. He was granted a commission in the artillery branch on the orders of the Directors.

An order cancelling commissions to other ranks in the artillery branch is indeed without parallel in the history of the British in India, and shows that the British were not prepared to take any chances with the artillery. Thereafter, they sent another letter (in January 1811) to the Madras Government. This concluded as follow:

> It is therefore our express desire that you should, in no case, fill up from the inferior ranks of artillery, or from the infantry or cavalry, the vacancies which may occur among the commissioned officers in your artillery.

It may seem anomalous that while the Directors were prepared to give commissions from the ranks to personnel of the cavalry and infantry, they would not permit this in the case of artillery despite the fact that they had some difficulty in getting an adequate number of officers to man their armies. Perhaps their policy was to have a smaller number of "proper" officers for this arm rather than to have larger numbers who could not meet the necessary qualifications, both personal and professional.

2. Dependability of Officers

In fact, due to the nature of the armament of artillery vis-a-vis those held by cavalry and infantry, the Directors had, from the very beginning, to depend on this arm even during peacetime to suppress any dissatisfaction or sign of unrest in their own armies. That is why as early as in 1753, they had spelt out that they were fully satisfied about "how great a share of our dependence must, in case of trouble, be on artillery and upon the skill of the people appropriated to its service."

This confidence was fully justified by the subsequent events of the history of the Company. In 1795, there was a great deal of discontent among the officers of the Company, as the officers of the King's army were deemed to be senior irrespective of the date of grant of rank. In Bengal there was almost a mutiny led by discontented officers and the situation was saved by the loyalty of the artillery arm.

Sir John Shore wrote to Lord Cornwallis on 26 April that :

> You will be surprised, mortified, and perhaps alarmed, at the accounts which you will hear of the state of the army. Their proceedings exceeded all bounds of decency or moderation...and, but for the firmness of the Artillery at Calcutta, and the manly resistance of several officers at Cawnpore, the army would have dictated to the Government their own terms.

Colonel Sir John Macgregor Murray, commanding the Presidency, placed Fort William in a state of defence relying on the "unshaken steadiness of the artillery which formed a large portion of its garrison."

The British were totally dependent on their army to achieve their political goals. Within the army they were dependent on the artillery arm in case of trouble; hence their sensitiveness to having "proper" officers for this arm. That this policy paid dividends is borne out by the subsequent history of events in that most mutinies and revolts which took place were in the cavalry and infantry units and the artillery arm was least affected.

3. Training of Officers

The training at Woolwich and Addiscombe was very thorough and cadets were trained in field fortifications, mathematics, geometry, works of defence and for offensive operations, in putting up gun platforms and parallels in siege warfare as well as in explosives and allied subjects. It was later felt that the training was too academic and therefore in 1839, tactical training was introduced through the use of sand models and outdoor exercises.

On arrival in India after commission, the artillery officers did not report direct to units but joined the Depot of Instruction established at artillery headquarters by each respective presidency. All officers had to be proficient in foot drill, horse riding, sword fighting and small arms.

On the 27th of January 1824, an institution was established at the headquarters of the artillery at St Thomas Mount for the purpose of completing the professional education of the junior officers of the corps, and imparting to the non-commissioned and privates a certain degree of theoretical knowledge of their duties. The following are extracts from the General Order issued on the occasion :

> The officer appointed to the charge of this institution will be designated "Director of the Artillery Depot of Instruction," and will have charge of the repository of models, and drawings of all ordnance carriages, and machinery attached to the artillery, as well as the patterns of stores of every description in use with that branch of the service : the institution to be formed and conducted under the immediate orders and control of the

Commandant of Artillery according to a plan which has been approved of by Government.

This office will also be considered the repository of all artillery experiments, and the proper place of record for all artillery practice : and it will be an important part of the duty of the Director of the Depot to arrange the results in such a manner as to be of most advantage, and of easiest access to the officers of the corps of artillery : not only of such practice as may now be on record at the Artillery Head Quarters, but such as may take place in future.

4. Artillery Officers as Engineers

When regular artillery units were ordered to be raised in 1748, the first Commandant of Artillery for all the three presidencies was also appointed as Chief Engineer His designation was First Captain & Chief Engineer. In a letter of February 1747, the Court of Directors advised that one Captain Delavaux was being sent for this appointment. This officer arrived at fort St. David early in 1748 but absconded to Pondicherry in May 1749.

Apart from the appointment of First Captain & Chief Engineer who was overall in charge, the actual officer commanding of each artillery company in the three Presidencies was also an engineer as is evident from his designation "Second Captain & Second Engineer"

In 1750, one Mr. Benjamin Robins arrived to replace captain Delavaux but died in 1751. His place was taken by Lieutenant Colonel Caroline Fredrick Scott of the infantry, as Commandant of Artillery & Chief Engineer. His designation was First Captain & Chief Engineer. This appointment is rather surprising, in that he was neither trained as an artillery man nor as an engineer; in fact his rank was too high for those days as there were hardly any lieutenant colonels in the army. Perhaps it was because he was earlier Aid-de-Camp to H.R.H. Duke of Cumberland that he got this appointment.

In 1756, Capt. Brohier, who was a qualified engineer and commanding the second artillery company in Madras, was sent for by Clive to serve in Bengal and in that capacity he planned and superintended the construction of Fort William.

In 1758, one Mr. John Call was appointed as Chief Engineer in the rank of Captain. Thereafter, a separate Engineering Department was raised and gradually artillery officers were replaced by engineer officers. However even as late as 1764, Captain Fleming Martin of the Bengal Artillery held the appointment of Chief Engineer, Fort William.

Although a separate Department of Engineers was opened, artillery officers continued to give engineering advice to the army when required. The reason for this was, that unlike infantry and cavalry officers, who had no formal training before being commissioned, artillery and engineer officers were trained together at Woolwich and Addiscombe with emphasis on engineering subjects. Thus, for any operation, whenever an engineer officer was not available, recourse was invariably made to the artillery officer for engineering advice.

5. Career of Officers

Artillery officers of the higher command as well as within the corps itself faced many problems with regard to their careers. It is indeed surprising that despite the fact that the artillery was paramount in the conquest and control of India by the British and that artillery officers were the best trained vis-a-vis cavalry and infantry officers, many hurdles were placed in their path to higher command outside their own arm. Such a conflict is often inevitable and it is difficult to pin down any single reason for it. For example, since officers of the cavalry were close friends and relatives of Directors, the latter tended to bring them up for higher command in preference to infantry and artillery officers.

The Directors however, while issuing their directive in 1748, did not lay any embargo at all. Para 37 is quite clear and reads :

> Those who serve in the artillery *may be promoted in other companies* in case of vacancies, as may who serve in other companies be promoted to vacancies in the Artillery Company, but not unless they have made themselves completely masters of the business and science of the Artillery in all its branches and give good proof of their knowledge and experience therein.

While this clearly implies that there could be an exchange of officers between the three principle arms, it did lay an indirect restriction on the transfer of cavalry and infantry officers to artillery due to the stipulation that the officers of the former two arms could only be promoted in the artillery if they were, in all respects, "masters of the business of artillery". Although the artillery was not classified as a technical arm like the engineering branch, it was relatively more technical and specialised than the very simple expertise required by the other two branches which, in practice, precluded them from commanding artillery units. And since officers of the cavalry and infantry in practice could not be promoted in the artillery on transfer, their officers were jealous when artillery officers on promotion were able to command the cavalry.

The first case of an artillery officer as force commander was that of Major Goodyear who was appointed as Commander of Bombay Forces as early as 1748. He died from wounds after the unsuccessful siege of Pondicherry. Another artillery officer, Capt. William Gibbs, was earmarked to replace him but he was not selected because he married a Roman Catholic. As laid down in Para 33 of the Directive, an artillery officer marrying anyone of that faith had to leave the service.

Again in February 1760, when Emperor Shah Alam attacked Patna, the British despatched a force of 200 Europeans, a battalion of sepoys and two guns, the whole force being under the command of Capt. Knox, an artillery officer. In 1764, Captain Jenning, an artillery officer, was made force commander of artillery, European Infantry and Native Infantry at Sawant, a cantonment of the British.

An interesting case involving Lord Clive relates to Sir Robert Barker, an artillery officer who had greatly distinguished himself during the siege of Fort St. George by the French General Lally. For this, Barker was created a Baronet. Clive wrote to the Directors on 27 April 1764, "To command your artillery, I would recommend Sir Robert Barker whose abilities in that department have been exceeded by no officer that ever was in your service." However there was no appointment of a lieutenant colonel in the artillery at that time. The officer was therefore given command of an army brigade but this was objected to by an infantry officer, Sir Robert Fletcher. Clive wrote to him :

> You think that he should remain in artillery. That would not have hindered him from commanding you upon all occasions when you were both upon service together. Indeed his rank is so high that he must always command wherever he is, if Carnac or Smith be not present which may seldom happen—except indeed by being an artillery officer, he should be thought improper to command the whole; and by that means an officer of his rank and merit would be deprived of acting in the field altogether.

Barker was promoted to a field command and commanded the Bengal Army from 1770 to 1773 in the rank of Brigadier General.

However, the Directors also felt that it would not be in the best interests of artillery officers to move them away from their parent arm when due for higher promotions, as this was against the interest of the arm itself. They therefore decided to create vacancies in the artillery. In 1767, the Directors approved the setting up of an HQ of artillery under a major with additional staff on the grounds that since the nature of service in the artillery excludes them from any pretensions of being removed for preferment into the battalions and that since the numbers are such that it requires an officer of that rank to head the corps.

On 29 December 1766, the government resolved to overcome some of the problems the artillery was facing. These included the following:

(a) The current companies of the artillery were inadequate in light of the commitment in the south, as well as the dispersal at fortifications and garrisons, with the result that none was left for service in the filed and in future emergencies.

(b) The duty and service of an artillery officer being distinct and different from other branches, officers could not

be removed for the sake of rank outside without prejudice to the corps itself.

(c) Feelings of dissatisfaction among artillery officers because of limited chance of advancement, and a sense that artillery officers should get a chance of advancement in their own corps in comparison to other branches.

In March 1768, the Directors ordered the formation of a battalion of five companies to be commanded by a lieutenant colonel, with a major as second-in-command. To exercise economy, these two officers also commanded companies, an anomaly which was removed later. At about the same time, the pay of captain's lieutenants and lieutenant fireworkers of artillery was increased. Interestingly, the pay of all ranks of the artillery was always higher than infantry. Cavalry personnel were also paid more but the officers and men of this arm were required to maintain horses and accoutrements at their own expense.

To further improve the career prospects, five captain lieutenants were promoted captains in July 1770 and in 1771, and the grades of second and third lieutenants were abolished.

In April 1775, an order was issued by the government that "officers of Artillery be in future considered, with respect to command of garrisons, in the same manner with the other officers of the army who arrive thereto according to the seniority of their commission." At about the same time, Lieutenant Colonel James was appointed to command the fort and garrison at Trichinopoly.

Although the above order pertains to the command of garrisons, it seems that it was liberally interpreted to include field command as in 1786. Col. T.D. Pearse, an eminent artillery officer of Bengal, was sent to Madras in 1780, with a force of artillery and five regiments of native infantry under his command.

Although artillery and engineer officers were trained together, the directors, when laying down instructions that artillery officers could command outside their own arm, said quite firmly that engineer officers may not be considered for such commands outside their own branch by a letter issued on 25 March 1772 which clearly stipulated that "....nor can we permit that Engineer Officers ever take command of our military either in field or garrison." Having thus excluded officers from Engineers for field command and allowed officers of artillery such command, there were still problems faced by artillery officers for command outside their corps. Part of the reason was that infantry and cavalry officers were seldom given command of artillery companies, battalions or garrison because of the specialised nature of the profession. For example in 1761, when Colonel Cailland was to proceed to Vellore, he recommended Capt. Barker to command his artillery in the rank of major and this was objected to by all captains of the 79th Regiment. Nevertheless the government maintained their position and Barker was promoted major.

The issue of field command was finally settled in 1840 when Major General Showers was appointed to command the Southern Division of the army and the Directors cancelled all orders and instructions regarding prohibition on artillery officers being given such commands.

6. Promotion within Corps

Although there was no bar to artillery officers holding higher appointments outside the corps as field and garrison commanders, it was found that even within the artillery arm gunner officers were getting less chances of promotion, as this arm could not be expanded the same way as infantry and cavalry because it needed special manpower and equipment. To keep pace with their counterparts in other arms, vacancies were created and the artillery was reorganised periodically to avoid dissatisfaction among the corps of officers. Appendix-A gives details of rank structure in relation to units of Bengal Artillery and indicates what kinds of attempts were made to solve this problem.

Before 1796, no officers of the rank of colonel were available in each of the presidencies. Thus it was ordered that the senior lieutenant colonel should act as the senior artillery commander.

Orders issued on 21 December 1792 in this regard were as follows :

> As uniformity of practice in the whole artillery upon establishment will always render it more useful upon the service, the Honourable President in Council is pleased to direct that the senior Lieutenant-Colonel of Artillery take immediate charge of all details of that nature in the battalions. The necessary orders to the other battalions for the present to be transmitted by the Adjutant of the battalion under the senior officer's own command.

Earlier, in 1795, since artillery officers had not yet reached the seniority of a colonel *vis-a-vis* other arms, the following orders were issue on 3 February 1795 to bring them at par in protocol with colonels of other arms.

> The senior Lieutenant-Colonel of the Madras Artillery shall in future be looked upon as the commanding officer of the whole corps. In order to give him respectability and enable him to defray the additional expense to which he will be exposed in that situation, he shall be permitted to draw allowances equal to those that would be given to a Colonel of the same quarters or cantonments, and he should be promoted to the rank of Colonel when all officers of infantry of the establishment present in India of senior standing in the service shall have obtained that rank.

Similar orders were issued in the Bengal and Bombay armies. It may be seen from Appendix-A that extra vacancies of lieutenant colonels and colonels were created and that in 1823 native battalions were also placed at par with European battalions. Whereas in 1818, a native battalion with 15 companies was commanded by a major, in 1827, 16 companies were formed into two battalions and given two colonels, two lieutenant colonels and two majors. The anomaly of course was in the earlier rank structure, in which native artillery units did not have a sufficient number of officers to command.

The increase in the number of vacancies in higher rank was to keep the artillery officers at par with other arms in promotion. In the army of the Company, there were very few vacancies of rank higher than that of a colonel and it was not obligatory that a particular formation be commanded by a specific rank as in modern armies. Much depended upon the seniority which a commander had achieved. For example the army under Lieutenant General Harris grouped for action against Tipu Sultan in 1799 had its brigades commanded as under :

(a) No. 4 Brigade — Lieutenant Colonel Gardiner
(b) No. 2 Brigade — Colonel Sherbrooke
(c) No. 1 Brigade — Major General Baird
(d) Commander Artillery — Colonel Smith

Again in 1825, the commander of the artillery division forming part of the force gathered against Bharatpore was Brigadier Macleod of the Bengal Artillery and the cavalry division having two brigades was commanded by a brigadier; in addition, its two brigades were also commanded by brigadiers.

Appendix 'A'

Pattern of Promotion of Officers in the Bengal Artillery

	Year	*Units*	*Rank Structure*		
			Col	*Lt. Col.*	*Maj*
(a)	1765	4 Coys	—	—	1
(b)	1770	1 Bn (5 Coys)	—	1	1
(c)	1778	1 European Bn (5 Coys)	—	1	2
		3 Native Bns	—	—	1
(d)	1779	2 European Bns (10 Coys)	—	2	2
(e)	1786	3 European Bns (15 Coys)	—	3	3
(f)	1796	3 European Bns (15 Coys)	3	3	3
(g)	1802	3 European Bns (21 Coys)	3	3	3
(h)	1806	3 European Bns (21 Coys)	3	6	6
		5 Native Coys	—	—	—
(i)	1818	3 European Bns (24 Coys)	3	6	6
		1 Native Bn (15 Coys)	—	—	1
		1 HA Bde*	1	2	2
(j)	1823	5 European Bns (20 Coys)	5	5	5
		1 Native Bn (20 Coys)	1	1	1
		3 HA Bdes*	3	3	3
(k)	1827	5 European Bns (20 Coys)	5	5	5
		2 Native Bns (16 Coys)	2	2	2

		3 HA Bdes*	3	3	3
(l)	1842	5 European Bns	5	5	5
		2 Native Bns (20 Coys)	2	2	2
		3 HA Bdes*	3	3	3
(m)	1844	6 European Bns (24 Coys)	6	6	6
		3 Native Bns (18 Coys)	3	3	3
		3 HA Bdes*	3	3	3

* Horse Artillery Brigade.

SPECIAL ASPECTS

We have examined the evolution of the artillery of the East India Company in respect of its organisation, equipment officer corps, training system and its philosophy in battle. Here, we look at some other aspects which may appear minor but were nevertheless important in terms of the overall impact they made on the morale and efficiency of the British artillery.

1. Guns as Colours of the British Artillery

The colours of a unit symbolised the spirit, traditions, honour and rallying point for the soldiers of that unit. British military history is full of innumerable examples where the loss of 'colours' or the flag was considered the highest form of disgrace and a number of lives were lost to protect them and recover them if captured by the enemy.

In the case of the British artillery, the gun symbolised the colours instead of the flag and it became the rallying point of the detachment, as well as its flag of honour. It was to this the men looked, this by which they stood, with and for which they fell. As long as the gun was theirs, they were unconquered, victorious; when the gun was lost all was lost.

British history of the artillery is full or innumerable examples where the loss of guns was considered a great dishonour for the battery and this was the main reason for the British not losing many guns in battle. If and when some lost, all efforts were made to recover them even at the cost of lives as is evident from some of following :

(a) During the wars with Hyder Ali, after the Battle at Virakandlur on 23 October 1782, the British lost one

gun but it was recaptured by the distinguished action of the whole of the Grenadier Battalion.

(b) Just before the battle of Plassey when reinforcements from Madras reached Budge Budge near Calcutta, they were attacked by the local Governor Manick Chand. The British had to withdraw. They suffered losses in men and abandoned the guns which were however later recovered by a body of volunteers.

(c) In October 1781, a British force was sent to intercept a force of Hyder's army but was itself surprised, losing 317 men and a gun which was captured. Caption J. Moore of the infantry and Captain Moorehouse of the artillery took a body of European and native sepoys and forced their way through the enemy and brought back the gun in triumph.

(d) During the Battle for Arcot in September 1781, when some of the guns were disabled, a whole battalion (14 carnatic) was left behind to cover the rear and protect disabled guns.

(e) During the Anglo-Sikh wars, in February 1848, at the Battle of Ramnagar, as the cavalry and horse artillery advanced towards Sikh positions, one of the guns got embedded in the sand. To cover the retreat of the rest of the artillery, a squadron of three Light Dragoons made a gallant charge on the Sikhs, who were trying to recover it but were held up by accurate artillery and musket fire. To recover the gun the whole of 14 Light Dragoon accompanied by five Native Infantry charged the Sikhs. The British lost 26 people and 58 were wounded the gun still left in the sand.

The above incidents clearly indicate the philosophy of the British in relation to their guns and artillery. This was quite unlike the case of Indian powers to whom the loss of over one hundred guns as in the Battle of Buxar was treated as one of the "fortunes of war". This also reveals their complete lack of understanding of the role of artillery in battle, something that led to repeated defeats at the hands of the British. To leave guns behind was considered the highest form of disgrace. In 1791, when Lord Cornwallis found it impossible to carry out the siege of Seringapatam because of the mortality of gun-pulling draught cattle, the failure of supplies, bad weather and the non-arrival of the Maratha army, he decided to withdraw. He could not take his heavy guns back due to the problem of draught cattle and therefore ordered these to be busted rather than let them fall into the hands of enemy

2. Protocol Seniority of the Artillery Arms

The British were extremely particular about protocol in all spheres, whether civil or military. Since ceremonials have always been part of all armies, it was essential to lay down the relative seniority of various arms. A doubt arose in 1790, when the army was being prepared and marshalled for war in Mysore. The following orders were issued by Major General Medows, the Commander-in-Chief in Madras, who was also to head the Grand Army for operations.

> His Majesty's Cavalry takes post of the Company's cavalry. His Majesty's Artillery of the Company's Artillery and His Majesty's Infantry of the Company's Infantry; but the Artillery takes post of the Infantry without considering the service to which they belong.

Thus the seniority of these combat arms became cavalry, artillery and infantry, in that order. Later, for a short period, this seniority was changed in England to artillery, cavalry and infantry but due to various pressures it was revised to horse artillery, cavalry, artillery and infantry, the former designated as "Right of the Line" when parading with their guns, always taking their place on the right. This protocol is still followed in the UK. The relative precedence given to the artillery by the British clearly indicates their philosophy of the role and importance of this arm in battle.

Lord Cornwallis also laid down that Bengal troops were always to take the right of those belonging to either of the other two presidencies. Thus Bengal artillery units would take precedence over the artillery of Madras and Bombay. On 24 May 1790, the Grand Army moved out with Madras artillery units grouped with the right wing. On 12 June while actually on the move, orders were issued for the Bengal artillery grouped with the left wing to replace the Madras artillery. The change involved the movement of 17 brigades of artillery and it is convincing proof of the battle procedure and discipline that a change so complicated was effected in so short a time.

The above incident indicates the extent to which the British artillery, unlike the Indians, had perfected their drills and procedures in moving their guns.

3. Role of Guns in Quelling the Mutiny

British guns were frequently employed, particularly against Indian soldiers of the Company, to quell mutinies and punish individual soldiers by "blowing him from the mouth of the gun". The latter form of punishment was invariably carried out in the presence of other native soldiers to overawe and frighten them.

As early as May 1764, when Major Munro assumed command of British forces in Oudh, he found that the native troops were very dissatisfied because of a lack of rewards, scarcity of provisions and the problems they faced because of the climate and disease. A battalion of sepoys left the camp but was pursued and brought back. Twenty-four of the ring leaders were "blown from the mouth of a cannon". Carnac writes that "no disposition to mutiny was thenceforth manifested. The same unit (9 Native Infantry Battalion) fought later in the Battle of Buxar in October 1764 and from all accounts did very well.

In 1775, Muctoom Sahib, Commandant of 9 Native Battalion, Madras army was charged with exciting his men to mutiny and persuading them not to embark. He was tried by courtmartial in February 1775 and "blown from a gun" in the presence of the battalion. The men afterwards embarked for Bombay quietly. The rank of Commandant was thereafter abolished in the army.

In 1828, 47 Bengal Native Infantry broke into open mutiny, as they were reluctant to proceed across the sea. The British moved a force of troop of horse artillery, a cavalry troop and two battalions of infantry at the place on mutiny. The whole of 47 Battalion and 120 personnel from 26 and 62 Native Battalions formed up to take on the British. The British horse artillery opened up with their guns and the mutineers broke up and fled. The British cavalry and infantry did not take part against the mutineers.

The British did not use guns to quell only the natives. In 1798, mutiny broke out in the 1st Battalion of Madras Artillery (British) due to some grievances regarding pay and issue of liquor. After the courtmartial, offenders were punished, one of them being ordered to be "blown away from a gun".

4. Personal Arms of Artillery Personnel

The personal weapon of an infantry soldier was a musket 4 feet 7 inches in length with a bayonet. The native sepoys were generally issued with matchlock or firelocks. It is interesting to note that as late as 1808, havildars of the native light infantry were carrying pikes; muskets being issued to them in November.

Artillery personnel, both of foot and horse, were issued with carbines to enable them to be more mobile on and around the gun during action as the guns had to be manhandled and had to change formations in battle. The gun was the main weapon of gunners in defence against infantry and cavalry charges, and guns were kept firing till the enemy had broken through and managed to get into the gun area which was invariably the forwardmost position (as otherwise the guns would mask of fire and movement of infantry and cavalry). It was only when guns could not be operated that the gunners fought with their carbines to defend their guns. Once the enemy moved away from the guns, the latter were used again to deal with him.

5. Casualties in Artillery

Unlike the current artillery guns, which had a range of over 30,000 metres and fired indirectly from depth positions, the limited effective range of guns of earlier days ensured that guns were invariably placed in the forefront for any operation. In defence, of course, they had to be placed ahead of the infantry and the cavalry; in attack, after the first engagement, they had to be moved forward and redeployed under and continuous enemy fire and during siege operations they were moved in a series of parallel positions to as close as 300 yards of fort walls to commence breaching operations. The casualties suffered by artillerymen and accompanying lascars were therefore quite high as the guns, apart from being prime targets, were also in close fire fights.

Some examples from operations are given below:

(a) During the Battle of Plassey, the gunners suffered the maximum casualties as the following figures show :

Arm	*Strength*	*Casualties*	*Percentage*
(a) Artillery	150	19	12 : 66
(b) European Infantry	750	7	0 : 93
(c) Native Infantry	2300	52	2 : 26

Four officers were wounded , three of whom were serving with artillery.

(b) On 1 January 1818, during the Anglo-Maratha wars, the British occupied a defensive position at Koregaum with a force of 600, including two six pounders manned by two officers and 27 men, and were attacked repeatedly by a strong force of the Peshwa (25,000 horse, 500 infantry and two siege guns). The Peshwa offered a reward Rs. 20,000 for the British guns. Out of a strength of 27 artillerymen the British lost 21 (9 killed and 112 wounded).

(c) In the Battle of Ferozeshah against the Sikhs, on 22 December 1845, out of 694 killed and 1729 wounded, the artillery had 118 killed, 20 missing and 7 wounded.

(d) During the siege of Delhi between 30 May and 20 September 1857, out of a total strength of 1350 all ranks, 365 artillerymen were killed or wounded as under:

	Killed	*Wounded*	*Missing*
(a) Officers	4	23	—

(b) Europeans (others)	43	216	—
(c) Native officers	1	1	—
(d) Natives (others)	26	49	2
Total	74	289	2

6. Interior Economy of Artillery Units

The British were extremely particular about the interior economy or administration of their units. Every single item held by them was accounted for in peace, during battle, and after an operation. The loss of a gun was of course considered a very serious matter and a dishonour. Everything relating to the gun and gun battery equipment was accounted for in great detail.

For example, during the siege of Ajigarh Fort in 1809, the artillery commander submitted a return of stores expended during the siege which lasted from 6 to 13 February. The report submitted on 17 February to higher authorties was as under :

Item		*Quantity*
Axes with helves	7	(missing)
Bags gunny for sand	897	
Bills hand	2	missing
Chalk	12	Chittacks
Cartridge 18 pounders	2053	
Cartridge 12 pounders	787	
Cartridge 18 pounders case	23	
Needles packing	3	Broke & lost
Needles sewing	5	Broke & lost
Pencils black lead	2	
Rammers earth	3	
Sights copper	1	lost
Twine, seers & chattacks	2111	
Shot 18 pounder	2053	
Shell 8 inch	268	
Shot 12 pounder	787	

The list contains over 30 other items, big and small, including the gunpowder consumed. It makes interesting reading, as apart from major items like ammunition, even details of sewing needles are included. Inclusion of such small items may appear trivial but in fact it was not so. Each battery had equipment tables duly approved by government which listed all items required by the unit for war and the absence of any one of them such as an axe or even pencil could seriously influence the operational efficiency adversely. It was therefore considered essential that full care was taken for their custody, serviceability and replacement.

There is no evidence available anywhere that the artillery units of Indian powers particularly methodical in looking after their equipment. Apart from other factors and reasons stated elsewhere in this study, a lack of working in detail was also one of the causes of the inefficiency of the artillery of Indian powers.

7. Procurement and Supply of Artillery Equipment

Board of Ordnance : In 1775, a Board of Ordnance was set up in Bengal by General Clavering, the Commander-in-Chief. Its duty was "all contracts for the supply of stores, proofs of ordnance and powder, plans for new construction of ordnance, reports of powder work, laboratory and arsenals were to be submitted. The Board did not deal with food and clothing but was concerned with supply of technical equipment. The Board first met in 1776.

Military Board : In 1785, the Board was designated the Military Board. It consisted of a Commander-in-Chief and the senior artillery officers of respective presidencies apart from other members such as the Quarter Master General and Adjutant General. In addition to other ordnance and technical functions, it also continued to perform the duties of provision of supplies till 1809, when the commissariat system was adopted whose main function was the supply of food and animals.

The preparation of all the artillery equipment was thus vested in the Board. However, due to the very technical requirement of the artillery, it was felt that the Board which had only one artillery officer as its member was not adequately equipped and supervise the requirements.

Supply of gun carriages and powder : In April 1782, Mr.

Thomas Powney was appointed an agent for the supply of gun carriages. In November 1783, these duties were taken over by Lieutenant Colonel P. Duff of the artillery. The gun carriage agency remained at Fort William when later in 1807 it was transferred to Cossipore. Earlier in 1800, Captain A. Glass was appointed agent for gun carriages and powder barrels.

Since all gun carriages were made of teak and then climate of Bengal was found to be unfit for seasoning wood, storage yards were found at Allahabad and Cawnpore in 1814. In 1825, Cawnpore was closed and moved to Fatehgarh. In 1829, Cossipore was also closed for the manufacture of gun carriages and shifted to Fatehgarh which became the sole manufactory of gun carriages and storage of material. Apart from technical and other considerations, the shifting to Fatehgarh was more prudent as the British army operations had now shifted towards the north. Cossipore yard then became a foundry for guns. Iron guns however continued to be supplied from England, as Cossipore supplied only brass guns.

Permanent Select Committee : In 1821, Lord Hastings formed a Permanent Select Committee of artillery officers to advise on artillery material and magazines. It was to consist of the respective Commandant of Artillery as the senior member assisted by Principal and Deputy Commissaries of Ordnance and agent for gun carriages. It was directed that no alteration in ordnance carriages of articles or artillery was to be made till they had been considered and reported upon by the Select Committee. The committee was found very useful in that, being a committee of experts headed by the senior artillery officer of the presidency, it would put forward the artillery's point of view. The Military Board was abolished in February 1855.

In Madras presidency, the gun carriages were manufactured in Seringapatam till 1830. In June, this was shifted to Fort St. George. In September 1832, this manufactory was placed under the control of Principal Commissary of Ordnance. Later in July 1840, the gun Carriage Manufactory became a separate department and was placed in charge of a Special Officer designated as "Superintendent of the Gun Carriage Manufactory".

5
Conquest of India

Although the East India Company had become, by 1765, an Indian power itself, its future as such was by no means safe. In particular, the economic base upon which its military, and hence political, strength was built was endangered by the rapacity of its own servants. In Madras this became known, from the nomination of the local currency, as the age of 'shaking the *pagoda*-tree', while the cry of 'Nizzy will pay' was used to justify all kinds of expenditure incurred by government in the name of the Nizam of Hyderabad. The position was most serious in Bengal, in that while revenues of this province were expected to be so profitable as to finance all British activities in India, they were actually being syphoned off, following the Mughal precedent, by the officers expected to collect them. Many of such officers, military and civil alike, were relatively new to Bengal, having been hastily appointed, or transferred from Madras or Bombay, to replace the experienced men lost in the Patna massacre. All hoped to make their fortune by private trade and the munificence of Indian princes or their courtiers, while the Directors continued to pay them low salaries on the assumption that the opportunities for local profit made anything more than what amounted to a retaining fee superfluous. The new opportunities for speculation enabled fortunes to be made in a far shorter time than previously, thus reducing the time that the Company's servants were exposed to the hazards of the climate and diseases of India, and so enabling larger numbers to return to the United Kingdom with enough money to buy country estates, seats in the House of Commons, and stock in the East India Company. By the first of these activities, the returning 'Nabobs' (as they were known, from the English corruption of the title *nawab*) aroused the envy of the landed gentry who formed the dominant class of Georgian England.[1] By the second, they threatened the political control by that class of the ruling ministry. By the third, they effectively became the masters of their own former employers. In 1764, disturbed by reports from Bengal that the activities of their servants there were so extreme as to be likely to kill the goose that laid the golden eggs, the Court of Proprietors (the stock-holders) proposed that Robert Clive, who had left India in 1760, and been enobled and promoted to major general in recognition of his services, should return as Governor and Commander-in-Chief of Bengal, and impose some kind of financial probity, or at least economy.

In the military sphere, the major economy to be effected was the reduction of *batta*. Mir Jafar, in 1757, had followed the example of Nawab Muhammad Ali in Madras by undertaking to pay to the Europeans employed in his support *batta* at the same rate as they received from the Company. When the revenues from which this was paid were assigned to the Company, the Directors saw no reason to pay the same allowance twice and instructed Clive to reduce expenditure under this head. Accordingly (after having taken about a year to sail from London to Calcutta), he ordered in December 1765, that troops in and around Calcutta, who were by definition not in the field, should receive no further *batta*. Those in cantonments further inland, were to be allowed half-*batta*, to compensate for the cost of obtaining essential supplies (including necessities such as, for a captain, 30 bottles of Madeira, 30 of beer, and 15 of spirits *per mensem*) and those in the field, full *batta*. In August 1765 Clive had re-organised the Bengal army into three brigades, each under a colonel, and each composed of a company of artillery and one battalion of infantry (all Europeans), with seven battalions of sepoys. He had also increased the established number of British officers in the Bengal sepoy battalions to a caption, two lieutenants and two ensigns, all of whom benefited from the existing *batta* regulations. The 1st Brigade, at Monghyr on the Ganges (some 250 miles inland from Calcutta), and the 3rd Brigade, another 100 miles up-river at Bankipur, near Patna, were now reduced from rates of double to half *batta*. The 2nd Brigade, at Allahabad, 200 miles further up-stream, on the River Jamna continued to receive full *batta* in cantonments and double *batta* in the field, as Allahabad (resumed by the Mughal Emperor from the Nawab of Awadh, with British military support), was technically a foreign country, where the Company was bound to pay *batta* once on account of distance and once more for the extra expense of field service.[2]

The consequence of these reductions was much the same as it had been in Madras fifteen years earlier, but on a large scale. Although the field officers (*i.e.* majors and above), most of whom had obtained their promotion to field rank through Clive's recent re-organisation, were thereby sufficiently well paid to accept the loss of *batta* without complaint, the captains and subalterns were not. When their initial letters of remonstrance were rejected, they made, in all three brigades, agreements to resign their commissions simultaneously unless the old rates of *batta* were restored. Those who refused were threatened with permanent ostracism by their fellows. Articles were drawn up, with the subscribing officers undertaking to contribute funds to buy commissions in the British army for any Company's officer whose resignation was accepted, or who was otherwise victimised for joining the combination. A large number of civil servants agreed to support this fund, as they had a grudge against Clive for his insistence that they should, as ordered by the Directors, sign a covenant not to accept presents from any person in India, so putting an end to the lavish subventions from Indian princes and their agents by which many a 'nabob's' fortune had been made.

Just as had been the case in Madras, the combination collapsed in the face of government determination. Few officers were prepared to press matters to extremes. Those in the 3rd Brigade at Bankipur never actually sent in their commissions, and those in the other two continued doing duty as volunteers while they waited for a government response to their action. At Monghyr where the rank and file of the European battalion fell in ready to support their officers, the officers declined to join them, and the authorities paraded sepoy battalions under

Indian officers with every intention of firing on the Europeans if need be. The idea of a fund to compensate anyone victimised collapsed when Clive threatened to give the Secretary at War the names of any officers dismissed for insubordination so ensuring that they would not be permitted to buy a commission in the British army, where, as he pointed out, they would in any case suffer a net loss of income. Meanwhile he asked the Madras and Bombay Councils to send him every officer and cadet they could spare (to replace Bengal officers who might resign), and European troops to counter any disaffection among the Bengal European soldiers. Private letters from Bengal officers to their colleagues in Madras were censored. Emergency commissions were offered to civil servants (only two accepted), and consideration was given to promoting sergeants and corporals. In the end, a few scapegoats were court-martialled and cashiered, though nearly all of these were eventually reinstated, among them Colonel Sir Robert Fletcher, Commander of the 1st Brigade at Monghyr, whose previous distinguished services did not save him from the charge of complicity because he had not reported all he knew of his officers' intentions. Those who had resigned their commissions had them restored, but as new appointments, thus placing them in seniority below those who had not resigned or who had come from Madras in response to Clive's appeal. The Company's officers thereafter were required to give an undertaking to serve for a minimum of three years and not to resign without giving a year's notice. This enabled the authorities to counter any future revival of the officers' claim that immediately upon resigning they ceased to be under military law, and could not be charged with failure to obey orders.[3]

In Southern India, the Madras Presidency embarked upon a war against Haydar Ali of Mysore. At first regarded by the English and the country rulers as something of an upstart, Haydar had risen in eleven years from the position of Commander-in-Chief of the army of the Raja of Mysore to being by 1766, the *de facto* ruler of the entire state. The Madras Council was at first disposed to a policy of appeasement, on the principle that he might prove a useful counterpoise to the power of the Marathas, then beginning to recover from their defeat at Panipat. Then, fearing that his growing strength and ambition would lead him to threaten the Company's protege Muhammad Ali, Nawab of Arcot, the Madras Council in November 1766 formed an alliance with the Nizam, who had, for his part, formed an alliance with the Marathas to secure Haydar Ali's downfall. All three allies then marched against Mysore early in 1767, but Haydar Ali delayed the progress of the Marathas by a scorched earth policy, and then bought them off with 35 lakhs of rupees. The Nizam then quite literally transferred his army from the British camp to that of Haydar Ali, in the anticipation that if the British were defeated in the field he could recover the Northern Sarkars which the Mughal Emperor Shah Alam had granted to the Company. The Madras army, commanded by Colonel Joseph Smith, defeated the combined forces of Haydar Ali and the Nizam at the battle of Trinamalai (26 September 1767). This had the effect of returning the Nizam to his alliance with the British and obtaining from Haydar an offer to make peace. His offer was rejected by the Madras Council, to which the Nizam had offered the *diwani* or civil government of all Mysore (which was not in his power to give). Haydar renewed the war, and displaying all the able generalship which had mad him such a feared opponent, made short work of the scattered British garrisons and other detachments. Smith, with the main force, was hampered by the presence of Nawab Muhammad Ali, whose troops were merely an added drain on the resources of the devastated countryside of which he was the nominal ruler, and by two members of Council (appointed by their colleagues as 'field-deputies'), who constantly interfered with his dispositions and questioned his orders. By February 1768, however, Smith had forced Haydar's army to retreat, but Haydar himself, with 6,000 horsemen, slipped away to re-appear outside the walls of Fort St. George. The Madras government seeing no end to a war which had ruined the revenues, and incurred military expenditure while destroying the means of paying for it, were happy to accept Haydar's proposals for peace, a mutual restitution of conquests and prisoners, and an agreement that each party would, in return for payment at fixed rates, send troops to support the other if it were the subject of aggression.[4]

The Madras government's conduct of this campaign drew much criticism. The Directors disapproved of the appointment of field-deputies : 'Our opinion is, that when the Company has made choice of a proper person to be a Commander-in-Chief, all trust and confidence should be reposed in him to direct the plans and operations of the campaign.'[5] Many of Smith's problems had arisen from lack of supplies and rations for his men. The Madras Council blamed the Nawab for failing to supply them, but it emerged that the councillors had since 1761, given themselves the contracts for army supply as a means of supplementing their income, and that no other tenders had been invited. 'We were yet much more astonished', continued the Directors, 'that of all the Members of our Council not one had honour or virtue enough to reject a proposal which was as wholly incompatible with their duty as it was unworthy their character and station to accept.'

While the Company's servants and shareholders grew rich, the Company grew poor. By becoming a territorial power it had incurred the burden of all the defence and other public expenditure inseparable from the business of a state. The war against Mysore had ruined Madras, and in 1770 a terrible famine along the lower Ganges plain, had the same effect on Bengal. The Directors were obliged to ask financial aid from the British government. This was granted, but only in terms giving the Cabinet more effective power over the Company's revenue, civil, and military affairs. This power was expressed in Lord North's 'Regulating Act' of 1773.[6] The Act replaced the Company's Governor of Fort William and his large council of ten or more, by a Governor-General and four councillors, initially nominated by the Crown, but still controlled by the Court of Directors. This Court was itself reformed by the same Act, to give it a greater element of continuity with a quarter of its members in future to be elected each year, and holding office for four years instead of all being elected for one year only. The Governor-General in Council was also given control over the power of the Madras and Bombay governments to engage in hostilities with country powers, except where grave danger would result from waiting for instructions.

In 1774, acting before the new restrictions upon their powers to wage war could come into force, the government of Bombay became involved in the struggle over the disputed succession to the Peshwa, Norayan Rao, the foremost of the Maratha princes. Anticipating benefits similar to those which had been gained by their colleagues in Bengal and Madras from similar interventions in Indian politics, the Bombay government agreed to support Raghunath Rao, uncle of the late (murdered) Peshwa, against a Regency ruling in the name of Narayan Rao's posthumous infant son. A force of some 2,500 men, consisting of four European companies and four sepoy battalions from the Bombay army, and two companies of European grenadiers and a sepoy battalion lent by Madras, marched towards Poona, the Peshwa's capital. A hardfought battle at Aras, on 18 May 1775, in which Raghunath Rao's contingent proved a useless rabble, while the Maratha cavalry and elephants destroyed the Madras grenadiers, was eventually won by the Company's troops. Raghunath thereupon assigned control of several valuable areas to the British, including the former Portuguese holdings at Bassein and Salsette. At this point orders came from the new Governor-General in Council of Bengal disavowing the alliance with Raghunath and ordering a suspension of hostilities.[7]

The new Governor-General was the former Governor of Bengal, Warren Hastings, whose anxiety to guard against the renascent power of the Marathas had involved the Company in the Rohilla War of February—April 1774. Hastings had a distinguished record as a Bengal civil servant, having fought at Plassey as a volunteer, and gained, in the subsequent decade, a reputation for incorruptibility. In 1773 he discontinued the payment of revenues from Bengal to the Emperor Shah Alam, on the grounds that the latter was passing the money on to the Marathas in return for their military support. While this was true enough, Shah Alam was entitled to his share of the revenue and to do with it as he chose. In this instance he used it to secure the ejection from Delhi of a Rohilla chieftain, who had been installed there by Ahmad Shah after the battle of Panipat in 1761. The Rohillas, descendants of earlier Afghan military adventurers had given their name to the neighbouring region, Rohilkhand, where they had obtained extensive grants from the Mughals. The Marathas, after recovering Delhi for Shah Alam, prepared to march into Rohilkhand. The Rohillas asked the Nawab of Awadh for aid, which he agreed to provide at a price, but when the Marathas, distracted by the succession to the Peshwaship, did not invade, the Rohillas refused to pay. The Nawab, long desirous of adding Rohilkhand to his own territories, made this a *casus belli.* In August 1773 he met Hastings at Benares and concluded a treaty of friendship which placed one of the Bengal army's three brigades at his disposal in return for Rs. 210,000 monthly. In consequence of this arrangement, which transferred some 30 per cent of Bengal's defence budget to that of Awadh, the brigade marched with the Nawab's army into Rohilkhand and secured a quick victory over their ill-organised opponents. Awadh, strengthened by the expropriation of the Rohillas, and safeguarded by its contingent of the Bengal army, became a strong buffer state against the Marathas and remained a loyal ally of the Company. The only protest in the Bengal Council came from the Commander-in-Chief, Brigadier General Sir Robert Barker, who had a number of personal grudges against Hastings. What he asked, if the Emperor, slighted by these proceedings, withdrew the *sanads* by which the Company held its rights in India? Hastings speaking more like a soldier than a civilian, replied that it was not *sanads* but the sword which had given the British the dominion of Bengal, and which alone would maintain it.[8]

Most members of the new Governor-General's Council then being set up by the Regulating Act took a different view of the episode. The new Commander-in-Chief of Bengal, and thus of all the Company's forces in India, Lieutenant-General Sir John Clavering, a British army officer, was named in the Act as successor to the Governor-Generalship if Hastings died or resigned. The other three Councillors were Philip Francis, an English politician with his own designs on the Governor-Generalship, Colonel the Honourable George Monson, who had been Coote's second-in-command at Pondicherry, and Richard Barwell, one of the Company's civil servants. The three newcomers saw their duty as the extirpation of misgovernment and oppression by the Company's servants, and formed the view, later to be shared by the Directors, that the campaign against the Rohillas, with whom the Company had no quarrel, was an example of both. They regularly outvoted Hastings in Council until Monson's death in September 1776, after which Hastings was able to use his casting vote. Prior to this Hastings had, in frustration, declared he would resign if the position remained unchanged. The Directors took this as a resignation and when the news reached Calcutta in June 1777, Clavering claimed the Governor-Generalship. Hastings denied he had resigned, and was supported by the Judges of the Supreme Court which the Regulating Act had set up at Calcutta. He and Barwell then voted Clavering's positions as C-in-C and Second in Council to be null and void, but were, in their turn, over-ruled by the Supreme Court. Clavering's death on 30 August 1777 brought this particular battle to an end and he was replaced by General Sir Eyre Coote, the victor of Wandewash.[9]

In August 1773, the Madras government sent its troops, led by Major-General Joseph Smith against the Raja of Tanjore, who was in dispute with their ally, the Nawab Muhammad Ali. Tanjore was stormed on 17 September 1773, the raja was made prisoner, and his territories were appropriated by the Nawab. In March 1774 news of this reached the Directors, who did not discuss the question until after the last ships of the season sailed for India three weeks later. Thus it was not until December 1775 that Lord Pigot (who had last been Governor of Madras twelve years earlier) arrived with orders to take over from the existing Governor, reprimand his Council, and restore the raja. He found that his Commander-in-Chief was Sir Robert Fletcher, who had appealed successfully against his dismissal following the mutiny of the Bengal officers in 1766, and had been appointed C-in-C Madras in 1772. There he had challenged the authority of Governor as the Commander-in-

Chief of Fort St. George, and returned home to resume his seat as a Member of Parliament before again being sent to Madras in succession to Major-General Joseph Smith.

Pigot's action in restoring the raja gained him the enmity of most of the Madras Council. He nominated one of his own supporters to be Resident at Tanjore, but Fletcher considered that his own second in command, Colonel Stuart, would be a better choice. Moreover, the appointment could then be combined with that of commander of the large garrison there, which the raja had agreed to accept and pay for, as the price of his restoration. The majority voted against Pigot, who then refused to sign the orders requiring the existing commandant at Tanjore, Colonel Harper, to hand over to Stuart. The majority ordered the Council's secretary to sign them in the Governor's name. Pigot then charged two of the majority with subversion, thus preventing them from voting, until their case was heard, and thereby gaining control of the Council by his own party. The original majority called upon the civil and military officers of the Presidency to obey the Council as previously constituted. Pigot ordered Fletcher's arrest for failing to obey him, as the Governor. Stuart, acting as C-in-C after Fletcher had developed a fever, then ordered his Adjutant-General to arrest Pigot. Pigot appealed to Admiral Sir Edward Hughes, commanding a Royal Naval squadron then off Madras, but the majority refused Hughes's orders to give him safe conduct to the flagship. Pigot declined the compromise offer of a passage on board an East Indiaman and remained under house arrest.[10]

Although Hastings and his Council, in a rare unanimity, supported the Madras majority, the Court of Directors insisted that the office of the Governor must be respected. They ordered the release and restoration of Pigot, to be followed by his immediate recall, and that of his entire Council, to London for an investigation, and by the court martial of the military officers involved. By the time the orders reached Madras both Pigot and Fletcher had died. Those who had formed the majority of the Council were eventually convicted and heavily fined, but Stuart (by then a Brigadier-General) and the remaining officers, successfully pleaded that they had been obeying the orders of the civil government of the day. The Madras command meanwhile devolved first upon Colonel Ross Lang of the Company's service, and then in February 1778, Major-General Hector Munro, the victor of Baksar. At the same time, Sir Thomas Rumbold, a Madras civil servant who had begun his career as an officer in the Madras army, and had fought as a captain at Plassey, arrived from England to replace Pigot.

A few months later, the outbreak of a new war between the British and French governments put the armies of all three Presidencies in India into the field. Pondicherry, restored to France after the Seven Years War, fell to the Madras army on 8 October 1778 after a month's siege. In June 1780 Haydar invaded the Carnatic, with 70,000 men, including sepoy battalions led by French officers. Within a month he was raiding the suburbs of Madras and had gained possession of almost every fort in the country. Those garrisoned by the British had been so ill provisioned by the civil authorities as to be incapable of resistance, and the gates of those held by the Nawab's own officers were in the Mughal tradition 'opened with a golden key', *i.e.* by bribing the commandant. The space of twenty-one days during August and September 1780 saw a reduction of British military prestige in India to a level lower than it had been since before Plassey. The war continued for another four years. In October 1780 Hastings sent Sir Eyre Coote, with every rupee and soldier he could spare, to take over operations in Madras. Hampered by lack of transport and supplies, Coote relieved the few garrisons still holding out, but undertook no major operations until the summer of 1781, when he gained a victory over Haydar at Porto Novo. Haydar, supported by a French brigade which disembarked in the Carnatic in March 1782, was able to keep the field with a large army, which included sepoys captured or deserted from the armies of Nawab Muhammad Ali and his British allies. Coote, quarrelling with Whitehill's successor, Lord Macartney, returned to Bengal in September 1782 to reassert his position as C-in-C of the army there. Haydar, despairing of eventual success in a war where, despite his continued victories on land, the power of the British at sea enabled them to continue the struggle, fell back from the Carnatic to consolidate his hold on the west coast. Five naval engagements fought during 1782, between the squadron of Sir Edward Hughes and the French admiral, de Suffren, had, in fact, left British control of Indian seas in the balance, and the arrival of reinforcements for the French army continued to distract the Madras government. Haydar died of blood poisoning in December 1782. Coote died in April 1783, suffering a stroke while his ship was pursued by two French men-of-war as he sailed back to resume command in Madras.[11]

On the British side, the war had been conducted in an atmosphere of continual constitutional crises. Lord Macartney, an ambitious Irish peer with a creditable record in British public life, was the first Governor of an Indian Presidency not to have risen from the Company's service. He took full advantage of the provisions of the Regulating Act which allowed the minor presidencies to make war independently of the Governor-General in Bengal in response to urgent local dangers. Coote, as C-in-C India, took a seat in the Madras Council when he was actually in the presidency but, while Macartney argued that he should be bound by the views of the majority in Council, Coote took the view that, in the conduct of the war, he spoke as a member of the Supreme Government in Bengal.[12] Coote also claimed that the Madras government's failure to provide him with the pack oxen and supplies he considered necessary prevented him from making any decisive moves against Haydar Ali.[13] Macartney replied that Coote seemed to consider that the Governor had no other part to play in the conduct of the war than to be a 'bullock agent' and openly expressed his disappointment that an army so expensively appointed had achieved so little.[14] He also mounted minor expeditions (including one led by the displaced Sir Hector Munro) without consulting Coote, while the latter was absent in the field with his main force. Coote, on his final visit to Calcutta, obtained from Hastings powers to act virtually as the military dictator of Madras, but died before the issue could be tested.

With Coote dead and Munro having returned to Europe, command in Madras passed to Major-General Stuart, the same officer who had arrested Lord Pigot. He had, since then, resumed his military duties, and had lost a leg in the war against Haydar Ali. Like Coote, he maintained that the C-in-C was, in all military matters, the sole competent authority. He went even further, by arguing that, as his commission was in the British army rather than the Company's army, he was, at least in his command of the British troops in Madras, not obliged to comply with the directions of the Company's civil authorities.[15]

Stuart continued to exasperate Macartney, who on 17 September 1783 used his own powers as Governor to dismiss him from the Company's service, on the grounds of disobedience. This had the effect of reducing him to his substantive position an as officer on the British half-pay list, since he held the rank of Major-General only by virtue of his employment as C-in-C of the Company's Madras army. He was thus disqualified from exercising authority over either British or Company's troops, and Major-General Sir John Burgoyne, the next senior officer of the British army then in Madras was ordered by Macartney to take over command of the British troops. Burgoyne, however, stated that he considered himself still under Stuart's orders, whereupon Macartney sent a Company's officer, with a party of sepoys to arrest Stuart and so physically prevent him from giving any orders at all.[16] At the same time he promoted Colonel Ross Lang of the Madras army tc be Lieutenant-General and commander of the Company's forces. Burgoyne assumed command of the British troops but, after countermanding orders issued by Macartney, was himself arrested on 31 December 1783, and replaced by Major-General Campbell, the next senior British officer. There matters rested until May 1785, when a British army officer, Lieutenant-General Sir John Dalling, arrived with authority to command all the troops in Madras. Lang retired with a special pension, and Burgoyne, acquitted by court martial, was recalled to Europe.[17] Macartney resigned in June 1785, and on returning to London was provoked into a duel, and wounded, by Stuart.[18] Hastings, who had, earlier, seriously considered suspending Macartney, a move which Stuart would have been only too happy to execute, himself resigned in February 1785.

The British had not only to deal with questions of civil-military relations, but with relations between the British and the Company's armies. After Stuart's arrest, the officers of British regiments in Madras refused to admit that Lang had authority over them in law, and declared that though they would follow his operational orders, they would do so as volunteers. The Company's officers, on their part, protested at the lavish grant to British army officers of brevet ranks (*i.e.* ranks higher than those permitted by the established strength of the army, to permit the holder to exercise higher powers of command). This had taken place during the Seven Years War, but the number of British troops in India, and the duration and scale of operations, had been much smaller than they were in the 1780s, and the grievance was not so greatly felt. In 1784, a petition by Madras officers to the Court of Directors pointed out that 4 British army colonels had become brevet major-Generals, 7 lieutenant-colonels had become brevet colonels, 6 majors and 3 captains had become brevet lieutenant-colonels and 1 captain a brevet major, whereas the Company's Madras establishment was only 1 major-general, 2 colonels, 4 lieutenant-colonels, and 4 majors of infantry (there was also 1 major of artillery).[19] This meant that, whether in the field or garrison, almost all the commands were taken, by virtue of their military seniority, by British army officers who had limited knowledge of Indian conditions. Their regimental duties were left to be performed by their junior officers, but even the most junior British army officer had seniority over the longest-serving Company's officer of the same rank. Colonel Fullerton of the 98th, who commanded in 1783-84 what was probably the most successful expedition in the war against Tipu, and who stood as Macartney's second in his duel with Stuart, recorded that the Madras officers had far more experience of independent command than their British equivalents, and were 'habituated to act in emergency with a facility that few subordinate officers in Europe ever have a prospect of acquiring'.[20]

The Company's officers, promoted in turn according to their seniority within the army, gained wide experience as they moved from post to post, so that when, usually after many years, they reached the rank of captain, they were fully competent in their profession. Lang, in his support for their petition quoted the case of a well-qualified captain with seventeen ears' service in the Company's army being obliged to serve under the orders of a newly arrived British captain of twenty-six month's service. An even more extreme case was that of a British army lieutenant aged fourteen, who took command of a picquet consisting mostly of sepoys whose own officer had been a subaltern for fourteen years.[21] A similar petition, signed by 132 Bengal army officers, and endorsed by Hastings in October 1783 protested that, notwithstanding the extent to which their service had grown into a large, regular, standing army, they were still obliged to defer to those of the same rank in the British service. They asked the Directors not to allow officers who had spent their lives in the Company's service to be subordinated to young British army officers 'many of whom have not been so long in Existence as the Dates of our Commissions'.[22] It was not until 1788, however, that some action was taken to remedy this grievance, and even then, only in connection with a quite separate constitutional issue.

Ten years of war had revealed the weaknesses of North's Regulating Act. It had required the Court of Directors to lay before the British government all correspondence with India dealing with foreign affairs, but provided no formal machinery whereby the government could control the orders which the Directors sent to their servants in India. It left the Governor-General, and the Governors of the minor presidencies, at the mercy of the majorities in their own Councils, and left the British military, sent to India in support of British foreign police, unclear of their exact constitutional position. The expansion of European power meant that British foreign policy in India could no longer be separated from that in the rest of the world. Moreover, in an age when patriotic Englishmen in America, and patriotic Irishmen nearer home had defied in arms the authority of the British government, there was some anxiety that yet another body of British citizens should be maintaining regular armies, fortifications and warships, not under the Crown's control. Charles James Fox, Lord North's ally in the

House of Commons, introduced a bill in 1783 to remedy this situation by giving to the government of the day the right to appoint all civil and military officers in British India. The prospect of any government having the patronage of India at its disposal, so that it could thereby secure so much support in the House of Commons as to maintain itself in power indefinitely, provoked the wrath of George III, who announced that anyone who voted for it would no longer be considered the King's friend. The Fox-North coalition fell, and William Pitt the Younger came to power, with the Indian question in urgent need of a solution.[23]

Pitt's India Act carried in 1784, established the constitutional framework by which British India would be governed for the next seventy-four years.[24] The most important feature was the establishment of a Board of Commissioners for the Control of India, presided over by a Secretary of State, who soon became, for all practical purposes, its sole member. The three senior members of the Court of Directors were formed into a Committee of Secrecy, which alone dealt with the Board, and relayed its orders in all matters of civil and military government of India. The patronage of India, including even the right to appoint and recall a Governor-General, remained with the court of all twenty-four Directors, although in practice, because the Act gave it a veto over these offices, the Board nominated the Governor-General, Governors and C-in-Cs. The number of members of the three Presidential Councils in India was reduced to four, composed of the Governor-General or Governor, the local C-in-C, and two others. The C-in-C India when in Madras or Bombay was to take the local C-in-C's place in Council with the local C-in-C then allowed to sit but not vote. C-in-Cs were not to succeed a Governor-General or Governor without express orders from the Court of Directors. At the other extreme, the Act provided that no cadets should be appointed to the Company's army under the age of 15 or over that of 22 (or 25 if they had previously served at least a year in the British army).

While the civil servant who had saved British India

returned home to face impeachment, the general who had lost America was sent to govern British India. Finding a successor for Warren Hastings was not easy for the Directors. The appointment was eventually accepted, by Lieutenant-General Lord Cornwallis who needed neither a title nor a fortune, and whose surrender at Yorktown was blamed upon his superiors. At his insistence, amending acts were passed enabling him to overrule his Council in emergency, and to hold the office of C-in-C India as well as that of Governor-General. Cornwallis thus took over from Macpherson and Lieutenant-General Sloper respectively in September 1786. The same principle, of combining the posts of Governor and C-in-C was applied at Bombay where Major-General William Medows was appointed in 1787, and at Madras, where he went on to hold the same two offices between 1790 and 1792. His replacement at Bombay by Major-General Sir Robert Abercromby placed all three presidencies for a time in the hands of military men.

The new Board of Control made the reorganisation of the military in India one of its first concerns. Henry Dundas, Pitt's tireless ally throughout his long ministry, was the architect of the ministry's Indian policy, and headed the Board from its inception. He decided that in future there would be a contingent of the British army stationed in India at all times, not only for the duration of hostilities with a rival European power. They therefore pressed for the transfer of the Company's European troops to the British army, and the grant of royal commissions to officers who remained with the sepoys. Cornwallis felt that fair consideration should be given to the officers.[25] Indeed he objected throughout his entire Indian career to the Directors' policy of paying low salaries to their civil and military servants alike, on the principle that they would make a good living out of the many opportunities, honest of otherwise, of profiting from their service in India, at least if they survived the effects of the climate and tropical disease. Probably the greatest achievement of his Indian administration was to secure an honest Civil Service by paying its officials so well that they did not need to be dishonest. Concerning the military officers, he wrote to the Duke of York on 10 November 1786 : 'they have no head to look up to; the promotion of rank has always gone by seniority; and the lucrative commands have been given to those who have had interest' (*i.e.* influence). 'Consequently there has been no spur to merit. The Company's officers have no regiments or governments to look forward to. . . If they cannot save some money, they must go home without rank or pay, condemned to disease or beggary. Under these circumstances, the most rigid general must relax a little and suffer practices that are in some degree repugnant to the nice feelings of a soldier.'[26] He recommended to Dundas that the Company's officers should take rank with those of the British army according to the date of their respective commissions within each rank. Their transfer to the British army would, he felt, weaken the control over them of the Company's local governments in India.

Dundas continued to advocate the replacement of the Company's European by British regiments.[27] In October 1787 he used the renewed tension between Britain and France as the occasion for informing the Directors that four new British regiments were to be raised and sent to India. Their officers were to be drawn equally from the British half-pay and Company's redundant officers, who would thus regain employment in their profession and cease to be an unprofitable charge on official funds. Only one of the four new lieutenant-colonels, however, was to be a former Company's officer, and even that would be in a regiment whose colonel, unlike most regimental colonels, would go with it in command. The Directors protested that this would adversely affect the interests of their own officers, of whom 600 were at the time surplus to establishment while the 1,800 in post stood to find themselves junior to officers of the new British regiments, 86 of them their own former comrades. The grievances sent home in the officers' petitions of 1783 were alluded to, and a delegation of the Company's officers then on leave in England waited upon the Court of Directors, to press their case.

As the international crisis waned, the Directors urged Dundas to cancel the orders for the new regiments, and allow the Company to recruit its own Europeans instead. When the Board of Control refused to bargain, the Directors voted against accepting the troops on their ships or paying them from Indian revenues.[28] Prior to 1781 the expenses of maintaining British troops in India had been borne by the British government, as they were sent there in furtherance of British foreign policy rather than the Company's interests. In 1781 it had been enacted that the Company would pay two lakhs of rupees per regiment per annum, but only for troops sent at the Company's request. The ministers responded with the Declaratory Act of February 1788[29] which gave authority to the Board of Control to order troops to India at the Company's expense irrespective of the wishes of the Court of Directors. Great opposition was encountered, however, even among the government's supporters, for fear partly of an extension of ministerial patronage, and partly of a tyrannical government raising troops from Indian revenues who could be used against the hard-won rights and liberties of Englishmen. Accordingly, provisions were added limiting the number of European troops that could be maintained in India to 8,045 from the British army and 12,200 from the Company's army. This had the effect of negating all the previous proposals of replacing the latter by the former.

The government went some way to redressing the grievance over relative seniority in 1788. Thereafter all the Company's officers were granted commissions by their Commanders-in-Chief giving them powers of command over British troops, in the East Indies only, and solely while in the service of the Company, with seniority according to the date of their commission from the Governor-General or Governors of Bengal, Madras and Bombay respectively, which gave them their power of command over the Company's troops. All brevets held by British army officers in India were cancelled, and no more granted, though British officers who had attained their substantive rank before the end of hostilities in 1783 were allowed to retain their seniority over all Company's officers of the same rank. These concessions did little, however, to address the problems caused by the rapidity of promotion in the British army permitted by the purchase system (and indeed thought to be one of its advantages, both for the officers and the army). compared with the slowness of that in any service where it depended upon seniority. Moreover, there were relatively few posts of field rank in the Company's service, as far the greater part of its 112,000 strong army consisted of sepoy battalions, which were commanded by captains. A newly promoted captain in command of a sepoy battalion was still junior to an equally newly promoted captain in command of a British company, irrespective of their individual length of service. Nevertheless, few wished to give up the actuality, or hope, of commanding a sepoy battalion, with all the military prestige and financial allowances that went with it, in order to become a junior captain in a junior British regiment, and when the four new regiments were eventually formed, they were officered mostly from the British half-pay (as Cornwallis had forecast would be the case).

Consideration of Indian army reform was postponed until Cornwallis returned to England in February 1794. He had sailed from Calcutta six months earlier, and was succeed as Governor-General by Sir John Shore, a Company's civil servant, and as C-in-C by Major-General Sir Robert Abercromby, a British army officer previously C-in-C at Bombay. In September 1794 Cornwallis was formally requested by Dundas to produce a plan for re-organising the army in India such as would improve the security of the British possession there, and would also bring to an end the friction between the King's and the Company's troops, and between the Company's own three presidential armies. His plan, submitted to the Board of Control in November 1794 recommended that all the Company's troops, native as well as European, should be transferred to the King's service, but the native troops should form a separate Indian army. European troops and their officers would simply become part of the British army, and, on doing so, conform to its existing rules for commissions and promotion. Offices of the Indian army would hold the King's commission and rise by seniority within their regiment to the rank of major, and thereafter, within their arm and presidency, by seniority as before. The ninety-five battalions of sepoys were to be reduced to eighty. The remaining units were to be formed into forty regiments each of two battalions. Each regiment would be commanded by a colonel, and each battalion by a lieutenant-colonel, as in the British army. The Company's officers were to opt to join either the British or Indian armies, and thereafter no exchanges would be permitted. Those who wished subsequently to sell their commission would be allowed to do so. Furloughs of up to three years would be granted without loss of pay, and officers could retire on full pay of their rank after six years' service as an ensign and on a scale proportionate to rank up to twenty-six years for lieutenant-colonels. Any brevet promotion which had been granted to all officers of the King's army would be matched by similar grants to officers of the Company's armies. To balance this, the double *batta* paid in Bengal would be abolished, as would be various other lucrative emoluments. Allowances for field service were to be standardised throughout the three armies.

Although this plan remedied many long-standing grievances, the time taken to prepare it, and the time it took for correspondence to pass between London and India, had an unsettling effect. Before leaving India, Cornwallis had circulated many of his ideas among the officers of the Madras army.[30] When the officers of the Bengal army, on whom they bore most hardly, learned of them from their Madras comrades, there was an immediate outcry. Committees were formed, petitions drawn up, and agents were sent to lay their case before the Directors. The officers of all three armies were opposed to promotion by regimental instead of army seniority, and to the introduction of British army officers into the European regiments (which would have been the consequence of absorbing these units into the British army). They insisted on the same rank being attached to the same level of command in the Indian as in the British service before any transfer from the Company to the Crown, and on the Indian army, including its European element, remaining separate from the British army.[31]

A pamphlet published by the Bengal officers early in 1794 condemned Cornwallis's proposals, and explained that because of the pay of the low rank to which they were restricted, the Company's officers were dependent upon the various allowances he proposed to abolish. They argued that whereas in the 80 regular infantry battalions of the British army (36,540 bayonets), there was 1 officer for every 14 soldiers and a general for every 430, in the Company's 95 battalions of infantry (59,280 bayonets) there were no generals, and only 1 officer (at least in Bengal) for every 48 sepoys. The weakness of this particular argument was that the Company's units also had a full complement of Indian officers in each company, but this was not remarked upon by either side in the dispute at the time. Unauthorised meetings and assemblies of officers continued in the Bengal army with increasing indignation on both sides throughout 1794 and 1795, and the wilder spirits even talked of arresting Shore and Abercromby, and ordering their own men to oppose movements by British troops. Shore was sufficiently concerned to order the admiral commanding the East Indies squadron to stand by to bring troops from Madras, and even contemplated the use of sepoys, and European mercenaries from the armies of friendly country powers. In January 1795, however, moderate opinion re-asserted itself, partly in response to Abercromby's assurances that something would be done to meet any legitimate grievances.[32]

Protracted discussions in London had resulted in significant changes to Cornwallis's original scheme. The Directors were initially cool towards their officers' complaints. Dundas was sufficiently concerned at reports of disaffection and agitation to meet a committee of offices, and to receive their formal objections to Cornwallis's plan, much to the latter's disgust. In January 1795 the Directors formally notified the Board of Control that they would on no account consent to the transfer of their army to the King's service.[33] The ministers, distracted by the spread of revolutionary ideas at home and abroad, and by the familiar tale of a British army being defeated in the Low Countries, felt the time was inopportune to force the issue. In April it became clear that they could not, in any case, command a majority in Parliament for the addition of 60,000 regular soldiers to those at the disposal of the Crown, for the very same reason that had brought them to power twelve years earlier. The patronage of India could not be entrusted to party politicians. Accordingly, when in January 1796 orders for the reform of the army were eventually sent to India, they contained nothing about amalgamating the European units with the British army, or transferring the sepoy units to the Crown. The main reform was the re-organisation of the infantry into forty regiments of two battalions, together with new provisions for paid furlough, pensions and promotion to general officer rank.[34]

The accompanying orders reducing *batta* and other allowances, and introducing promotion by seniority within the new regiments provoked a storm of protest in Bengal, even from the former moderates. Once again petitions and protests were drawn up. The reduction in officers' allowances without fully compensating increases in the level of their rank was compared unfavourably with the lavish increases by which Cornwallis had brought out the corrupt practices of the Indian civil service. The introduction of promotion to field rank by regimental seniority, and to subsequent command by selection was condemned on the grounds that this would allow promotion to be affected by chance (if casualties occurred more frequently in one regiment or another) or favouritism (if officers were selected on the subjective grounds of supposed merit rather than the objective ones of length of service, for which all had contracted on accepting their commissions).

Shore and Abercromby together formed the view that there was nothing to be gained by driving the Bengal officers into a refusal to obey orders. While any insurrection would have easily been put down, for the officers of Madras and Bombay, while content to benefit from any concession secured by those of Bengal, were not willing to join them in a mutiny, the very possibility was enough to waken the efficiency and loyalty of the Bengal sepoys, and, in turn, the security of British possessions in India. Moreover, with the war against France continuing to go ill for the British, an efficient Bengal army led by well-motivated officers was infinitely more useful than one reduced to inefficiency by the mass resignation of its officers, or even their departure to a rival Indian employer. Accordingly in May 1796, Shore and Abercromby decided to hold up the introduction of regimental promotion, and, while complying with the letter of their orders to end the specified allowances, followed the precedent set by the Madras government in paying separate new allowances equal to those which were discontinued.

Once again the ministers turned to Cornwallis. After being appointed Governor-General for a second tour, in February 1797, he again put forward his old proposals for bringing the company's European units into the British army, for regimental promotion, and for filling commands by nomination rather than seniority. With Dundas's approval, he demanded that his instructions from the Directors who were, constitutionally, his employers, should give him absolute power to re-organise their army as he saw fit.[35] When the Board of Control formally supported him, the Directors responded by calling a meeting of the Court of Proprietors, on 5 May 1797. This voted against giving Cornwallis the instructions he wanted. Once again disasters nearer home, including mutinies in the Fleet, distracted the Cabinet from taking issue with the Company, and in August Cornwallis resigned, going to Ireland in 1798 to deal with the rebellion which had broken out there.[36]

The only part of his Indian army reforms to be implemented against the wishes of the local officers was the creation of the new regiments, and the introduction of regimental promotion. This meant the separation of the European from the Native line in the infantry, though not in the other arms, as there was no European cavalry in the Company's service, and all gunners, European or Native, continued to belong to their respective single regiments of artillery at each presidency. Infantry officers permanently posted to a native regiment feared a loss of prestige, while those remaining in a European regiment feared a loss of command opportunities, with their chances of extra income and greater distinction. The introduction of retirement pensions, and the prospect of promotion offered by the increased number and rank of the officers authorised for the new regiments, made this reform the easier to accept. For every regiment of 2 battalions, each of 10 companies, there was a colonel, 2 lieutenant-colonels, 2 majors, 7 captains and a captain-lieutenant, 22 lieutenants and 10 ensigns. This meant that each battalion had 2 field officers, 4 captains and 16 subalterns, in place of the 1 captain and 8 subalterns previously allowed.

The extra British officers were also expected to make the sepoy battalions more combat-worthy, as, in the campaigns against Mysore and the Marathas, sepoys were thought to have performed better when led by British rather than native company officers. Insofar as there was an average qualitative superiority, the British derived it partly from at least a notional study of their profession (easier for those with a Western ducation than for those without), partly from their identification with the regime for which they were fighting (whereas the native officer had no vested interest other than his pay, and its arrears) and partly because promotion by seniority, although it prevented corruption, meant that promotion was just as slow for the native as for the British officer. In a society where men grew, and felt, old more quickly than in Europe, a sepoy was likely to be a grandfather sooner than becoming a subedar. Those who still retained their physical and mental energy were often regarded with suspicion. The native commandants of battalions had been abolished in 1781, on the grounds that, if feeble they were useless, and if influential, they might exert their influence against their British paymasters. The addition of so many more British company officers left the native officers (one subedar and one jemadar per company) with nothing to command. Although in battle they remained as courageous as anybody else, in barracks they became more like welfare officers or trade union officials, mediating between the troops and officers who became, paradoxically, the more remote as they became more numerous.

A series of wars between 1799 and 1805 left the British masters of Mysore, where Haydar's son Tipu Sultan fell fighting to the last, and victorious over the Marathas. Cornwallis was again sent out as Governor-General and C-in-C, but died soon after arrival in India. His successor, Sir George Barlow, the last civil servant to hold this office under the Company's rule, faithfully implemented the court's instructions to make peace and reduce defence expenditure.

In Madras the new local C-in-C, Sir John Cradock decided that, with the coming of peace, it was time to smarten up his army. Regulations were published banning the personal ornaments and coloured marks upon their foreheads which sepoys had customarily worn in military as in civil life, banning the beards which to many was an outward sign of their virility, and ordering moustaches to be trimmed to a specified pattern. Worse still, with the enthusiasm which peace-time commanders so often display for military tailoring, Cradock devised a new pattern of head-dress, designed, like the other changes, to make his men look more like British soldiers. This had an unsettling effect on the troops. The displacement of so many princes in so short a period had revealed to everyone the true extent of British power in South Asia. Although the presence of Christian missionaries (the 'padres' as they were called by Indian, irrespective of sect) in British India was always discouraged by the East India Company, everyone knew that Christianity was a missionary religion , and also that Indian rulers such as (Tipu Sultan), zealous in their own faith, had been known to order the forcible conversion of their subjects. Making men look like Christians through the adoption of the uniform of Christian soldiers was feared to be a step to making them become Christians, so facing men with a choice between pollution and ostracism on the one hand, or the loss of the economic and social benefits of military service on the other.

At Vellore (Vellur) where the survivors of Tipu's family had their residence, there was a combination of irreconcilables who saw no reason why the dynasty so recently displaced should not rise again, and of sepoys suspicious of the intentions of their British employers. In May 1806 19 grenadiers of the 2nd Battalion 4th Madras Native Infantry refused to wear the new head-dress, and only submitted after two of their number received 900 lashes each. Statements obtained by the British from local spiritual leaders that the new head-dress infringed neither Muslim nor Hindu codes went unheeded. Other noly men preached resistance, and it was rumoured in the bazaar that after fifty years the end of British dominion was at hand. Discipline, which Cradock's regulations had been intended to tighten, in fact began to crack. In June 1806, a sepoy, Mustafa Beg, warned his colonel that a mutiny was being planned, but as his story was referred for investigation by a board of native officers who were involved in the plot, he found himself thrown in the cells, as a troublemaker. He was still there on 10 July 1806, when the mutiny broke out.

The Vellore incident differed markedly from all previous sepoy mutinies. These had all been concerned with purely military grievances, connected with arrears of pay, or conditions of service. Indeed, only eight years earlier the European artillery at Madras itself had mutinied over these very questions, settled only after the authorities had hung three of the ringleaders and blown away one from a gun in the old Mughal custom. Previous action had taken the form of desertion, or seizure of government property. At Vellore, for the first time, the issue raised was one of religion. For the first time too, the return to power of an Indian regime was envisaged. Led by native officers, sepoys of the garrison opened fire with musketry and artillery on barracks where 370 men of the 67th Foot were asleep, killing or wounding nearly 200 of them. The British rushed the magazine, but finding it empty , took refuge over the main gateway, suffering more casualties, including all the surviving officers, in the process. Inside the fort, Tipu's old flag was hoisted in place of the British colours.

Sixteen miles away at Arcot news reached the commander, Colonel Rollo Gillespie, some three hours after firing started. At the head of a troop of his regiment, the 19th Light Dragoons, he reached Vellore within two hours, and climbed up a rope of buckled belts to take command of the gateway until his horse artillery arrived. Like most South Asian fortresses, Vellore had no defences to pretect its gates against cannon fire. The usual procedure when a siege was anticipated, that of bricking them up, had been pre-empted by Gillespie's rapid response. His guns shot the gates away and the cavalry rode in, trapping the mutineers, who lacking any clear leadership of their own, made little resistance. Some four hundred were killed in the fort, and of the remainder who fled or surrendered, seventeen were executed after a drumhead court-martial. About six hundred men who had not been taken in arms, but who had at best remained as bystanders, were dismissed. Tipu's family was removed to Calcutta. The rest of the Madras native army remained obedient to orders. Sir John Cradock and the Governor of Madras, Lord William Bentinck, were recalled. The new Governor, Sir George Barlow (whom the Board of Control had refused to confirm as Governor-General) blamed missionaries for disturbing the army, and continued to discourage their activities.[37]

In response to demands for military economies which Barlow ordered while acting Governor-General, both Bentinck and Cradock had agreed that the Madras army's tent contract system could be abolished. This system was merely an additional allowance to commanding officers, in peace and war, for providing their regiments with tentage which was only needed, and therefore only provided, in war. Colonel John Monro, Quartermaster General of the Madras army, on being ordered by Cradock to investigate the system, reported that it gave officers a strong personal inducement to neglect their duty and that, from his six years' experience of it, the disadvantages of this were obvious. This brought a storm of protest from officers who accused Monro of imugning their honour. Monro denied such an intention, but the officers called for him to be court-martialled. On Cradock's recall, the post of C-in-C Madras had been given to Major-General Hay Macdowall, but without the seat in Council that normally went with it. In the spring of 1809 he had resigned over this issue and was awaiting passage home, while his relations with Barlow, whom he blamed for his exclusion from the Council and for excessive military retrenchment, sank to ever lower levels. The judge advocate general of the Madras army, to whom the question of Monro's conduct was referred, ruled that there was no case to answer.[38]

The officers thereupon withdrew their demand for a court-martial, and prepared a memorial to the Court of Directors, asking for an investigation to clear their name of any suggestion of misconduct. Barlow, however, refused to forward it. Macdowell ordered Monro's arrest, and refused to forward his subsequent appeal to the Governor. Barlow, nevertheless, learned of the arrest and ordered Monro's release. Macdowell then published a General Order, reprimanding Monro for appealing to the Governor, and accusing him of insubordination and disrespect to military authority. Barlow then suspended from their position in the Company's service both Major Bowels, the over-zealous deputy Adjutant-General who issued the general order in Macdowell's name, and Colonel Capper, the Adjutant-General, who, though, absent when the order was published, insisted on being held responsible for his deputy's actions. A group of officers then presented Bowles with an address commending his conduct, and subscribed to a compensation fund for him, and prepared a memorial to be sent to Governor-General Lord Minto.

Three months later Barlow responded by suspending, without trial or warning, several senior officers for encouraging the address to Bowles and for signing the memorial to the Governor-General, of which Barlow had obtained a copy, although in fact it had not actually been sent. He also congratulated the officers stationed at Hyderabad for their good conduct in refusing to be associated with these protests. This provoked these officers into threatening to march on Madras unless Capper and Bowles were reinstated and their replacements dismissed. The European regiment at Masulipatam, on being ordered to sea as marines, refused to go. Its officers arrested their colonel and made common cause with those at Hyderbad, Barlow ordered all officers to sign a document asserting their loyalty. Only 150 of the 1,300 officers in the Madras army signed, as even loyal officers objected on the grounds that a signature implied their own loyalty had been in doubt.[39]

Even more serious incidents occurred before discipline was restored. British regiments were moved to where they could overawe the Company's Europeans. Proclamations were issued to the native officers and sepoys pointing out that their British officers' quarrel was a private one with the government which controlled the pay and pensions of all ranks. Nevertheless, at Seringapatam, the European officers, on being informed by Barlaw that, as punishment for failing to sign the document of loyalty, they would be removed from their regiments, drove a British detachment out of the fort, seized the treasury, and prepared for a siege. Two sepoy battalions marching to join the mutiny were attacked by government reinforcements, and lost about two hundred before a sally from the fort allowed them to join the garrison, which then turned its guns on the loyal troops. Then, despite troops from Jalna and the Northern Sarkars being on their way to join them, the officers of the Hyderabad committee decided that matters had gone too far. They all signed the document and sent messages to officers of the other stations encouraging them to do likewise. Seringapatam surrendered , and by the time that Minto arrived at Madras on September 1809, intending to quell the mutiny in person, he found that all was quiet. Twenty-one officers who had been the most active in the mutiny were tried by court-martial or summarily dismissed. Papers were called for in the House of Commons. The Directors approved all Barlow's actions except for the suspension of Bowles and the removal of the other officers without proper evidence or trial.[40] The affair ended Barlow's prospects of succeeding Minto as Governor-General, which he had been promised, and he was recalled in 1812. Macdowell was blamed for encouraging the officers in their resistance to Barlow's economies, but as the East Indiaman on which he had sailed for England was lost without trace, he never received this censure. Never again, however, was a Commander-in-Chief appointed without a seat in the Governor's Council.

Far away , at Badajoz, Lord Wellington, the sepoy general who had learnt in India many of the campaigning skills that would bring him victory in Spain, wrote to his old Indian comrade Sir John Malcolm, that nothing could have been more absurd than the pretext for the officers' action. Monro, he said, should not have been court-martialled for giving his opinion, harsh though it was towards his brother officers, but rather, court-martialled had he *not* given it when ordered. As to whether the governor had the right to protect Monro from his C-in-C, this was a question upon which :

> no man can have a doubt who has any knowledge of the constitution of Great Britain, and particularly that of the Indian governments. I who have arrived pretty nearly at the top of the tree should be the last man to give up any point of right or military etiquette. But I have no doubt whatever, not only that it was the right, but that it was the duty of the governor in council to interfere to save Colonel Monro.[41]

The emergence of the British as the paramount power in South Asia came with the campaigns of the Marquess of Hastings. Governor-General and Commander-in-Chief from October 1813 to January 1823, he held the latter appointment longer than any other officer, and the former longer than anyone except Warren Hastings, its first holder. Hastings, unlike his predecessor Minto, who had been previously President of the Board of Control, had no knowledge of India and little of public office. His military career had been unremarkable, and his appointment, at the age of fifty-eight, was thought to owe more to the influence of his friend the Prince Regent than to his perceived merits. He soon had the chance to show his ability as a strategist when the revival in 1814 of a long-standing dispute over the old northern borders of Awadh led to war with Nepal. After initial disasters including the defeat and death of Major-General Gillespie, the hero of Vellur, the superior resources of the British brought them success in 1816. Nepal ceded territory and accepted British protection, but without the requirement for a subsidy. Nepali Gurkha soldiers, who had, man for man, proved themselves a match for British soldiers and Bengal sepoys, were enlisted into the Bengal army.[42]

At the end of 1817 the Maratha princes, determined to resist further British expansion, gathered their men for their last great battles. At Poona, the Peshwa Baji Rao II attacked and burnt the British Residency, only to see his army defeated by the Bombay troops at Kirkee (Khadki) on 5 November 1817. The Bhonsla Raja of Nagpur attacked the British Residency there, before going down to defeat at Sitabaldi on 27 November 1817 and outside Nagpur itself on 16 December. Holkar's army, despite the effectiveness of its seventy well-served guns, was smashed by Hislop at Mahidpur on 20 December. At Koregaon, on 1 January 1818, less than 1,000 Bombay sepoys and 24 Madras European gunners held off the Peshwa's last army, 20,000 strong. At the end of hostilities the British were unchallenged.[43] The Peshwa and Bhonsla were deposed and their dominions annexed by the British. Holkar, Sindia, and the Gaekwar of Baroda accepted British protection, and control of their foreign and defence policies. Hastings, conscious of the consequences of his campaigns, ordered that the Mughal Emperor should no longer be presented with the formal gifts of honour rendered by a subject to a sovereign. Although until 1835 the Company would continue to strike currency bearing his cipher, India was now subject to a new empire, and a new military system

REFERENCES

1. L.S. Sutherland, *The English East India Company and Eighteenth Century Politics,* Oxford, 1952, *passim.*
2. F.G. Cardew, *A Sketch of the Services of the Bengal Native Army,* Calcutta, 1903, pp. 30-4; A. Broome, *History of the Rise and Progress of the Bengal Army,* Calcutta, 1850, pp. 550-9; V.A. Smith, *The Oxford History of India,* Oxford, 1923, p. 478; H.H. Dodwell, *The Cambridge History of India, Vol. V. British India 1497-1858,* Cambridge, 1929, p. 179.
3. A. Broome, *op. cit.*
4. H. Beveridge, *A Comprehensive History of India,* London, 1865, Vol. 2, pp. 272-82.
5. Court of Directors to Governor and Council of Madras, 15 September 1769, *cit.* in W.J. Wilson, *History of the Madras Army,* Vol. 1, Madras, 1882, p. 278.

6. 13 Geo. III, c. 63.
7. P. Cadell, *History of the Bombay Army,* London, 1938, p. 86-90.
8. Beveridge, *op. cit.,* p. 325.
9. Dodwell, *op. cit.,* Vol. V, pp. 228-9; Beveridge, *op. cit.,* pp. 421-8.
10. Wilson, *op. cit.,* Vol. 1, pp. 340-1; Beveridge, *op. cit.,* pp. 396-7.
11. E.W. Sheppard, *Coote Bahadur : A Life of Lieutenant General Sir Eyre Coote KB,* London, 1956, p. 178; H.C. Wylly, *A Life of Lieutenant General Sir Eyre Coote,* Oxford, 1922, p. 361.
12. Beveridge, *op. cit.,* pp. 501-2.
13. Governor-General in Council, Bengal to Governor in Council, Madras 11 March 1782, *cit.* in Wylly, *op. cit.,* pp. 272-3.
14. Keay, *Honourable Company,* London, 1991, p. 417.
15. Beveridge, *op. cit.,* p. 509.
16. Wilson, *op. cit.,* Vol. II, pp. 82-4 and Wilson, *op. cit.,* Appendix O.
17. Wilson, *op. cit.,* Vol. II, p. 136.
18. Keay, *op. cit.,* p. 418.
19. Wilson, *op. cit.,* Vol. II, pp. 117-19.
20. *Cit.* in Wilson, *op. cit.,* p. 120.
21. *Cit.* in Wilson, *op. cit.,* p. 121.
22. *Cit.* in R. Callahan, *The East India Company and Army Reform 1783-1798,* Cambridge, Mass, 1972, p. 87.
23. J. Steven Watson; *The Reign of George III,* Oxford, 1960, pp. 263-7.
24. 21 Geo. III, c. 8.
25. Callahan, *op. cit.,* pp. 43, 104.
26. Cornwallis to Duke of York, 10 November 1786, *cit.* in Callahan, *op. cit.,* p. 24.
27. Callahan, *op. cit.,* p. 79.
28. *Ibid.,* pp. 92-3; Archbold, *op. cit.,* p. 92.
29. 28 Geo. III, c. 8.
30. Callahan, *op. cit.,* p. 120.

31. *Ibid.*, pp. 132-3.
32. Beveridge, *op. cit.* p. 675; Wilson, *op. cit.*, pp. 280-3; Callahan, *op. cit.*, Ch. 7.
33. Callahan, *op. cit.*, pp. 144-45.
34. Wilson, *op. cit.* Vol. 2, pp. 280-8; Cardew, *op. cit.*, pp. 66-9; Cadell, *op. cit.*, pp. 123-4.
35. Beveridge, *op. cit.*, p. 676; Callahan, *op. cit.*, pp. 201-5; J. Steven Watson, *op. cit.*, p. 382.
36. *Ibid.*
37. 'Report of a Commission on the Vellore Mutiny, assembled 9th August 1806'. Return to an address of the House of Commons 15 May 1861. (Parliamentary Papers 1861, Vol. XLII). A.D. Cameron, 'The Vellore Mutiny', unpub. Ph.D. thesis, Edinburgh, 1984, *passim*; Beveridge, *op. cit.*, pp. 811-16; Wilson, *op. cit.*, Vol. 3, Ch. XVIII.
38. Beveridge, *op. cit.*, pp. 840-5; A. Cardew, *The White Mutiny, London, 1929, passim*; Wilson, *op. cit.*, Vol. 3, Ch. 20.
39. *Ibid.*
40. *Ibid.*
41. Wellington to Malcolm (pte) 3 December 1806, *cit.* in Beveridge, *op. cit.*, p. 846.
42. F.G. Cardew, *op. cit.*, pp. 117-27; V.A. Smith, *op. cit.*, pp. 565-7; P.J. Marshall, *New Cambridge History of India*, II. 2., Cambridge, 1987, p. 44; Dodwell, *op. cit.*, pp. 378-9.
43. Cardew, *op. cit.*, pp. 128 ff; V.A. Smith, *op. cit.*, pp. 567-71; Cadell, *op. cit.*, Ch. VIII; Dodwell, *op. cit.*, pp. 379-83.

6
The Revolt of 1857

With the end of the Anglo-Sikh Wars in 1849 the British became the virtual masters of India. Between 1849 and 1857, they were mainly involved with the warlike tribes of the North West Frontier and in the Second Burmese War. However both these events are outside the scope of this study.

The Revolt of 1857 or the so-called Mutiny has been a subject of considerable research and study. Notwithstanding many political and other factors, it has been clearly established that the final outcome of the Mutiny was decided only by a clash of arms between the British and the forces opposing them. The role played by the artillery in suppressing the revolt can be taken for granted and there is no need to go into the details of various tactical battles. However, it is important to examine the extent to which the past policy of the British in keeping this arm firmly under their control contributed to their success in quelling the revolt.

The following facts stand out on examination of the sequence of events :

(a) *Manning of cavalry and infantry.* These arms were predominantly manned by natives, the proportion to European manned units being sometimes as high as 10 to 1.

(b) *Manning of artillery.* This arm was overwhelmingly manned by Europeans, the proportion being sometimes 3 to 1 in favour of Europeans.

(c) *Units in revolt.* The artillery arm was least affected by the revolt. The number of native artillery units which revolted was much smaller in relation to their overall strength, whereas in the case of the other two arms the proportion was very high.

(d) *Discipline.* Even when a unit revolted, there was not a single case where the native gunners killed their own officers whereas in the other two arms, killing and massacre of officers was a common occurrence.

(e) *Professional competence.* Native artillery units, whether remaining loyal or going in for the revolt, displayed a very high degree of professional competence in battle and their performance could not be faulted, whereas in the case of cavalry and infantry their reliability was always suspect whether fighting for or against the British.

1. Strength of Combat Arms

In 1856, the strength of the army of the Company was as under :

(a) Europeans	—	48,319
(b) Natives	—	2,75,304
Total	—	3,23,623

The cavalry and infantry units were overwhelmingly manned by natives. In 1856, the state of units in the Bombay army was as under :

	European	*Native*
(a) Cavalry	—	8
(b) Infantry	3	32
(c) Artillery (foot)	12	12
(d) Artillery (horse)	4	—

The overall strength of artillery units on the eve of the revolt was as under :

(a) Foot artillery	*European*	*Native*
Bengal	24	18
Madras	16	6
Bombay	12	12
	52	36

(b) Horse artillery

Bengal	9	3
Madras	4	2
Bombay	4	—
	17	5

It was only in the Bombay army that native artillery units were almost at par with European units, the balance being slightly maintained in favour of Europeans. The proportion of native units in cavalry or infantry was as high as 8 to 10 times whereas in artillery the strength of European units was still higher (16 against 12).

In the final analysis, the overall proportion of artillery in 1857 of the army of the Company was as under :

(a) Foot artillery

(i) Europeans	—	62%
(ii) Natives	—	38%

(b) Horse artillery

(i) Europeans	—	70%
(ii) Natives	—	30%

We have seen earlier, that for various reasons, the British were compelled by circumstances to have more native artillery units despite the higher policy. However, the expansion was kept strictly under control as on the eve of the revolt, the artillery arm was mainly manned by Europeans. To offset any unbalance in foot artillery, the strength of European-manned horse artillery was kept at a much higher percentage. The horse artillery, due to its very high mobility and shock action, was to play a significant role in suppressing the revolt and disarming the native cavalry and infantry units.

2. Units involved in the revolt

Out of a total strength of 36 foot companies and 5 horse artillery troops manned by natives, the following number were involved :

	Strength	Revolted
(a) *Madras artillery*		
(i) Foot companies	6	—
(ii) Horse troops	2	—
(b) *Bombay artillery*		
(i) Foot companies	12	2
(ii) Horse troops	—	—
(c) *Bengal artillery*		
(i) Foot Companies	18	6
(ii) Horse troops	3	1

The higher number from the Bengal artillery is mainly due to two reasons. First, the Bengal army was much more affected by the revolt than the other two armies and second the strength of this army was the highest as is evident from the figures as on 1 January, 1857 :

(a) Natives	—	1,70,000
(b) Europeans	—	59,486

It is of significance that although the native artillery of Madras helped to suppress the revolt, not a single unit actually took part in it. Again, in the case of Bombay artillery, which was also employed by the British in the area of disturbances, only two out of the 12 companies were involved. These were :

(a) *Bombay artillery*

No. 3 and 5 companies of No. 4 Artillery Battalion revolted in Sind. Both were newly raised in 1843 and 1846 respectively (Earlier 8 companies were raised in 1826-1827). In 3 company, only a few men were involved and the revolt in this company was quickly overcome.

(b) Bengal artillery

(i) No. 4 Troop of No. 1 Horse Artillery Brigade revolted at Nimach on 3 June.

(ii) The following companies of No. 7 Battalion were involved :

(aa) No. 2 at Nasirabad

(bb) No. 3 at Delhi

(cc) No. 5 at Faizabad

(dd) No. 6 at Kanpur.

(iii) No. 6 company of No. 8 Battalion revolted at Bareilly.

(iv) No. 4 company of No. 9 Battalion revolted at Nowgong.

Interestingly, Subedar Muhamad Bakht of the Company which revolted at Bareilly later became the Commander-in-Chief of Emperor Bahadur Shah at Delhi and in that capacity fought with exemplary courage and devotion in the famous siege of Delhi by the British. His exploits have been described in great detail by Savarkar in his book "The Indian War of Independence—1857".

Taking into account the total strength of the native artillery units and the number involved in the revolt in relation to the other two arms, the native artillery was least influenced. No native artilleryman, though otherwise involved in revolt, murdered his own officer although the massacre of British officers in native infantry and cavalry units was commonplace. This speaks highly of their sense of discipline and loyalty. As mentioned earlier, the officers were very carefully selected, as the British even during peace time had to depend largely on the loyalty of their artillery arm in case of trouble, or when the other two arms gave cause for anxiety. The extreme loyalty of artillery officers over the period must have inculcated the same virtues and values in native gunners.

3. Professional Competence

An analysis of the performance of the artillery that remained loyal to the British and the one that joined the opposite camp reveals that native artillery on both sides showed competence of a high order and unlike their counterparts in cavalry and infantry, the artillery of the mutineers was always handled with great professional pride, whereas the performance of the other two arms in a fight against the British could never be relied upon. Similarly the performance of the native artillery who remained loyal to the British was exemplary. The following excerpts confirm how well the artillery of mutineers fared in battle :

(a) The skill and courage with which the mutineers' artillery had been served through the campaign made such a deep impression on the British authority that it was determined that there should be no more native artillery except for the odd 4 batteries for service in the Frontier.

(b) In June 1857, General Hope Grant directed a surprise attack at Nabobganj near Lucknow on the mutineers. Writing later about the artillery opposing him he stated:

They brought two guns in the open and attacked us in the rear. In the first instance they attacked Hodson's Horse who would not face them and by their unsteadiness placed in great jeopardy the two guns attached to the Regiment. I ordered 7th Hussars and 4 guns to within 500 yeads of the enemy and opened fire of grape which mowed them down with a terrible effect like thistles before scythe. Their chief, a big fellow, nothing daunted, caused two green standards to be placed close to their guns and used them as rallying points. But our grape fire was so destructive that whenever they attempted to save their guns, they were struck down. Two squadron and more now came up to our side and forced the survivors to retire. Around the 2 guns alone there were 125 corpses.

(c) In May 1857, the revolutionaries met the English army at Alipore (Delhi). The Delhi artillery was so powerful that the English artillery could do nothing against it. While the artillerymen and officers of the English were following, the Delhi artillery became more and more fearful.

(d) Writing about the defence of Lucknow by the British in July 1857, Savarkar says : "Before the terrible daily fire of artillery and guns, the English found it unbearable to hold out much longer".

(e) The eminent historian, Wilson makes following observations on the performance of the native artillery:

This measure, which was part of the general policy of Government, deprived the country of an excellent and efficient body of artillery, maintained at comparatively small cost, and which had rendered good and faithful service from the time of the first war in Burma up to that of Mutiny in Bengal during which it distinguished itself on every opportunity which occurred. Their gallantry during the actions at Cawnpore on the 26th, 27th and 28th November 1857, and subsequently in the Operations under Lord Clyde, which resulted in the final defeat of the mutineers near Cawnpore on 8th December of the same year, elicited the thanks and commendations both of the officer commanding the Brigade, and of Major-General Dupuis, commanding the Royal Artillery.

In looking at the performance of the native artillery who remained loyal to the British, the following cases and events cited by Indian and British historians lead us to confirm the facts that its competence was beyond doubt :

(a) No. 5 Troop of No. 1 Horse Artillery Brigade took part in almost all operations and probably had the distinction of winning the highest number of decorations given to a native unit. It won the following awards :

(i)	Order of British India, 1st Class	—	1
(ii)	Order of British India, 2nd Class	—	2
(iii)	Order of Merit, 1st Class	—	1
(iv)	Order of Merit, 3rd Class	—	84

Considering that the strength of natives in a troop was 141, 88, the awards are high by any standard.

(b) During the critical siege of Delhi by the British, a total of 1350 officers and men were involved from the artillery, both native and British. The performance of

native gunners was as good as that of European artillerymen. Out of the total casualties of 365, 79 were natives.

(c) No. 4 Troop of 3rd Brigade Horse Artillery, the only artillery unit based at Multan, took part in disarming of mutinous sepoy regiments supported by only one European company and a unit of irregular company.

(d) In June 1857, the British came to know that a large contingent of native infantry located at Mian Mir, near Lahore, was likely to revolt. They had them fall in as for normal parade and then ordered their artillery to be in readiness to fire. The confused thousand sepoys, indignant with rage but overawed by the strong force of artillery, threw down their arms and without a word walked down to their lines.

(e) Speaking of native artillery during the siege of Delhi, where they were manning a battery, Forrest writes : "The natives excelled in steady and unparalleled bravery. When man after man was killed, they would keep up their work. If the man in front was killed by a bomb, they would stop for a moment, shed a tear or two for the dead, put the new body in the line of corpses and begin work again in that terrible place."

4. Conclusion

The Revolt of 1857 was a watershed in the history of India. Whatever may be other factors in the final suppression by the British, we must be very clear that the final outcome was decided purely by a clash of arms between the victorious and the revolutionaries. Ever since their first victory at Plassey in 1757 to their final victory at Gujrat in 1849 the British were greatly dependent on the loyalty and professional competence of their artillery arm both during peace and war. We have also analysed and studied how they managed to keep that arm firmly under their own control given the requirements of expansion. Although native manned units had to be raised, their number was never allowed to reach a figure which would be dangerous to their goal of conquest of India and retention of their power.

One does not have to delve deep into historical research to guess what would have been the likely outcome of revolt, if the native artillery of the British had gone across to the side of the mutineers in large numbers (as in the case of cavalry and infantry) or if the proportion of native to European gunner units was the same as in the other two arms of the British.

It is indeed a great credit to the astuteness and far-sightedness of the British Directors and Government sitting over 6,000 miles away, that for 100 years from 1748 to 1857 they never once wavered from their policy of keeping firm control of artillery in their hands and keeping the natives "off" the art and science of this arm as far as possible. Of course, they went even further in not allowing Roman Catholics and Europeans of doubtful loyalty in this arm.

The British policy and its implementation must be a unique case in military history where the main principle of war, *i.e.* "Selection and Maintenance of the Aim", has been pursued relentlessly for over 100 years; in fact over 190 years (from 1748 to 1935) as after the revolt, the native artillery was totally disbanded except for few mountain artillery units used in the defence of the Frontier.

In conclusion, the following excerpts from the recommendations of the high level inquiry ordered on the subject of reorganisation of the armies of India confirm the views of the Government.

(i) Profiting from the experience of the past year, it is proposed to transfer the mass of the artillery from the hand of the natives to those of European gunners. A small European force with a powerful artillery should be irresistible and no mutiny of a native army without guns could hope to be successful.

(ii) It is scarcely necessary to make any allusion to the artillery branch of service. In no way in future should the natives of the country be entrusted with British

> artillery, nor should any native of India be entrusted in the use of such dangerous weapons.

The Indian artillery as such was thereafter raised only in 1935. It is interesting that whereas Indian officers for cavalry and infantry were accepted in the early nineteen twenties and for the Indian Air Force in 1932, artillery officers were last to be inducted in 1935.

7
End of the Company Rule

During the second quarter of the nineteenth century, British India became not merely the strongest but the paramount power in South Asia. Through a combination of military victories over the remaining country powers that offered opposition, and military protection to those that offered submission, the East India Company succeeded the Mughals as the next Indian empire. Paradoxically, the greater its power in India grew the more its freedom of action was constrained by the authority of the British government in London, while the same Indian soldiers who had conquered their own subcontinent in its service became alarmed at the consequence of their own achievements. The Company's regime would eventually be brought down by a combination of these two processes, but like a falling star, blazed most fiercely as it approached its end.

The administrative institutions to support the establishment of the new empire were already in place by the beginning of this period. As early as 1763 the business of the Bengal authorities was divided between a Secret Department, which dealt with military plans, operations, and the conduct of relations with the country powers, and a Public Department, which dealt with all other matters, including military appointments and fortifications. The Select Committee, which had been set up by Clive to conduct secret business disappeared in 1774 and its function was taken over by the Secret Department. Although the records of the two departments were separate, both were headed by the same permanent secretary until 1783, when a separate official was appointed to each. A Military Department was created out of the Public Department at the end of 1776, to deal with all matters of military expenditure, returns of casualties recruits, lists of officers, and any other question of pay, pensions, and promotion.[1]

Another Military Department, was set up in 1786, as part of of the Secret Department, and took over control of matters affecting officers' promotions and appointments. This was abolished in 1790 and the original Military Department, which had in the interim been known as the Military Department of Inspection, resumed its original title, which it would retain until 1906. Various other changes culminated in Wellesley's reorganisation of 1798, by which time the three Secret, Political, and Foreign Departments had become separate though all were still headed by the same permanent secretary. The first to hold this combined office was a military man, Lieutenant-Colonel William Kirkpatrick, and most of the residents at Indian courts with whom these departments dealt were also soldiers. Kirkpatrick's successors, however, were civil servants, as were the secretaries of all the other departments except the Military Department, where the secretaries continued to be military officers.[2]

The East India Company's home establishment in London developed along broadly similar lines. Until the beginning of the nineteenth century all reports from their servants in India reached the Court of Directors through their Committee of Correspondence which had its own permanent secretary. Secret matters, including operations of war, were with by the court's Secret Committee in consultation with the Board of Control which also had its own permanent officials. In 1804 a separate Military Department was established at the Company's offices in East India House, to hondle all business with the military departments of the three Indian presidencies. A permanent secretary was appointed to this department in 1809. The first incumbent was a former captain in the Bengal army. He was restored to his military position, and remained as secretary of the Military Department until he retired, with the rank of major-general in 1837. His successor, Philip Melvill, a civil servant held the post until it was abolished in 1858. In 1834 the Committee of Correspondence (composed of the Chairman and

Deputy Chairman of the court and the next 9 senior of the 24 Directors) disappeared. The number of non-secret committees was reduced to three, of which one, the Political and Military Committee, dealt both with the conduct of diplomacy with Indian states, and the administration of the army.[3]

The Company continued to depend upon the Charter Acts for its legal existence, and each renewal made changes to take account of the shifting political position in the United Kingdom and in India. The Act of 1793[4] passed at a time when the attention of most British statesmen was turned to the threat of invasion from Revolutionary France, gave the Board of Control the power to divert the whole of the Company's revenue to defence if it thought necessary, without leaving a single rupee for other purposes of government, still less of dividend. In the negotiations, which lasted from 1808 to 1812, leading to the Act of 1813,[5] Dundas made his last, unsuccessful attempt to combine the Company's army with that of the Crown in India. Under the provisions of this act, the patronage of Indian appointments remained with the Company and training colleges were set up for its future civil and military officers, at Haileybury and Addiscombe respectively. The number of British troops that the Board of Control could order the Company to pay for (unless the Directors actually asked for more, which was generally considered to be an improbable contingency), was raised to 20,000 officers and men. Any others would have to be paid by the British taxpayer, if voted for by a watchful Parliament.

The Charter Act of 1833[6] brought further changes. The Company lost the right to carry on commercial activities in India or anywhere else. Thus it ceased to be legally known as 'the United Company of Merchants of England trading to the East Indies' and became officially, as it long had been in ordinary usage, merely 'The East India Company'. Its Indian administration was to be headed by a Governor-General in Council, replacing the Governor-General in Council of Bengal, heading a new government of India, in which 'the superintendence, direction, and control of the whole civil and military government of all the said territories and revenues in

India' was vested. Below this government were to be four presidencies, each with a governor and council of three members. The four presidencies were the existing ones of Madras and Bombay, and two new ones, Bengal and Agra formed by the division of the existing Bengal presidency. Notionally this might have led to the creation of a fourth army and C-in-C for Agra. Certainly it was envisaged that the C-in-C India would henceforth be separate from the C-in-C Bengal, as the Act provided that when there was no C-in-C India, or when the office was combined with that of the Governor-General, the C-in-C Bengal should take the place of the C-in-C India as an extra-ordinary member of the Governor-General's Council. Local C-in-Cs were likewise extra-ordinary members of their respective Governor's Councils so that, without its own C-in-C, Agra would not have enjoyed the equality of position with the other presidencies that the Act envisaged.

When these orders reached India, Bentinck, the Governor-General and C-in-C, India was at Ootacamund (Utakamand) in the Nilgheri hills of the Madras presidency. He delayed the implementation of those setting up the new Agra presidency long enough for there to be a change of view in London, and in 1835 a new Act[7] allowed the Directors to appoint a Lieutenant-Governor for Bengal and Agra respectively, selected from any of their servants who had been ten years in India, instead of Governors and Council. As this was a cheaper alternative, it was readily adopted, and the first Lieutenant-Governor of the North West Provinces (Agra) was appointed in 1836. The Governor General of India continued to act as Governor of Bengal until a Lieutenant-Governor was appointed there in 1854, and all the military and political business, which in Madras and Bombay were devolved to these local governments were, for Bengal, exercised by the government of India. The 1833 Charter Act also added a fourth member of the Governor-General's Council, to provide expert advice on drafting Indian legislation, a power which was by the same Act taken away from the local governments. The remaining three members were all to be servants of the Company, and the practice began of including among them an army officer who could provide expert advice from the point of view of the Indian military, as the C-in-C India was always at this period a British army officer usually with limited local experience, and in any case often absent from the seat of government on campaign or tours of inspection.

The expansion of the company's territorial possessions in South Asia had been matched by the increase in the size of its armies. By 1823 Bengal and Madras each had eight regiments of sepoy cavalry and Bombay had two.[8] These regiments were paired to form brigades, which were administrative rather than tactical formations, each under a Colonel conforming to the system in the infantry, where Colonels commanded regiments each of two battalions. Each of the three armies retained its European artillery and infantry regiments, but the sepoy element in both these arms steadily expanded. In 1803 the totals of sepoy infantry battalions were 38, in the Bengal and Madras armies, and 9 (including one of marines) in the Bombay army. In 1813 the totals were 54, 50, and 18 respectively, and, by 1823, 60, 50, and 24.[9]

In 1824 each of these units became a separate corps.[10] The cavalry regiments retained their existing numbers and names, while each infantry battalion became a regiment. Those which had existed prior to re-organisation by Cornwallis in 1796 were renumbered in their original sequence and the remainder in order according to the date of their being raised. The military justification for this step was that under the Cornwallis system the authority of the lieutenant-colonels commanding units was weakened by the powers of administrative control held by the colonels of cavalry brigades or infantry regiments. The units were rarely co-located either in peace or war, just as was the case in the British army, and the need for a battalion commander to refer matters such as recruiting, leave, or promotion to his distant regimental colonel caused exasperation to the officers and puzzlement to their sepoys. A further unsettling effect was the movement of officers between units, for, as their promotion took place by regimental seniority, a vacancy in one battalion might be filled by an officer from another. Cross-postings, to take account of consequential promotion in the subaltern ranks, brought officers to command men who were strangers to them, although the turbulence caused by promotion according to army seniority, in the system abolished by Cornwallis, had been even greater, especially with a smaller number of British officers in each battalion. The most potent reason for re-organising the armies into single-unit corps was to ease the blockage of promotion which arose from officers staying in the service as long as possible in the hope of promotion to senior rank, and of eventaully retiring with a higher pension. Doubling the number of corps doubled the number of colonels, and gave immediate promotion to one lieutenant-colonel, one major, one captain, one lieutenant, and one cornet or ensign in every unit, while all the others moved up one place in the seniority lists.

In addition to these troops, the Company raised numerous irregular corps. These performed a variety of auxiliary roles, and were particularly useful in supporting the administration of newly acquired territories, assisting in the collection of revenue, the suppression of disorder, escorting officials, guarding public buildings, and the like. The mounted units provided an alternative to the native light cavalry. By 1857 there were eighteen regiments of Irregular Cavalry in the Bengal army and seven of Irregular Horse in that of Bombay. Although the dress and side arms of the men conformed to Indian rather than European pattern, the significance of the term irregular lay in the way in which these units were officered and organized. They had no permanent cadre of British officers and could therefore be raised without the administrative problems that occurred when regular units were affected. *Irregular* regiments had only four appointments for Europeans. These were the commandant, second-in-command, adjutant and surgeon. As the combatant officers belonged to regular corps, which, with an establishment of 24 officers each in the cavalry and 26 in the infantry could easily spare them, no financial outlay was involved apart from the extra allowances which they received for filling these staff posts. The officers benefited not only from the extra pay, but from a higher status and more professionally satisfying duties than were available for them as junior officers in their regular regiments.

Irregular regiments of cavalry adopted the Mughal *silladari* system of the irregular mounted units. A *silladar* or 'man-at-arms' was paid higher wages than a regular sepoy, in return for providing and maintaining his own horse, weapons, clothing and equipment. The state thus in effect contracted out these functions to the silladari regiments, as for the sake of uniformity the men were required to obtain them through regimental sources. To cover the cost of initial outlay, the soldier lodged a deposit or *asami* (literally a 'place' or 'billet') with the regiment, refundable on death or retirement, but forfeited in case of desertion or dismissal, so ensuring a high quality of recruit and discipline. If a horse was killed or hurt on duty, a replacement was provided from regimental funds. If it went lame or sick from neglect, the soldier's pay was reduced to infantry rates until it recovered or he supplied another. Wealthy troopers were, subject to numerical limitations, allowed to provide *asamis* for men who could not afford their own. These men, known as *bargirs,* were often younger members of their own family, or others who gave part of their pay to their sponsors, in effect as interest on the loan of their deposit.

The sea long remained, to the majority of South Asians, an alien and unknown element. Most of the great Indian empires were land powers, and few, even those with extensive coastlines, maintained navies or exercised control over the sea lanes of the Indian Ocean. In the classical Hindu period, ships sailed from South Asia east and west to Indonesia and the Red Sea,[11] but by the time of the early Muslim invasions, advances in ship design by Arab and Chinese naval architects had made Indian vessels unprofitable. Moreover, with increasing stress being laid upon the importance of performing every detail of prescribed ritual, religious authorities had come to teach that sea voyages, if only because conditions on board ship did not allow food to be prepared and consumed with the proper observances, would result in irretrievable pollution for members of the *brahman* and *ksatriya* classes. This religious objection to sea travel was the more readily accepted by those to whom the sea was an object of fear and suspicion. South Asian seamen, drawn from the lower two classes, continued to display their courage and resourcefulness, but to the law-givers, sailing the ocean sea was an activity perilous to body and soul alike. 'The Muslim invasions encouraged xenophobia, and the people who had planted their colonies from Socotra to Borneo became, with religious sanction, a nation of land-lubbers.'[12]

So it was that when the East India Company began to recruit sepoys from the men of high religious class whose homes lay in what had become the centre of Hindu culture, it found them reluctant to embark upon its ships. With Muslim and lower-class Hindus there were no religious scruples to overcome, but sailing in the late eighteenth century was like flying in the late twentieth, statistically safe, but with occasional disasters whose dramatic effect outweighed that of more familiar accidents. It was therefore particularly unfortunate that, although in 1767 three battalions of sepoys had sailed from Bengal to the Northern Sarkars, to support the Madras troops engaged with Haydar Ali, two companies of grenadiers were lost without trace on their way back in 1770.[13]

Thereafter, whenever Bengal troops were needed outside their own presidency, they generally marched overland, despite the delays, desertions and expense involved. If men were required to travel by sea to a theatre of war in India or elsewhere, the usual practice was to raise new units, made up of volunteers from existing battalions. The move by sea to Madras in 1790 of the 1st Bengal Cavalry was made easier by most of the men in this arm being Muslims. Men who volunteered for these new units received substantial bounties, so that this system was more costly than that which obtained in Madras and Bombay, where existing units were simply ordered to embark, though only after their formal consent was obtained in each case. The Bengal army raised a battalion of marines in 1795 (converted to the line in 1803), who had no objection to seaborne duty, but in the same year the 15th Battalion of Bengal sepoys stationed at Midnapur, after volunteering to sail with the expedition to Malacca, mutinied when ordered to march to its embarkation point.[14] It was dispersed by the 29th Battalion with its accompanying light guns. The 29th became very unpopular with other battalions for its part in suppressing this mutiny (resulting in the disbandment and disgrace of the 15th) and in an unsuccessful attempt to force the government to disband it four units subsequently refused orders to march to the Northern Sarkars.[15] The grudge may have arisen from the perception that the 15th had been punished for refusing to embark and that the 29th were men who would force others to do so.

A generation later, the objection by Bengal sepoys to go on board ship was as strong as ever. On the outbreak of the 1st Anglo-Burmese war in 1824, the British, appreciating the difficulties of the country where Bengal and Burma meet, decided to make use of their naval power and so sent a force which landed at Rangoon. Only one battalion of sepoys (the former Marine regiment), together with two British regiments, came from Bengal, while Madras sent seven battalions of sepoys and three of Europeans.[16] The war did not at first go well for the British, despite their superior technology, including the Company's new paddle-steamer, *Diana*, which it was hoped would overawe the superstitious by moving up the Irrawaddy without sails or oars. It was therefore decided to open a second front in the Arakan. Reports of the terrible climate, of disease, of Burmese skill in jungle warfare, and of the superhuman powers of the Burmese General, Maha Bandula, depressed morale among the troops assembling for the new campaign, and a higher than usual number of desertions were reported among sepoy battalions en route from Hindustan to lower Bengal. At Barrackpur, the large military station fifteen miles from Calcutta, the newly renumbered 26th, 47th and 62nd Bengal, Native Infantry, were told that, to avoid going to Arakan by sea, they would march there overland. In India, sepoys customarily provided their own carriage for their personal effects, including the heavy brass cooking and drinking vessels which each man used to avoid the risk of ritual pollution. In this instance, as the road to Burma lay through strange and dangerous country, the normal operation of market forces meant that the contractors who supplied pack bullocks would only do so at high prices. The troops therefore asked for the provision of carriage by the government, or for additional pay and allowances to cover the extra cost of providing their own in the usual way. When these requests were refused, gatherings took place at which men agreed not to march until their demands were met. Subsequently, some bullocks were found for them, and advances of pay were offered. The Indian officers of the 47th, the first regiment warned for duty, reported it ready to march, and told their men that when the Company went to war they ought not to shrink. According to the sepoys, they added that the regiment was going to Rangoon by ship.

The subsequent refusal by the 47th to parade for inspection in marching order brought the Commander-in-Chief, General Sir Edward Pagat, up from Calcutta with a squadron of Indian cavalry (the Governor-General's Bodyguard), two British battalions, and a troop of the Bengal Horse Artillery. The 47th presented him with a petition to the effect that they would not go on board ship, nor march anywhere for that purpose.[17] They asked only to be allowed to take their discharge. Paget, a one-armed veteran of the Peninsular War, replied that there was no intention of sending them to sea, but he would have no negotiations with them until they returned to duty. The 47th, joined by groups from the 26th and 62nd fell in, without the Indian officers, at dawn on 2 November. Pagat addressed them through an interpreter, but was met with further protests.[18] He then ordered them to ground arms, and when only one man obeyed, the gunners suddenly revealed their presence and opened fire. The leaderless sepoys fled without resistance. Eleven were killed in the cannonade and pursuit, many were arrested, some were later hanged and others sentenced to the chain gang. The native officers were dismissed and the 47th's name was deleted from the Bengal army list.

Paget's action was not well received by the Bengal army. There was feeling that, left to themselves, Bengal officers could have persuaded the men to obey orders, and that Paget's approach, based upon British notions of discipline, disregarded the local ways of settling disagreements. A court of enquiry's findings hinted that Paget, by concealing his guns behind his other troops, had not given the sepoys a fair chance of appreciating his intentions and that they would have surrendered in the end. They also pointed to the fact that the sepoys, though each had the full regulation sixty rounds in their pouches, had not loaded their muskets and did not return fire. Their action, said the court, was 'an ebulliation of despair at being compelled to march without the means of doing so', and if proper carriage had been provided at the right time, none of the other complaints would have been made 'and the late 47th regiment would now have been contending against the enemies of the state'.[19]

Paget had little sympathy with this attitude. The sepoys he said were not less mutinous for not having loaded their muskets, and he had no intention of giving them the chance to do so. He returned to England to become Governor of the Royal Military College at Sandhurst, and later gave evidence to a House of Commons committee on Indian army discipline.

> There is a great spirit of insubordination in the army, at least in that which I had the opportunity of more particularly seeing, which is the Bengal Army. A sort of spirit of independence prevails among the officers, which is totally inconsistent with our ideas of military discipline. I had abundant opportunities of seeing it myself and had the proofs before me of that spirit; and I have reason to think, from what I have subsequently heard, that it is by no means subsiding.[20]

Wellington at much the same time was equally suspicious of the Indian army's officers and sepoys alike. In 1826, commenting upon proposals by Sir John Malcolm's recently published proposals advocating the amalgamation of the three presidential armies, he wrote, 'My opinion is not altered by perusal of Malcolm's. He is a very clever fellow, and has considered these subjects more than I have', but, he added, the sepoys and their officers had a record of mutiny, 'and seeing what armies have done in different countries of Europe, and are capable of attempting, and knowing them as I do, and knowing moreover the sort of men whom you must employ to manage them, I cannot but think it fortunate that they are three separate and distinct armies.'[21]

Only two years later, the officers of the Bengal army were again at odds with their employers over the *batta* question. In 1801 Shore had averted the threat of a mutiny of officers, whose *batta* the Court had ordered him to reduce, by in fact continuing to pay it, whether they were in the field or cantonments, in the guise of an accommodation allowance. In return the officers were required to provide their own accommodation at all times. Officers' quarters were sold by the government to their occupants, who in turn sold them on to their successors. The Court of Directors repeatedly ordered that in the stations nearest to Calcutta, this allowance was to be at half the normal rate, but both Hastings, and his successor, Amherst, returned the orders to London for reconsideration, so delaying implementation by at least a year every time this was done. The cost of the eventual British victory in Burma led the Court of Directors to look for economies, and *batta* again became an issue.

In 1828 a new Governor-General, Lord William Bentinck, arrived. Twenty years earlier he had been recalled from Madras after the Vellur mutiny, and now military discontent again threatened to blight his administration. His orders were to effect retrenchment in government expenditure, starting with the reduction of officer's *batta.* The Commander-in-Chief, Lord Combermere (who, as Sir Stapleton Cotton, had commanded Wellington's cavalry in the Peninsula) resigned in protest, and the two remining members of the Governor-General's Council signed the order introducing half-*batta* only because, as its civil servants, they felt obliged to carry out the Company's policy. One of them, Sir Charles Metcalfe, nevertheless minuted his view that the allowances of officers even on full *batta* were barely sufficient, and that any reduction would cause suffering to the individuals affected, and injury to the public good. This view was held, and expressed, even more strongly by the officers themselves. The usual protests were drawn up and memorials presented to the C-in-C for submission to government. Bentinck himself let it be known that he would be glad to rescind the order if the Court of Directors agreed (though this did not save him from ostracism by Calcutta society, or the nickname 'The clipping Dutchman').[22] The Court, however, would not hear of it, and denounced the tone of the memorials as contrary to military discipline. The officers, together with the civil servants who suffered similar reductions in income, had no choice but to accept, and wait with increasing impatience for promotion or transfer to posts which carried other allowances.

Increasing attention was paid at this period to retirement on pension as promotion prospects worsened. There was still the chance of an occasional campaign, such as that against Bharatpur which Combermere had stormed in 1826, where Lake had failed. In general, however, most operations were against local rulers or peasants resisting the collection of the revenue, and these did not result in either the glory or the consequential promotion through battle casualties that large-scale conventional wars provided.

As the British came to replace the Mughals as holders of the empire of India, their attention turned towards the north west, from which invaders had come to overthrow so many earlier Indian empires. Even the Mughals themselves had been brought down not so much by the British as by Nadir Shah of Iran and Ahmad Shah of Afghanistan. To the long-established fear of invading hordes from Iran and Central Asia was added a new anxiety that, arising from the extension of European power into Asia, these hordes would have the benefit of European military assistance. By the 1820s, just as they would in the late 1940s, the Russians had changed, in the perception of British public opinion, from being the brave allies, the endurance of whose people and the skill of whose armies had delivered Europe from a dictator, into the evil empire which practised tyranny at home and encouraged it abroad. Moreover, an army which in the space of two years had pursued the forces of Napoleon back from Moscow all the way to Paris, just as its successors would those of Hitler from Stalingrad to Berlin, was one to be taken seriously, even if the assistance it gave was limited to military advice and training.

In 1839, therefore, to counter a threat (which had actually

disappeared) that Iran, under Russian influence, would occupy Herat and from there re-assert Iranian control of Afghanistan, a British Indian army marched through Sind to Kandahar and Kabul. Shah Shuja-ul-Mulk, the last of Ahmad Shah's dynasty, was restored to his throne with British support, and the Amir Dost Muhammad, who had replaced him, was deposed. The Amir had offered the British an alliance but only at the price of their support in recovering the province of Peshawur, which he had lost to Ranjit Singh, Maharaja of Lahore. As the British wanted the alliance of this powerful neighbour even more than that of the more distant Amir of Kabul, Shah Shuja (who had alrady conceded Peshawur to Ranjit Singh in return for his promise of support) was their preferred choice. He was not, however, that of the Afghans, and a widespread rebellion in 1841 led to the notorious 'retreat from Kabul', an episode as potent in the folk memory of British soldiers as that of the retreat from Moscow a generation earlier had become in that of the French. The fact that most British garrisons in Afghanistan held out, that it was the cold of the Afghan winter rather than the weapons of the Afghan tribesmen which destroyed the Kabul troops (scarcely a brigade strong), and that in 1842 two British divisions marched from opposite ends of the country to meet in Kabul itself, cannot destroy the image of an entire British army destroyed, and all its military and diplomatic staff killed or held hostage.[23]

As the British would find again in 1879-81, and the Soviets would a century later, the brilliance of victory was dimmed by the dust of the cost of occupation, while any ruler installed in Afghanistan with the aid of foreign troops was instantly seen by his subjects as the puppet of a foreign ruler. In October 1842 (much as in 1881) a change of government in London resulted in a change of policy in India, and the army was recalled, leaving Dost Muhammad to resume his throne.

Lord Ellenborough, who replaced the discredited Lord Auckland as Governor-General in February 1842, was more successful in his wars. Sind, occupied by the British in 1839 on the grounds that it had once been part of the empire which they were restoring to Shah Shuja, was annexed after a brief campaign culminating in the battle of Miani (February 1843). General Sir Charles Napier, the conqueror of Sind, remined there for four years as its governor, holding both the civil and military authority there. Though subsequently both the government and garrison of Sind were made subordinate to Bombay, this unification of civil and military command long remained a feature of the administration of Sind. Until 1877 the political superintendent of the Upper Sind Frontier commanded the (predominantly cavalry) Sind Frontier Force, conducted British foreign policy with the neighbouring, and independent ruler of Baluchistan, and was also chief magistrate of the district.

The annexation of Sind brought two military problems to the British. The first was that they now had a permanent border with the independently minded and warlike tribal communities of the wild country between South and Central Asia. The inhabitants of this country, long accustomed to raiding their more settled neighbours continued to do so when these became British subjects. In 1844-45, Napier waged a successful campaign, in which, by the employment of novel devices such as mountain artillery and a camel corps for operations respectively in the hills and deserts of this frontier, he demonstrated that well-led regular troops could secure victories over ill-armed tribesmen regardless of terrain.[24]

The second problem was that of finding regular troops willing to serve there. To the Bengal army, Sind was a foreign country, with an objectionable climate. The reduction in *batta* that followed the annexation of Sind (which thereby ceased to be a 'foreign' station, though still just as expensive to live in) made service there even less popular. When in 1844, Bengal troops were ordered to go there, 190 sepoys in the 4th Native Infantry, and 90 in the 69th applied for their discharge and were granted it even though hostilities were in progress. The 7th Light Cavalry and 34th Native Infantry refused to march, and the former changed its mind only when the latter was disbanded and its men dismissed for mutiny. The 64th agreed to march only when its commanding officer promised them that full field *batta* would be paid. When they reached Sind, and found that he was in error, they refused to accept their pay, the conventional method of protest among troops with a grievance, but no intent to mutiny. Subsequently, however, men stoned their brigade commander, with the result that about seventy were dismissed and the regiment deprived of its colours, while its colonel was cashiered for misrepresentation and inefficiency.[25]

The last independent Indian power was the kingdom of Lahore. Neither the geographical term 'the Punjab', nor the religious one 'the Sikhs' are accurate synonyms for this state, as not all its dominions lay within the Punjab—the Five Rivers Land—nor did all the Punjab come under its sway. Likewise, not all its subjects were Sikhs, nor did rule over all Sikhs, nor even over all territories under Sikh princes. After the execution by the Mughal authorities in 1715 of Banda Singh ('the false Guru'), his surviving followers fled to the Himalayan foothills. 'The Sikhs, it was thought, had been hammered out of existence. But the hammering did not in fact reduce them to a pulp, but hardened a remnant to tempered steel.'[26] After the invasions of Nadir Shah and Ahmad Shah weakened Mughal control of the Punjab, Sikh war bands reappeared in the plains, gaining recruits and converts, and forming political entities which spread from the Indus almost to Delhi itself. In 1799 Ranjit Singh, the teenage head of one of these groups, obtained from the Mughal Shah Zaman a sanad recognising him as ruler of Lahore. From here he went on to capture Amritsar in 1802, Ludhiana in 1806, Multan and Kashmir in 1818 19, Ladakh in 1833, and Peshawar in 1834, so establishing a kingdom whose population, though largely Sikh, comprised a large proportion of Hindus and Muslims, both Punjabis and Afghans. Sikh states on the east side of the Satlej managed to avoid absorption by accepting British protection.

This state was built up and defended by an army which, by the time of Maharaja Ranjit Singh's death in 1839, amounted to some 75,000 men. About half of these were contingents furnished by eminent landholders in accordance with the traditional system of military tenure. Others were Akalis or

Sikh zealots. The true strength, however, lay in the 35,000 regular soldiers, organised in the European manner, and trained by European officers, including a number of Napoleon's veterans. The infantry and artillery, dressed in imitation of the Company's sepoys, were at least their equal in terms of drill, equipment, and morale.

In the struggle for power at Lahore which followed Ranjit Singh's death, the regular army assumed the role of a Praetorian Guard, giving its support to whichever of the contending parties offered the best terms. While observing the existing chain of command for discipline and training, each regiment had a soldiers' committee or 'panch' (literally, a 'five'), based on the pattern of the councils by which Indian villagers had managed their own local affairs, independent of kings and governments, since classical Hindu times. The committees decided whom to support, and officers led the regiments accordingly. In 1845 the ruling party at Lahore, headed by the Rani Jindan (acting as regent for her infant son Dhalip Singh), Lal Singh (the Wazir or Finance Minister), and Tej Singh (the Commander-in-Chief) decided that their best hope of survival ay in a war with the British. If the army won, its attention would be distracted from politics, and its appetite would be met by the proceeds of new conquests. If it lost, the British would ensure it was reduced to a manageable size, a step which no ruler at Lahore dare take and expect to live. At any event, the Rani and her advisers were sure that if they crossed the river they would destroy a great army.

On 11 December 1845 the Lahore troops crossed the Satlej river into British-protected territory. Although the invasion was not unexpected (indeed one reason for Ellenborough's campaign against Sindia in 1843 was to ensure that he would not be a threat if war came with the Sikhs) and the British had 40,000 men stationed between the Satlej and Delhi, it was a tactical surprise and a brief but bloody campaign ensued. Both sides were handicapped by civil-military problems in their respective commands. On the Sikh side, the army, with good reason, had doubts about its leaders' desire to win. Neither Lal Singh nor Tej Singh trusted each other's whole-hearted devotion to securing a victory. On the British side, Sir Hugh Gough, the C-in-C, was hampered by the Governor-General, Lieutenant-General Sir Henry Hardinge, a veteran of 'The Hundred Days'. Hardinge, as a serving officer, volunteered to serve under Gough, an offer which could scarcely be refused, but which made for difficulties when, as Governor-General, he was able to overrule the C-in-C's strategic plans, on political grounds. Gough's standard tactic, a frontal attack by infantry against an unshaken enemy, cost his own army dear at Ferozeshah on 19-20 December 1845, but a victory by Sir Harry Smith at Aliwal on 28 January 1846, and another by Gough at Sobraon on 10 February 1846, finally drove their enemies back to Lahore.

After the first shock of defeat, a mood of resistance to British control developed in the kingdom of Lahore. When Sir Henry Lawrence, the British Resident, became President of the Regency Council, and it was announced that British garrisons would remain by its invitation for a further eight years, he appeared as the representative of an occupying power, and the chiefs who supported him were stigmatised as collaborators. Reforms aimed at benefiting the cultivators alienated the great landholders. Above all, the army, like the German army after World War I, felt that it had not been defeated but stabbed in the back. Unemployed and disbanded soldiers blamed the British for their plight, and those still in the service made common cause with their old comrades. When, in April 1848, two British officers were murdered by dissidents at Multan, a local act of defiance became the first clash in a new war. Troops loyal to the government, led by British officers, failed to capture Multan, and in September a much larger body sent as reinforcements went over to the other side.

The course of what then became the Second Sikh War in many ways resembled that of the war which was to come in the plains of Hindustan nine years later. There was the same discontent among the leading classes in society at the assumption of rule by the British, the same anger among men thrown out of work, despite previous honorable service, by a government policy of reducing the number of those employed by the state, the same unease among the population as a whole at reforms which seemed to threaten long-established religious and cultural practices, and above all the same kind of enemy, well-armed regular soldiers trained in the most up-to-date Western tactics.

There was the same hard level of fighting too. Hardinge had returned to the United Kingdom at the end of 1847, to succeed Wellington as C-in-C of the British army. His successor, Earl Dalhousie, at the age of thirty-five the youngest Governor-General ever, combined great personal energy with a firm belief in the superiority of Western over Indian values. He readily accepted the challenge of a new war and Gough marched to re-establish British supremacy. At Ramnagar on 22 November 1848, he was nearly defeated. Chilianwala (13 January 1849), was another Ferozshah in the scale of its casualties and the doubtful nature of its outcome. At Gujarat, 'the battle of the guns', on 21 February 1849, Gough at last used his superiority in artillery and secured a decisive victory. Dalhousie, on his own initiative, annexed the kingdom of Lahore to British India as the new province of the Punjab.

Although the Second Sikh War was fought, by the British, without the civil-military difficulties of its predecessor, the immediate aftermath contained a full measure of them. The news of Chilianwala was greeted in London with a general outcry at Gough's poor generalship. Yielding to popular opinion, the Court of Directors appointed Sir Charles Napier to succeed him. In the ten weeks between Napier leaving England in late February and reaching India in early May (travelling by steamship through the Mediterranean and the Red Sea, and overland through Suez) Gough had triumphed at Gujarat and the war was over. Dalhousie was as jealous of his own position and prerogatives as Napier was of his. The 68-year-old veteran, the conqueror and former governor of Sind, whose officials freely contrasted their own achievements favourably with those of the the Punjab which Dalhousie had made his own, was warned by the imperious young nobleman at their first meeting to keep in his place. Both were individuals of determined character, and each soon developed a strong dislike of the other's personality and proceedings.

Their final clash arose from the ever-vexed question of *batta.* When the Punjab was annexed, it ceased to be a foreign country, and therefore the allowances paid to troops serving outside British territory were discontinued, just as they had been in the case of Sind, and with just the same result. The sepoys perceived that the consequence of their victory in battle was diminution in their pay. Only those stationed on the border with Afghan territory, the new North West Frontier of British India, were exempt, being virtually on permanent field service against the continual risk of Pathan tribesman raiding from the hills. In serveral units, including the 13th, 22nd, and 32nd Bengal Native Infantry, sepoys made the conventional protest of refusing to accept pay they considered to be below the proper rate. At Amritsar, the 66th Bengal NI refused to perform duty. Napier, who had experienced much the same problem in the midst of his hill campaign in Sind, acted with his characteristic decisiveness. The regiment was marched to Amballa, where all its non-European personnel wee discharged, and its colours and number in the Bengal army list were handed over to the Nasiri Gurkha Battalion, which had fought well in the recent wars.[27] Napier's aim, apart from showing how he would deal with insubordination, was to demonstrate to the Hindustani Purabiyas that he could easily find other troops to replace them if they did not wish to serve on the offered terms. There were already six regiments of Sikh infantry (raised in 1846) and twelve Punjabi regiments, cavalry and infantry in the British order of battle. To Napier's chagrin, those belonging to the Punjab Frontier Force came under the government of India in the foreign department (*i.e.* the local political authorities) not under him as C-in-C India. His, actions, changing the composition of the 66th from Purabiya to Gurkha, and recruiting the Nasiri Gurkha Battalion to full strength to replace the men remustered in the 66th, were carried out without reference to the government of India. Although within his legal powers, it had political implications, and Dalhousie expressed his disapproval at not being informed of these orders before they were given.

While firm in his response to insubordination which it

provoked, Napier had no sympathy with the order to withdraw *batta*, and by taking an opportunity of countermanding it, brought about his own downfall. While Dalhousie was at sea, and without the agreement of the other members of the Governor-General's Council, Napier suspended the orders reducing the Punjab *batta*. Dalhousie responded with a formal letter from the government of India in the Military Department to the Adjutant-General of the Bengal army stating that the Governor-General in Council (one of whose members was the C-in-C), viewed the C-in-C's orders on the Punjab *batta* with regret and dissatisfaction, and that the Governor-General in Council would not again permit the C-in-C to usurp its proper authority by issuing orders changing the pay of the troops. Napier responded to this public rebuke by submitting his resignation and returned to England in March 1851. He subsequently published a book The Defects, Civil and Military, of the Government of India, in which he paid off old scores against the East India Company, its policies and employees. His criticisms of the Bengal army, in particular, were to be proved only too well founded, by the disaster which overtook it in 1857, four years after Napier's death.

With the Punjab secured, Dalhousie went on to take every opportunity of annexing other Indian states, which were too weak to offer military resistance. Satara (created by Lord Hastings in 1819 as a principality to be held by last descendant of Sivaji), Nagpur, Jhansi, Sambalpur, and a number of others were annexed on the failure of natural heirs to their respective thrones. Awadh, whose rulers had long been faithful and generous allies of the British had been an independent Muslim Shi'a kingdom since 1819 when, with British encouragement, it had created to acknowledge Mughal soverignty. Protected by British troops against the consequence of misgovernment, but refusing to accept the advice of British residents to improve their administration, successive Kings of Awadh had been criticised for tyranny, oppression or neglect. Nevertheless, as in 1809 half of Awadh had been ceded to the Company in return for a guarantee of protection of the other half, against internal and external enemies alike, the British had no claim on Awadh.

Its annexation in February 1856 on the grounds that the British government, if it did not stop maladministration, would be seen as party to it, was generally regarded as an invasion. The monarch, Wajid Ali Shah, had been a patron of learning, and his court at Lucknow (Lakhnao) had become a centre of Urdu culture. His subjects had not invited the British to liberate them. Many of those who had loyally served the state as soldiers, scholars or administrators, or in humbler capacities, lost their livelihood, as the new rulers introduced a ruthless and short-sighed policy of reducing public expenditure in order to reduce taxes. The cultivators saw no improvement in their lot, and the many Purabiyas recruited from Awadh lost the privileged position which they had enjoyed locally through their connection with the British. Indeed, they, like all Awadhis, also lost their independence.

The Bengal sepoys soon had a more personal grievance. In the spring of 1852 a second Burmese War had begun. One division from the Bengal army, including some of the recently raised Punjabi units, and another from Madras, supported by nineteen steamers mounting 159 guns between them, waged a campaign in the jungles and paddy fields of lower Burma. Pegu was annexed to British India, and the entire Burmese coastline came under British rule. The 38th Bengal Native Infantry refused to embark for the war, but the new C-in-C, General Sir William Gomm, was no Napier, still less a Paget, and no disciplinary action followed. The subject was on of those covered by Dalhousie in the series of nine memoranda on army organisation which he submitted to the Court of Directors, and the question was one of the first to be resolved by his successor, Lord Canning, who assumed office on 1 March 1856.

Later that year, he directed that all new recruits for the Bengal army should be enlisted for general service only (as was already the case for those of the Madras and Bombay armies). Even Muslim sepoys, who had no religious scruples about going to sea, were adversely affected by this, as they had benefited equally with their Hindu comrades from the bounties offered to those who would embark for overseas duty. To those Hindus whom no amount of money would induce to sail, the new regulation meant that their sons would be cut off from a form of honorable and lucrative employment that men of their communities had followed for generations. There were no other large armies in South Asia in which the Purabiyas could enlist as an alternative to the East India Company's service. Even those who were already serving, on whom the new conditions were not binding, feared that they would be subject to moral pressure to embark, and find themselves at sea, unable to perform their ritual ablutions, or prepare their food properly, or becalmed and obliged to eat salt beef. Some even feared that there was a a scheme to pollute men through sea travel, and oblige them to become Christians : people who ate and drank all kinds of impure things without discrimination, and who had few rules of religious hygiene.[28]

It was a conflict between old religion and new technology that led to the outbreak of mutiny in the Bengal army in 1857. Soldiers had known since classical times that to impart spin to a projectile would improve its range and accuracy. In the design of firearms this is best achieved by cutting a spiral groove (rifling) in the bore of the piece through which the projectile is driven by rapidly expanding gasses when the weapon is fired. Experience in the Crimean War of 1854-56 had shown the British that the Minie rifle, issued to selected regiments, was superior to the old smooth-bore musket, and accordingly the new small-arms factory at Enfield Lock, in the countryside ten miles north of London, went into full production with an improved version. The East India Company, so that its army should have the same modern equipment as the British army for which it was a local substitute, ordered large quantities of the new Enfield rifles and dispatched them to India. The Enfields were muzzle-loaders, like the smooth bores which they replaced. Their ammunition came in the form of paper tubes (cartridges), each containing the standard charge of gunpowder, and lead bullet. The cartridge was opened by soldiers using their teeth, since one hand was required to hold the weapon, while the other held the cartridge. The cartridges of the new Enfields were greased, using tallow or lard, to lubricate the rifling. The composition of the grease was a matter of importance to men who would be defiled by putting into their mouths either beef, sacred to Hindus, or pork, unclean to Muslims. The rapidly spreading belief that fats from these nimals were indeed used in the manufacture of the new cartridges, either deliberately to destroy men's religion, or at best indiscriminately by defence contractors using the cheapest material in their usual greed for profits, caused deeply felt alarm.[29]

At first it seemed that a simple solution could be found. In January, 1857, Major Bontein, commanding the Arsenal of Dum Dum, near Calcutta, where details from each regiment were being sent to learn the new drill, learnt of the discontent. He paraded the men and asked those who wished to complain to step forward. About two-thirds did so. In a disciplined manner they stated their religious objections, and suggested that beeswax or coconut oil would be an equally effective, but acceptable, substitute. These alternatives indeed later were authorised, while in Madras the cartrides would be issued ungreased, and the sepoys bought *ghi* (clarified butter) from the bazaar to use as the lubricant. In Bengal, however, even the new shiny paper of the cartridges was feared to be manufactured from forbidden animals, while as new rumour spread that the English were grinding up cow and pig bones to mix with the flour sold in military bazaars.

The 34th Bengal Native Infantry was at this time due to march from Barrackpur, near Calcutta, to relieve the 19th at Berhampur, a hundred miles to the north. An advance party reached these on 24 February, and enjoyed the hospitality usual on such occasions. On 26 February, men of the 19th Bengal Native Infantry refused to accept the issue of even the old pattern cartridges. In the evening they seized their arms and refused all orders. The garrison commander, with only native artillery and cavalry left at his disposal, neither of which were useful in the dark, decided not to force the issue, and the regiment returned to duty on condition of not being ordered to take suspect cartridges.

Canning determined to make an example of the 19th, on the grounds that whatever the sepoys' fears, nothing could excuse mutiny under arms and open defiance of their officers. The 84th Foot was recalled from Burma, and was sent with the 53rd Foot and two troops of Bengal Horse Artillery to Barrackpur. The 19th Bengal Native Infantry was marched there from Berhampur. Two days before its arrival Sepoy Mangal Pande called on his comrades of the 34th, still at Barrackpur, to rise and assist him in killing their European officers. He succeeded in wounding his Adjutant and Serjeant-Major before being arrested by a Muslim sepoy of the same regiment. The guard, led by Jemandar Iswari Pande, turned out but made no attempt to assist. The two Pandes (a common name among Purabiyas, and one subsequently used by the British as a synonym for Hindustani mutineers), were tried by a court-martial of native officers and sent to the gallows, but as every sepoy knew that native officers only brought in the verdict they thought that their British officers expected, it was widely felt that they were martyrs. Much the same was felt when the 19th Native Infantry was disbanded after arrival at Barrackpur, as was the 34th on 4 May 1857.[30]

At Mirath (Meerut) near Delhi, the skirmishers of the 3rd Bengal Light Cavalry were ordered to parade on 24 April to demonstrate to the rest of their regiment the new drill for breaking instead of biting the cartridges. Only five out of the ninety accepted the cartridges. A court of inquiry found that the action of the remainder stemmed from fear of public opinion only. A native court-martial, with one member dissenting, convicted them to ten years' hard labour. On Sunday 9 May the eighty-five troopers, the elite of their regiment, many of them old soldiers, some with medals from the First Sikh War, were put into chains in the presence of the whole garrison, and led off to prison, while some of their comrades began to consider plans for an appeal.[31] That evening, while the European troops fell in, without arms, for church parade, there began an appeal to the sword. Some of the cavalry broke open the city gaol to release the skirmishers, letting out every other prisoner as well. Sepoys of cavalry and infantry alike, joined by the city mob, attacked European officers, civilians, women, children, Indian shopkeepers, servants, and anyone who got in their way. Others did what they could to protect their own officers. Some decided to remain with their regiments, right or wrong. Some just made themselves scarce.[32]

During the night the mutineers marched to Delhi, where the three sepoy battalions there, among them the same 38th which had refused to go to Burma, joined them, as did every criminal who hoped to profit from a breakdown of order, and every patriot who desired a restoration of Mughal power. All Europeans, and many Indian Christians, were attacked, regardless of age or sex. Some escaped, helped by local people, some were robbed, some were murdered, with little effort made to protect them by Bahadur Shah, the old and irresolute Mughal monarch. Nine British members of the Bengal Ordnance Department defended the great magazine before blowing it up, five surviving to win the recently instated Victoria Cross for valour. Bahadur Shah sent a camel rider to Agra to notify the Lieutenant-Governor of Bengal's North-Western Provinces that mutineers had taken Delhi. Then he waited for the British to come and restore order. When they did not come, he endeavoured to rule despite the indiscipline of the sepoys, the ambition of his sons, and the uncertain loyalty of his subjects.[33]

North-west of Delhi lay the recently conquered province of the Punjab. There, the Chief Commissioner, Sir John Lawrence, and a band of fifty-six officers selected from the best volunteers of the Bengal Civil Service and army, governed a population that had no special reason to support the continuation of British rule. It was for this reason that it had a garrison of 60,000 men, of whom 36,000 were Purabiyas with the rest either Europeans of Punjabis. News of the events at Mirath and Delhi reached Lahore by telegraph on the morning of 12 May. It was decided that the risk of a new Punjabi rising was less than that of a spreading sepoy mutiny, and action was at once taken to disarm the Hindustani regiments. On 13 May the three battalions and one cavalry regiment at Mian Mir piled arm without incident.

The Punjab proved to be an unlooked-for source of strength to the British cause. Punjabis had no great reason to support the British who had defeated them barely a decade earlier, but even less to sympathise with the Purabiya sepoys who had contributed so conspicuously to that defeat and made up so large a part of the army of occupation. Sikhs especially had only ill feelings towards the Mughal dynasty whose rulers had persecuted the later gurus and their followers. Young men, whether Sikh, Punjabi Muslims, or Pathans from the hills, saw glittering prospects of looting Delhi and the other great cities of Hindustan, if they joined the British side. Punjabi princes also threw in their lot with the British, or at least refrained from any movement against them. The British had the weapons and officers of disarmed units with which to arm and lead the new ones they raised from Punjabi recruits (including old soldiers of the Lahore army). Hindustanis who mutinined, far from home, found every man's hand against them, and only made their escape if well-armed and moving in regimental groups.

Delhi remained the critical point of the whole campaign. When days went by with no sign of the British Bahadur Shah accepted with some reluctance the reins of authority pressed into his hands by the sepoys and attempted to set up some kind of government, to which those holding *jagirs* in his kingdom rallied with their military contingents. The British troops at Mirath had been unable to pursue the mutineers to Delhi without leaving their own civilians at the mercy of the city mob, which had committed the worst of the attacks on Europeans, and which normally would have been suppressed by the very troops that had mutinied. General Anson, the C-in-C India, was 150 miles away with most of his European troops, in the Himalayan foothills, where they were stationed for the hot weather. Before he could take the field he had to organise transport and supplies. When he did march it could only be at night, as movement by European troops by day in the plains during the hot weather was liable to put most of them out of action long before they encountered the enemy. Anson himself died of cholera en route to Delhi.[34]

His successor, Sir Harry Barnard, a Crimean veteran, joined forces with the troops from Mirath, encountering opposition from mutineers along their line of march, and winning the first major engagement of the war at Badli-ki-Serai, five miles from Delhi, on 8 June. They then encamped on the ridge overlooking Delhi, so denying the opposition of any chance of establishing a secure seat of government. The first group of reinforcements, the Corps of Guides, arrived on 9 June, after a march of 580 miles from Peshawur, but the British were too few to invest the city, still less to attack fortifications they had themselves modernised. Barnard died of cholera on 5 July. His successor, Major-General Reed, was invalided to the hills eleven days later and command passed to Brigadier-General Wilson. Large-scale reinforcements fought their way down from the Punjab to arrive by mid-August but not until the arrival on 3 September of the siege train from Ferozepur, despite desperate attempts by their enemies to intercept it, were the British able to take the offensive.[35]

The fate of Delhi had the greatest consequences. The final attack included a week's continuous bombardment, before the city walls were stormed on 14 September. Six more days of street fighting followed before resistance was ended. The four months' fighting cost the British side 3,537 dead and wounded, out of a total of 11,200 soldiers (3,300 Europeans, 7,900 Indians). A total of 3,500 casualties, over 20 per cent of those involved in the assault, were suffered on 14 September alone. The defenders, who included large numbers of religious warriors and armed retainers of chiefs loyal to Bahadur Shah, as well as mutineers of the Bengal army, suffered even heavier losses, as did the unfortunate inhabitants of Delhi in the subsequent sack of their city. The Mughal princes surrendered. Three were shot to forestall any rescue, twenty-three were later hanged as rebels and Bahadur Shah, who had been given a promise that his life would be spared, was put on trial for rebellion.[36]

If Delhi was the head of the insurgency, Hindustan was its heart. After three weeks of rising mistrust and tension between the British (whose intelligence officers warned that the example of the Mirath and Delhi mutineers might be followed anwhere), and the Bengal sepoys (who feared that British precautionary measures would lead to their own immediate or eventual destruction), both sides were proved right. During the night of 30 May, a mutiny broke out at Lucknow. Loyal men of the 13th and 71st Bengal Native Infantry, fighting alongside the 32nd Foot, defeated the mutineers, who then marched to Delhi. Those of their number who had been taken prisoner were tried by court-martial and hanged. Elsewhere in Awadh, however, the newly installed British administration collapsed, as the garrison of the various district headquarters joined the mutiny. As had been the case at Mirath, in some cases, the soldiers ensured that no harm came to their officers. In others, Europeans including women and children were murdered, with civilian rioters joining in the attacks. In yet others, local landholders protected European refugees and helped them escape before going themselves, with their retainers, to fight against the British who had, the year before, taken their country. At Banares, on 5 June, the 37th Bengal Native Infantry was in the process of being disarmed when shooting started, and the sepoys were dispersed by Colonel Neill and his Madras European Fusiliers, rushed up bv steamer and the first few hundred miles of railway in India. The Allahabad garrison mutinied the next day, and many Christians, and Hindu pilgrims too, died at the hands of local criminals. Neill reached Allahabad and relieved the fort there on 11 June. The many acts of reprisal which he and other British officers authorised began to have a counter-productive effect, for as they were imposed with little regard for guilt or innocence, most of the local population fled on his approach, making it difficult to obtain the local labour, transport and supplies on which his troops depended.[37]

The next garrison up the Ganges was at Kanpur (Cawnpore). The commander, Major-General Sir Hugh Wheeler, an ageing but able veteran of the Maratha wars, appreciated that if his sepoys mutinied, they would desert and march to Delhi. He therefore built field works outside the city into which, when the mutiny did occur on 4 June, the European community and loyal elements moved. The mutineers (2nd Bengal Irregular Cavalry, 1st, 53rd, and 55th Native Infantry) were, however, joined by the forces of Nana Sahib, adopted son of Baji Rao II, the last of the Peshwas, deposed by the British in 1818, and holder of a *jagir* near Kanpur until his death in 1851. Nana Sahib, to whom the British had declined to allow either the Peshwa's titles or his allowances, then led the combined force against Wheeler's entrenchments.[38] After three weeks' desperate resistance, and influenced by the plight of his non-combatants, Wheeler accepted Nana Sahib's promise of safe conduct by river-boat to Allahabad and surrendered on 27 June. After reaching the boats, he and the remnants of his command were attacked. Of those who survived, the men were shot and the women and children taken back into Kanpur.[39] On 30 June, Major-General Havelock, a 65-year-old veteran of campaigns against the Afghans, Punjabis, and most recently Iranians, with 42 years commissioned service to his credit, arrived to take over command from Neill at Allahabad. He marched for Kanpur on 10 July, hoping to rescue the European women and children, but fought his way into the city a week later only to find that all had been murdered just before his arrivel.[40]

He pushed on through the mid-summer heat to Lucknow. There the British community, increased by refugees from elsewhere in Awadh, had been under siege since the beginning of July, following the defeat of an ill-starred effort to counter the mutineers approaching from Kanpur. The Residency, the seat of British government, was well-fortified and stoutly defended by a mixed force of British regulars and volunteers, strengthened by loyal sepoys and military pensioners. Nevertheless casualties steadily rose. Women and children suffered, like the men, from disease, the heat, and enemy artillery. The Commissioner was killed by shellfire. Supplies of food, munitions and medical supplies steadily dwindled. Havelock's own force reduced by fighting and sickness to 1,364 rank and file and ten guns, fell back towards Kanpur on 30 July to await reinforcements. Neill, holding Kanpur with the aid of a policy of frightfulness, told Havelock he should have pressed on, and that this retreat was a blow to British prestige. Havelock answered that he stood in no need of such advice from an officer under his command, and that, but for the military emergency, he would have placed Neill under arrest.[41]

On 3 August, after receiving a few reinforcements, he resumed the offensive, only to be forced back to Kanpur where Neill needed support against another large force of insurgents. This was defeated at Bithur on 16 August, but, with his own force reduced to barely 700 effectives, and further disturbances lower down the Ganges, Havelock, despite his unbroken record of victory whenever he had actually encountered his opponents, could do no more until reinforcements arrived.

They arrived at Kanpur on 15 September, led by Sir James Outram. He, though the senior ranking of the two generals, lived up to his reputation as 'the Bayard of India' by ceding command to Havelock, and accompanying the troops only in his capacity as civil Commissioner.[42] Nevertheless, but for the long-standing personal friendship between the two men, civil-military relations would have proved just as difficult as when a military Governor-General and a C-in-C India were in the field together during the first Sikh War, for Havelock was bound to move his army in accordance with Outram's political directions. Nevertheless, Outram's decision gained the concurrence of both the Governor-General, and of the newly arrived C-in-C India. This was Sir Colin Campbell, a Highland officer who had served in the Peninsular War, the West Indies and the Punjab. Re-employed on the outbreak of the Crimean War, he commanded the 'thin red line' at Balaclava, a battle from which he was one of the few British generals to emerge with his reputation enhanced.[43] On 19 September, as the weather was becoming cooler, and reinforcements arriving at Calcutta, the British again advanced from Kanpur. They fought their way into Lucknow a week later, losing 31 officers and 504 men killed and wounded out of 3,197 with Brigadier-General Neill among the fallen, but the Residency was reached. It was however, reinforced rather than relieved, and the siege continued, with the besiegers defiantly proclaiming the restoration of the former dynasty. It was not until 17 November that a relieving force led by Cambell himself, and including a brigade of heavy guns manned from HMS *Shannon,* finally reached Lucknow. The fighting was still by no means over. An army composed of Nana Sahib's men and mutineers of the

Gwalior contingent, led by Ramachandra Panduranga, better known as Tatya Tope, a general of the late Peshwa's service, was still in the field, and succeeded in recapturing Kanpur, on 27 November.[44] Campbell abandoned Lucknow and after sending his non-combatants to safety, turned to face this new threat. Tatya Tope was defeated on 6-7 December, and Kanpur was re-occupied by the British. A column of British troops from Delhi then fought its way eastwards to join forces with Campbell on 4 January 1858.

Lucknow was now as politically significant as Delhi had been in the first phase of the war. It was a focus of loyalty for the mutineers of whose country it was the capital, as of the Awadhi landholders *(taluqdars)* whose king had ruled there until the previous year. They had proclaimed the restoration of the dynasty, they still had a formidable power in the field, and they still challenged the legitimacy of British dominion over Hindustan. It was not, however, until the campaigning season was almost over that Campbell was able to begin his offensive. He marched from Kanpur on 27 February 1858 and, after a carefully conducted ten days' siege, took Lucknow by storm on 21 March. As retribution for the sympathy which so many of them had displayed for the insurgents, Canning proclaimed to the landholders of Awadh that, with the exception of only six named individuals, all were deemed to have forfeited their grants and would have to rely upon the mercy and justice of the the British government for the retention of life and liberty. On the evidence of British policy during the previous decade, most landholders assumed this meant general confiscation, and rather than tamely lose their place in the world, many who had previously remained neutral now rose in arms against the British. It was not until February 1859 that Awadh was reconquered, and even then a few desperate bands held out in the jungle-clad hill areas on the borders of Nepal.

The third major campaign of the war was in Central India.[45] Jhansi, a small state in Bundelkhand, had been ruled by a Maratha prince, Maharaja Gangadhar Rao, a friend of the British until his death in November 1853. In March 1854 Dalhousie had set aside Gangadhar Rao's dying request that the state be ruled by his widow, Rani Laksmi Bai, in the minority of his adopted son, and annexed Jhansi under the doctrine of lapse. The troops maintained by the late Maharaja were disbanded, and their place taken by the 12th Bengal Native Infantry, which was still stationed at the city Jhansi three years later, and which mutinied on 5 June 1857. The British officials and clerks held out for four days in the fort, but having neither provisions nor any hope of relief, came out hoping for safe conduct, only to be killed with their women and children. Some fifty-five people were murdered, the worst massacre in the whole Indian Mutiny, except for those at Kanpur.

Sixty miles north west of Jhansi, the Gwalior contingent, the subsidiary force of Company sepoys imposed upon Sindia after his defeat in the campaign of 1843, mutinied on 14 June 1857. Europeans who escaped the massacre there found refuge with the maharaja, and were subsequently escorted to Agra, sixty miles to the north. Sindia temporised with the troops of the contingent until September 1857, when Tatya Tope arrived in person and persuaded them to join the operations against Kanpur that caused Campbell to abandon Lucknow at the end of the month.

The column of troops from the Bombay army, led by Major-General Sir Hugh Rose, reached Jhansi on 21 March 1858. By this time all in the British camp were convinced of the Rani's treachery, while she and her people were determined to resist the return of British rule by force of arms. On 31 March an attempt by Tatya Tope to relieve the city was defeated, and Jhansi was stormed on 3 April, with much slaughter. The Rani escaped, through the self-sacrifice of her Afghan bodyguard, and joined Tatya's army. This force crossed into Gwalior, hoping that Sindia would at last make common cause with Nana Sahib, who, having taken the title of Pehswa, claimed the leadership of all the Maratha princes. Sindia's army went over to the invaders, but he himself refused to join them, and fled to the British at Agra. Rose, pursuing Tatya, captured Gwalior on 20 June. The Rani of Jhansi was killed in a skirmish with the advancing British forces on 17 June. On 29 June, Rose handed over command to his chief of staff, Robert Napier, who pursued Tatya Tope and what was left of his army across the Chambal into Rajasthan. Tatya Tope, betrayed and captured in April 1859, was hanged as a rebel, though this was something of a technicality as he was a subject of the last acknowledged Peshwa, Baji Rao II, until his death in 1851, and had sworn no oath to the Company. His master, Nana Sahib, escaped to Nepal jungles with a lakh of rupees on his head. His fate remains unknown to historians. Jung Bahadur, ruler of Nepal, told the British that his officers believed the Nana Sahib died of fever on 24 September 1859. Other witnesses claimed to have seen him alive after that date, in Nepal or even, as late as 1895, in India itself, in the shape of a wandering mendicant.[46]

REFERENCES

1. A. Farrington, *Guide to the Records of the India Office Military Department,* London, 1982.
2. *Ibid.*
3. *Ibid.*
4. 33 Geo. III, c. 52.
5. 53 Geo. III, c. 155.
6. 3 & 4 Will. IV, c. 85.
7. 5 & 6 Will. IV, c. 52.
8. *East India Registers,* London, annually 1804-1858.
9. *Ibid.*
10. F.G. Cardew, *A Sketch of the Services of the Bengal Native Infantry,* Calcutta, 1903, pp. 142-3; p. Cadell, *History of the Bombay Army,* London, 1938, pp. 165-6.
11. A.L. Basham, 'Notes on Seafaring in Ancient India', *Art and Letters (Journal of the Royal India, Pakistan and Ceylon Society*), London Vol. 23, 1949, p. 60; R.K. Mookerji, *History of Indian Shipping,* London, 1918.
12. A.L. Basham, *The Wonder That Was India,* London, 1954, p. 231.
13. Cardew, *op. cit., p.* 36.
14. Cardew, *op. cit.,* p. 66.

15. R. Callahan, *The East India Company and Army Reform 1783-1798*, Cambridge, Mass, 1972, pp. 174-5.
16. Cardew, *op. cit.*, p. 146.
17. H. Beveridge, *A Comprehensive History of India, London*, 1865, Vol. 2, p. 159.
18. *Ibid.*, p. 160.
19. *Ibid.*, p. 161.
20. *Ibid.*, p. 162.
21. Wellington to the Rt Hon. Sir Charles Wynne (pte) 7 August 1826, *Despatches, Correspondence and Memorials of Arthur, Duke of Wellington*, London, 1856.
22. V.A. Smith, *The Oxford History of India*, Oxford, 1958, p. 587.
23. T.A. Heathcote, *The Afghan Wars 1839-1919*, London, 1980, pp. 32-67.
24. H.T. Lambrick, *Sir Charles Napier and Sind*, Oxford, 1952.
25. Cardew, *op. cit.*, p. 202.

26 V.A. Smith, *op. cit.*, p. 610.

27 Cardew, *op. cit.*, pp. 241-2.

28 'A few words relative to the late Mutiny of the Bengal Army and the rebellion in the Bengal Presidency. By Shaik Hedayut Ali, Soobahdar and Sirdar Bahadoor, Bengal Seikh Police Battalion commanded by Captain T. Rattray', *cit.* in M.R. Gubbins, *An Account of the Mutinies in Oudh*, 3rd edn., London, 1859, pp. 533, 560; J.W. Kaye, *A History of the Sepoy War in India*, 3 Vols., London, 1877, Vol. 1, pp. 466-9.

29 G.W. Forrest, ed., *Selections from the Letters, Despatches, and other State Papers preserved in the Military Department of the Government of India 1857-1858*, 3 Vols., Calcutta, 1893-1902, Vol. 1, pp. 1-5, pp. 227-41.

30 S.N. Sen, *Eighteen Fifty Seven*, Delhi, 1957, pp. 50-4; Trial of Jemadar Issuree Pandy, 10 April 1857, *cit.* in Forrest, pp. 177-207.

31 Sen, *op. cit.*, pp. 57-8.

32 Sen, *op. cit.*, pp. 60-2.

33 *Ibid.*, pp. 70-3.

34 Kaye, *op. cit.*, Vol. II. pp. 168-71.

35 Cardew, *op. cit.,* pp. 271-2.

36 *Ibid.*, pp. 272-5; Sen, *op. cit.,* pp. 79-118.

37 Sen, *op. cit.,* pp. 154-6.

38 P.C. Gupta, *Nana Sahib and the Rising at Lucknow,* Oxford, 1963, pp. 68-9.

39 Sen, *op. cit.,* p. 157.

40 Sen, *op. cit.,* p. 158.

41 *Ibid.*, p. 206.

42 *Ibid.*, p. 218; J.C. Pollock, *Way to Glory : The Life of Havelock of Lucknow,* London, 1957, p. 219; Divisional Order by Maj. Gen. Sir James Outram dated 16 Sept. 1857, *cit.* in W. Brock, *A Biographical Sketch of Sir Henry Havelock, KCB,* London, 1858, pp. 219-20, and in A. Forbes, *Havelock,* London, 1890, p. 179.

43 A. Forbes, *Colin Campbell, Lord Clyde,* London, 1895.

44 Sen, *op. cit.,* Ch. 4; P.C. Gupta, *op. cit.,* Ch. 5; Kayel *op. cit.,* Vol. II, Book V, Chs. 1-4; Forrest, *op. cit.,* Vol. 2. Chs. 1-7.

45 R.G. Burton, *The Revolt in Central India 1857-58,* compiled in the Intelligence Branch, Army HQ India, from the dispatches of the campaign, Simla 1908; Sen, *op, cit.,* Chs, 7-8; G.W. Forrest, *A History of the Indian Mutiny Reviewed and Illustrated from Original Documents,* 3 Vols., Edinburgh and London, 1904-1912, Vol. 3, Chs. 1-7, 19.

46 Gupta, *op. cit.,* pp. 200-203.

8
Conclusion

The research, cannot be confined only to one aspect as the subject by its very nature is related to other factors such as the structure at organisation of armies and their relation to the state. The period covered (1757 to 1857) was critical in our history as, for the first time, the whole of India came under the sway of a single power, whereas earlier the political geography was a patchwork of states under different rulers, some of them owing a loose form of allegiance to a central authority but trying all the time to break away.

The reasons for the conquest of India by the British and their overcoming all major powers like the Moghuls, Marathas and Sikhs have been gone into by historians. Indian scholars, particularly, have stressed that the British supremacy was due to deceit, intrigue and political chicanery. They have however failed to comprehend that the British wrested control purely by military means. Politics and intrigues may have played their role as always happens, but the final issue as to who was to rule was always decided in the field of battle by a clash of arms. In fact, the history of India has largely been influenced by the military factor. Even the recent events since our independence in 1947 (our military action in Jammu and Kashmir, Junagadh, Hyderabad, Goa, NEFA, and wars of 1965 and 1971) would confirm this.

Although military history is such an important subject, Indian scholars have generally turned away form a serious study of the art and science of war and its influence on history and society. It is essential for all our citizens, whether in uniform or otherwise, to know our military history, understand the true causes of our defeats and victories and draw lessons from it.

Only then will our leaders be able to ensure that our defence policy is sound and that past mistakes in organisation, strategy, tactics and weaponry are not repeated.

In the current study, a number of selected battles have been described in detail. For a military student, battle or campaign history is considered more important than other branches of military historiography as it is not what armies are, but what they do that is important.

The introduction of the artillery in battle made a battlefield much more complex, as previously the fighting was mainly hand to hand combat and there were only three main types of combat :

(a) Infantry versus infantry;

(b) Infantry versus cavalry;

(c) Cavalry versus cavalry.

Artillery not only multiplied the number and types of engagements by it also made the tactics more complex due to its long range and much greater destructive potential. The number of possible encounters increased to six with the addition of following new types :

(a) Artillery versus artillery;

(b) Artillery versus infantry;

(c) Artillery versus cavalry.

In actual fact, the number of possible encounters was mush more, when one or more arms were combined to gather in an attack by the artillery/cavalry combination on infantry or by the artillery/infantry combination over cavalry. All this implied that the leaders in battle not only had to be more knowledgeable about the battle tactics but much sharper in their decisions, the timings and weight of various engagements in the thick of battle. The handling of artillery particularly required special experience as not only was it capable of causing greater destruction on fortifications and massed cavalry and infantry, but its ability to fight at longer range outside the orbit of hand-to-hand fighting, which was characteristic of infantry and cavalry, gave it a great significance. The human mind generally takes its own time to grasp new ideas and tends to stick to well proven and defined theories and practices. Indian leaders (with the exception perhaps of Ranjit Singh), whose armies were based mainly on cavalry, were reluctant and slow to appreciate the potential of artillery and subordinate the "glory" of cavalry to a new arm. The statement of Prince Azam Shah in 1707 that "to fight with artillery was a stripling's pastime, the only true weapon was the sword" does not represent an isolated Indian philosophy of warfare. The bane of thinking of Indian leaders regarding warfare was that, in fact, they really never understood war. It was not that they did not want to. It is just that the whole system of government of which the army formed a part was ad hoc without any philosophy about how to run a state. A well-known English historian and analyst has made the following comments :

> No one had really given a thought to the philosophy of running a state. Political chaos is the most grequent condition. Empires and states rise and fall, wars roll across India but it is hard to see any principle. The issue is usually whether one man shall rule or another, as often as not the battle is between brother and brother or father and son. In all this confusion there was very little thought about the nature of state and no one really gave serious thought as to how best to provide an army which could protect the state faithfully or to finding a system that would bring victory.

In all this political confusion, it is not really surprising that the Indians, who had never studied war seriously in all its ramifications, invariably came out as losers when their armies faced the British.

The above fact is all the more unfortunate as almost all foreign observers of those days are unanimous in their opinion that man for man an Indian soldier, both mounted and dismounted, was superior in skill at arms and in personal courage was equal to the British. It is a reasonable deduction that both Indian soldiers and their leaders, who were used to deciding the issue of battle by close hand-to-hand combat, invariably got confused and demoralised when highly skilled British guns fired at them at long range (without themselves being under effective fire). The only antidote was, of course, a charge of cavalry on the guns or counter-fire by guns which, when applied, were ineffective due to reasons brought out in this study.

The case with which the armies of the East India Company overwhelmed the armies of Indians despite being outnumbered and the apparent invincibility of the British artillery merited detailed investigation and this study has attempted to bring out the reasons for our defeats. Some historians have ascribed the victories of the British to their technical superiority, which in those days implied artillery with its guns, ammunition and accessories. But was it really so? India had been using guns long before the arrival of the British in the country. Babar won his victory at the Battle of Panipat in 1526 due to the use of his artillery. In his memoirs, he has mentioned in some detail the manufacture of guns by his chief of Artillery, Ustad Quli Khan. In 1540, Humayun used various types of guns at the Battle of Kanauj. Akbar called his guns "locks and keys of empire". Hyder Ali and Tipu often had more guns than the British. In 1763, at the Battle of Gheria the artillery of Mir Kasim organised by Gurkhin Khan was the best that any Indian prince ever possessed and in no way was it inferior to that of the English as far as its weapons and ammunition were concerned. As late as in 1803, the Marathas at the Battle of Assaye had excellent artillery. The Sikhs under Ranjit Singh had brought up their artillery virtually to European standards.

What then could be the reasons that, when facing British artillery even though outnumbering it in numbers and weight of metal, the Indians invariably could not match the artillery of the former despite having good guns and ammunition? The truth really is that they had never given any thought to war and all that it implies in its multiple variables of organisation, tactics, command, essence of inter-arm cooperation and weaponry. They had never bothered to ponder whether it was possible by better drill and organisation to increase the rate of fire of a gun from 4 to 8 rounds or even more per hour. British light guns like 6 pounders could fire as many as 5 rounds a minute but for safety and technical reasons, fired 2 rounds a minute for a long period. Thus a battery of 8 guns could fire as many as 288 rounds on the attacking infantry and 88 rounds on the attacking cavalry from the time the latter two moved for assault to the time they reached the defences, changing the type of ammunition in between. Depending upon the distance, they started with spherical shot and finished with case shot (case full of bullets) as the enemy closed on the guns. The greater rapidity of fire was essential in the battlefield as the role of artillery was to create firepower at selected points, to first neutralise the enemy, then demoralise him and finally destroy him. Although there can be no mathematical equation, it would probably not be an exaggeration to say that one European gun in action was equal to twenty manned by Indian gunners due to the higher achieved rate of fire. No one has cared to study why it was necessary tactically to concentrate maximum fire on a given portion of the battlefield. Tactics imply the best and timely use of firepower and manoeuvres to defeat the enemy. Firepower was the preserve of artillery. Infantry and cavalry were required to manoeuvre in conjunction with firepower; in fact the artillery also manoeuvred its firepower to assist the movement of the other two arms. This required a very high standard of battle procedure by the artillery and a sense of cooperation by all three arms. All this could only be achieved by constant practice in peacetime as well as understanding of war. There is no historical record to prove that apart from Ranjit Singh, any other leader ever carried out practice during peace time in combined manoeuvres.

The other aspect which put Indians at a great disadvantage was the system of the organisation of armies due to the nature of the political set-up. Whereas the artillery arm was kept central under the kings or chiefs, the infantry and cavalry were generally gathered under the banner of their chiefs, owing allegiance to their over-lord just prior to the impending battle, with the result that during the actual battle there could be no coordination of fire and movement. Guns were just placed to fire as long as they could, dispersed all over the front with no central brain to guide them for maximum effect. Maybe the reason for this lack of mutual support and cooperation between the artillery and other two arms was due to the examples set by the political chiefs of India who could seldom put up a united fron against a common enemy and spent more time in infighting than trying to get together.

Another revealing feature of the battles fought by the British for supremacy over Indians is that for the first 50 years from the time they raised their regular armies in 1748, the British won their battles mainly by the use of their artillery and infantry against Indian powers whose armies predominantly consisted of cavalry with their artillery and infantry employed in a secondary role. For the first 50 years the British did not even raise their cavalry arm in any worthwhile strength, so much was their faith in the influence of their artillery in battle. This itself is a fascinating study of human behaviour in battle. The current research has already revealed that Indian soldiers seemed to have an inborn fear when facing guns. Analysts have generally been baffled by this. As one historian speaking of 1760 has stated, "Nothing is so ruinous to their military affairs as the false notion which is generally entertained by them and chiefly their commanders in relation to artillery. They are terrified with that of the enemy and foolishly put a confidence in their own and what is the most fatal mistake, they place their most dependence on the largest pieces which they know neither how to manage nor to move".

As regards the fear of Indian cavalry to close with guns it was not based so much on fear for their lives as for their fortunes which were all laid out in the horse they rode. The horse and the weapon being the property of the individual and not the the state, the mounted soldiers were extremely unwilling to bring their horses within the reach of British guns. If a man had his horse killed or wounded, no compensation was paid to him by his chief. He not only lost his animal but also his allowance; as such he was careful to preserve both.

The armies of Indians were composed of nobles and

chieftain who joined together at the time of war under a common banner. The soldiers were not professionals but only part-time fighters and when the need of their chiefs was over, they returned to their homes and occupations. Even in such a highly organised professional army as that of the Sikhs, it has been brought out that as late as in 1848, gunners were not kept in peace time but were enlisted and discharged according to the position of affairs. Since there was no continuity of military service, there was no attempt to study the technique of battle. The soldiers were incapable of carrying out anything but the simplest movements. Whereas the artillery arm was kept central under the Moghul kings and the other two arms brought to battle by various mansabdars, there could be no understanding at all of combining their functions in battle. The guns were scattered untactically all over the front and failed to make an impact except on a very weak enemy.

The Marathas did make great efforts later to reorganise their armies on the European model by having trained and disciplined artillery and infantry but they still did not shed the old tactics, resulting in a compromise. It is not easy to change the philosophy of warfare overnight. It was only Ranjit Singh who, understanding human nature, decided to go slow to enable his chiefs to absorb the new system and also give time to himself to study and understand the European model.

The British clearly understood that if they were to be the future rulers of India, application of superior military power would be its main instrument. They also appreciated that they would invariably be outnumbered in battle in all the three arms. They therefore concluded that their main plank to tilt the outcome of a battle in their favour was the powerful arms of artillery. When raising their regular armies in 1748, composed mainly of artillery and infantry, a categorical policy on their artillery arm was issued by the Directors in England to the following effect :

(a) No native is to be employed in their artillery.

(b) Natives are to be kept ignorant of the theory and practice of the artillery branch.

(c) No deserter from any nation is allowed to serve in artillery, even if a British subject.

(d) No Roman Catholic is allowed to serve in this arm and he is to leave this arm if he marries a person of that religion.

(e) No native is to be allowed to come near or set foot in the laboratory or military magazine.

It may even strange that whereas natives were allowed to man their cavalry and infantry, they were not permitted in the artillery. Whereas deserters and Roman Catholics could join the other two arms, their employment was forbidden in the artillery. In fact, later the Directors even did not permit the artillery to have officers commissioned from the ranks, whereas there was no such embargo on the other arms. The main reason for such severe restrictions on artillery was that the British were not only extremely sensitive to its role in battle but also in peacetime to quell mutinies and unrest within their own army. They wanted to be sure that this arm was kept totally reliable and loyal. As early as 1753, the Directors had spelt out "how great a share of our dependence must in case of trouble lie on the Artillery and upon the skill of people appropriated to its service".

It has been brought out that earlier British would not even allow two light guns held on charge of native infantry battalions to be manned by natives. They were either withdrawn or ordered to be manned by Europeans. We have seen the vicissitudes of native artillery of the Company and how, after their initial raising in 1777, due to the compulsion of finance and shortage of European manpower, they were periodically disbanded and raised because of the fear of natives manning guns as their cavalry and infantry arms were mainly composed of native soldiers. If such a dangerous arm like the artillery was allowed to be manned predominantly by natives, the very existence of the British in India would have been in jeopardy.

It was only from 1806 onwards that the native artillery came to stay due to the compulsions of expansion. Even then, the British ensured that European-manned units were always in a majority. Horse artillery, whose influence in peace and war was very important, had a much higher ratio of European units. On the eve of the revolt, the proportion of natives to Europeans in the other two arms was as high as 10 to 1 whereas in the case of both foot and horse artillery, European units were in preponderance. This was one of the major factors leading to the suppressing of the Revolt of 1857. The British would have certainly lost their future empire if their artillery arm was also Indianised to even half the extent of the cavalry and infantry and if they had allowed the policy of 1748 by the Directors in England to drift due to the compulsion of events.

They remained very clear in their appreciation and conclusion that it was better to have lesser artillery units which were wholly reliable, trustworthy and effective in battle than to have more units whose reliability was suspect.

Of all the three native manned arms of the Company, the artillery was the least influenced by the revolt. Not only was this a major saving factor for the British but it was also found that native artillery units which did not go across to the other side, thereafter proved themselves to be completely reliable and their battle performance was praiseworthy, unlike the case of the other two arms whose loyalty and battle performance could never be relied upon totally till the issue was finally decided.

This study covers a span of over 100 years. Considering the length of this period, there were any number of major changes in higher policy relating to army, politics, trade, government and other related spheres. In the case of manning of their artillery arm by natives, the stand remained unwavering. It is to the credit of the British from their point of view that their stand on this policy was fully vindicated by subsequent historical events.

After the revolt, a high powered committee met in 1858 in England to give recommendations for reorganisation of the army in India. It questioned a large number of army and civilian officers to get their opinion. The inquiry found conflicting views on the size, composition, armament, organisation and other related aspects. However, every single witness gave the same opinion in respect of the artillery branch, that it was wholly to be manned by Europeans and natives must not be allowed to man such a dangerous arm. They were united in their view that a small force with a powerful artillery in India would be irresistible and no mutiny of a native army without guns could hope to be successful, a policy which stood the test for the next 80 years. The British allowed only four mountain batteries manned by natives for the defence of the Frontier, but also stipulated that they will not be moved out from that area.

It is not surprising, thus, that even some Indian historians have written that the artillery was one of the key forces that ensured the supremacy of the British in India.

The aim of current research was to cover a lacuna in the history of India and to highlight how the handling and control of weapon systems can influence the history of a nation. The study, in addition, brings out some important aspects of the military history of India between 1757 and 1857. It has attempted to highlight in a chronological and comprehensive narrative the evolution of the artillery of the British and Indian powers of the period and show how it influenced the balance of power.

It is hoped that all Indians concerned with the policy of defence of India will be able to draw important lessons from the analysis so that they can understand the past and plan for the future. It has rightly been said that those who do not study and understand the past can neither handle the present nor creatively plan for the future.

Appendices

APPENDIX—I

GUIDE TO THE RECORDS NATIONAL ARCHIVES OF INDIA, NEW DELHI

(A) MILITARY DEPARTMENT—ITS PREDECESSOR BODIES/ARMY DEPARTMENT/DEFENCE DEPARTMENT/WAR DEPARTMENT/MINISTRY OF DEFENCE

I. ORGANISATIONAL CHANGES

It is perhaps incontrovertible that the superstructure of the British Empire built in India was mainly the work of the British Army. The strength and efficiency of the British Army in India was demonstrated in an ample measure right from the Company Period to the end of the British Rule. History of the British India is replete with instances when a handful of the British Army defeated the massive native armies in pitched battles. This was attributed to the exemplary discipline and excellent organisation of the British Indian Army. Not only as a superior striking force but the superiority of the British Army was also exhibited in other spheres of British administration in India. There is an unending list of militiamen providing outstanding administrators, prolific writers, archaeologists, cartographers, geologists and what not. The soldiers of the Indian Army fought in many campaigns overseas also where they won laurels.

The shape and size of the Military organisation in India, however, varied at different intervals. During the initial stages of the rule of the East India Company, there was required only a small army of soldiers for the defence of the Company's possession. But with the conquest of more and more territories, the size of the Army had to be increased and consequently due also to the changing trends of the methods of warfare, the Army administration underwent tremendous changes.

The genesis of the administrative history of the Military Department of the Government of India goes back to the early days of the East India Company in 1644, when Fort St. George was built to protect the Company's property in Madras. The original garrison of Fort St. George in 1645 consisted of a mixed body of Englishmen, French and Dutch deserters, Portuguese, and Negroes, numbering in all about hundred men. To this promising force may be traced the origin of what till 1895 was the Madras Army.

The next English Commercial Centre was the East India Company's factory at Hugli established in 1652 under an Agent who was permitted by a *farman* of the Mughal Emperor to have a small personal guard of honour of an "ensign and thirty men". Such was the origin of the celebrated Bengal Army. For various reasons the chief centre of the Company's commercial activities in Bengal was transferred in 1689 to Calcutta and the Agent's guards were increased to 100 men. In 1696, however, the Agent, Mr. Charles Eyre applied to the local Nawab for permission to fortify his factory at Calcutta. He was granted permission to defend himself, and the fort thus constructed was named as the Fort William, in honour of King Wiliam III.

Bombay was the next foothold acquired by the British in India in their chronological order of possession. In 1662[1] the Island of Bombay became the property of King Charles-II ceded to him by the Crown of Portugal as a portion of the marriage settlement of the Queen Catherine of Braganza. A detachment of King's troops, subsequently augmented by a few Europeans of various nationalities collected locally was its garrison which became the embryo of what in course of time grew to be the Bombay Army. In 1668 the garrison of Bombay consisted of 5 officers, 139 commissioned officers and men, 54 Topasses, apart from 2 gunners and their 21 pieces of cannon. All the men were Europeans except the 54 Topasses, who were half-castes claiming descent from the Portuguese and were so called from the form of the headgear which they used. This was the largest of the military bodies at that time in India.

The Council set up at Fort William for the management of Company's affairs commenced recording the proceedings of the meetings from the year 1704. But the Council's proceedings prior to 1748 are not available in the National Archives of India.

The conflict between Nawab Siraj-ud-daulah of Bengal and the Council created a new situation for the English in Bengal. The Nawab captured Calcutta on 20 June 1756, and the members of the Council made their escape lower down the Hooghly river at Falta. There the members appointed from themselves a Secret Committee with Roger Drake Junior, as the President to conduct the political and military affairs of the Company in Bengal, and to maintain their secrecy. The sittings of the Secret Committee were held from 22 August to 10 December[2] 1756.

Meanwhile the impending war with France led the Court of Directors to appoint a Select Committee[3] to deal with Company's political and military affairs. Roger Drake was appointed its President and it replaced the Falta Secret Committee.

The political eclipse of the English in Bengal was not much prolonged. They recovered Calcutta on 2 January 1757, concluded a treaty with Siraj-ud-daulah on 9 February 1757, and defeated his army at the Battle of Plassey on 23 June 1757. The Company's position in Bengal, henceforth, underwent a rapid change. The Select Committee held its meetings from 21 February 1757 to 28 December 1762, when the functions were taken over by the Council of Fort William.

The functions of the Council, so far, were not organised into regular departments. A single Secretary's Office was simply sufficient for the transaction of all business of administration of the Council. The Council's proceedings did not bear the heading of any department except "Fort William", till December 1763. But when armies were raised, and political relations established with the Princely States, it became necessary to establish new departments for the despatch of the business. Moreover, due to political instability prevailing at that time, and the exigencies of war with Mir Kasim, the official work of the Council for the first time was divided between two distinct departments—"Public", and "Secret", in accordance with the resolution of the President-in-Council, dated 3 November 1763 (see Appendix-I). The resolution, however, was to take effect from 1 January 1764, but the records of the "Public" and "Secret" Departments were actually separated from 8 December 1763. This division of functions gave rise to two distinct series of records in the Council, each bearing the name of the respective department. The Public Department continued to deal with all affairs, except diplomatic and political and the Secret Department was entrusted with all military plans and operations and matters relating to diplomatic and political. The "Public" and "Secret" Departments though distinct and separate, however, continued to be held by a single Secretary named, John Graham.

The Secret Department operated for a little more than sixteen months when its functions were taken over by a new Select Committee constituted[4] on 7 May 1765 by Lord Clive on his arrival for the second time as the Governor of Bengal and the President of the Council. Clive's object of constituting the new Select Committee was in fact to centralise authority in the office of the Governor, and Select Committee held full powers to regulate the political and military affairs of the Company in relation to the Indian States.[5]

The East India Company secured the Diwani of the provinces of Bengal, Bihar and Orissa[6] from the Mughal Emperor Shah Alam II in August 1765. A formal distribution of work between the Select Committee and the Council took place on 21 December 1765, Clive specified the powers exerciseable by them. The Select Committee was vested with vide powers to conduct the political and military affairs and collection of the revenue arising from the grant of Diwani. The Council, on the other hand was left with the management of the trade, the Zamindari of Calcutta and the assigned districts of Burdwan, Midnapore and Chittagong.

The relative position of the Select Committee and the Council, however, changed and the powers of former were curtailed after Clive left India in February 1767. The Secret

Department in the period of interlude did not function from 7 May 1765 to August 1768, and was revived[7] by a resolution of the Council, dated 22 August 1768 under the charge of the Secretary in the Public Department. The Secret Department, henceforth, was concerned with political and military matters generally as opposed to trade, revenue etc. and the secret matters which did not come under the purview of the Select Committee. The Select Committee was dissolved on 20 October 1774.

The Public Department was also concerned with the military administration, such as conduct of warfares, discipline, executive control, maintenance etc., till a separate agency known as the "Controlling Military Committee" was formed[8] at Calcutta on 21 march 1771. John Cartier was appointed its President. The functions of the Committee were to inspect, control and regulate all affairs concerning the military activities of the Company. But the Committee was short-lived and abolished in 1774, perhaps due to the creation of the Offices of the Quartermaster General in Bengal in December 1773[9] and that of Adjutant General to the Bengal Army in February 1774.[10] In April 1775 a Board of Ordnance[11] was established with the object of regulating military expenses. But even so, the Public Department did not cease altogether to identify itself with the military affairs, particularly in respect of local matters and the internal defence of the country until 1786, when the military secretariat was reorganised.

On 30 October 1776,[12] Warren Hastings laid before the Council a plan by which the management and direction of all military affairs of the Company was to be in the hands of a new Military Department with the Town Major of Fort William as the Secretary. The duties of this new department were to include the recording of orders affecting the army passed in other departments, of all General Orders of whatever nature and of all memorials of officers respecting rank. The suggestion was given effect to two months later when a Military Board which was in fact the Military Department consisting of the Governor General and other members of the Council was formed. It met for the first time on 22 January 1777. This new department was considered as a part of the Public Department and continued as such till 1786 when it was merged in the newly created Secret and Military Department.

During the years that followed, the secret and political business in the Secret Department increased greatly on account of growing settlements and augmentation of the army and it became difficult for one Secretary in the Public Department to bestow proper attention on the double duties both in the "Public" and "Secret" Departments. By a resolution of the Council, dated 23 September, 1783,[13] Warren Hastings appointed a Secretary in each department. William Bruere and Edward Hay were made the Secretary in the "Public" and "Secret" Departments respectively. Edward Hay who was a civilian, took over the charge of the Secret Department on 3 December 1783.[14]

Certain other important changes were made both in the civil and the military administration of the country as a result of the orders contained in a despatch from the Court of Directors dated 21 September 1785 (received in May 1786). The Court ordered in the despatch that the Government should be carried on by the Governor General-in-Council through the medium of the following Boards :

1. Board of Council.
2. Military Board.
3. Board of Revenue, and
4. Board of Trade.

The Military Board was to act as an expert advisory and inspecting body of the Government on all military affairs, the supreme military authority being vested in the Board of Council. The Directors clearly defined the powers of the Military Board in the following words : "We mean them as a Board of reference and report for the purpose of inspection, and to prevent abuse and deficiencies". It held its first meeting on 25 May 1786.

The year 1786 saw some important alterations in the Secret

Department. The business in that department had increased tremendously. Edward Hay, the Secretary, therefore, proposed that the functions of that department be divided into four distinct departments[15] (see Appendix-II).

(i) Secret and Political Department—to deal with all subjects of a political nature.

(ii) Secret and Military Department—to deal the all subjects of military affairs.

(iii) Secret and Foreign Department—to deal with the European powers in India and other foreign nations, and

(iv) Secret Department of Reforms—a temporary Department to deal with all matters relating to the general retrenchment of expenses, both civil and military.

This division took place with effect from 31 May 1786 and a new series "Secret and Military" were started. From 15 May 1789 the title "Secret" was dropped and henceforth the series came to be known simply as "Military". Thus a distinct Military Department came into existence[16] on 15 May 1789, although the records were separated from the Secret Department only from January 1790. The Office of the Quarter Master General which was abolished[17] on 28 September 1785 in order to curtail the military expenditure was reconstituted[18] in May 1786.

In addition to the departments mentioned above, a separate "Military Department of inspection" was formed[19] on 2 August 1786. The duties of the new Department were to include "all memorials laid before the Board respecting military rank; all appeals from the audits of the Commissary-General upon military accounts and charges, but which were still to be transmitted through the prescribed channel of the paymasters and Commissary-General; all military contracts and agencies; and all correspondence with the Military Board established by the Company's orders of 21 September 1785". Lieutenant Colonel Kyd was appointed the Secretary to this Department. The records of this Department are not available in the National

Archives of India. However, the Military Department of Inspection was abolished[20] on 3 June 1793 as a result of the death of Lieutenant-Colonel Kyd and its work was distributed among the Secretary to the Government of India in the Military Department, the Adjutant General and the Town Major of Calcutta.

A Hospital Board was constituted[21] for the Bengal Presidency on 23 May 1786 for the direction, superintendence of the Company's military hospitals. It was superseded by a Medical Board[22] on 24 June 1796, which had the control of the medical affairs both in the civil and military lines. The Medical Board was abolished with the appointment of Surgeon J. Forsyth as the first Director General of Medical Department[23] who took charge on 18 January 1858.

A Marine Board was created[24] on 6 April 1795 under the control of Board of Trade for marine affairs of the 'Supreme Government' and the transactions of the Governor General-in-Council on marine business were recorded in the Public Department. A separate series of Marine consultations commenced[25] from 1 May 1838, but the marine administration was re-absorbed by the Home Department when it was constituted on 1 May 1843. The marine business was ultimately transferred[26] to the Military Department in 1867.

The Charter Act of 1813 provided for the appointment of a Bishop at Calcutta to meet the religious needs of the Europeans. Consequently on the appointment of the Bishop of Calcutta in May 1814, the matters relating to the duties or concerns of clergy came to be recorded separately as the "Ecclesiastical Proceedings" in the Public Department from 1 November 1815.[27]

The ecclesiastical matters were previously administered by the Public as well as the Military Departments. This was due to the fact that all the clergy at that time were considered as Military Chaplains, those attached to the Churches in Calcutta being under the control of the Governor General, and those stationed at other places received their orders directly from the Commander-in-Chief. By the appointment of the

Bishop at Calcutta, the Military Department was relieved from all correspondence relative to the Clerical establishment of the Bengal Presidency, which henceforth became the responsibility of the newly created Ecclesiastical Department.

The mode of supplying the army with clothing by the contract system having proved inconvenient, the Court of Directors in their despatch dated 8 April 1807, ordered that the system of Agency might be adopted and the supply of clothing to the army be entrusted to an officer of the General Staff, namely, the Adjutant General, Quarter Master General or one of their deputies. Thus the adoption of a system for victualling the European troops and supplying to the army studs by an agency led to the establishment of a Commissariat[28] Department on an extended scale on 1 February 1810. It was placed under the direction and control of Commissary-General with the rank of Lieutenant Colonel assisted by one Deputy Commissary-General holding the rank of Major. The main function of the Commissary Department was to supply provisions, for troops, cattles etc. and arrange for transportation of troops and stores at the Presidency. On 1 May 1816, a Clothing Board was constituted[29] to conduct all the business connected with the clothing and half mounting of the army. The constitution of the Clothing Board comprised the General Officer Commanding at the Presidency, the Commandant of Artillery and Military Auditor General. On 10 March 1817 the constitution[30] of the Board was revised and it was ordered that all General Officers in the Company's Army who had the rank of Colonel and who were posted in the Bengal Presidency should be considered as members of the Board. The Board was abolished on 1 June 1854 and its duties were entrusted to an officer styled as Superintendent of Army Clothing.

It would be worthwhile to mention here that mostly the office of the Secretary to the Military Department was held by the civilian officers till 1817 and the last civilian incumbent to the post was C.W. Gardiner. Captain James Young was the first military officer who was appointed[31] as the Military secretary in July 1817 and rank of Lieutenant Colonel was conferred on him. The post of Deputy Secretary was also created in the same year with the rank of a Major. In 1823 an order[32] was passed to the effect that the officer holding the office of the Secretary in the Military Department should vacate his seat on promotion to the rank of Major General and that the office of Deputy Secretary was to be vacated on promotion to Major General, Regimental Colonel or Lieutenant Colonel etc.

On 1 June 1818, the administration of the Surveyor General Department hitherto dealt in the Military Department was transferred[33] to the Public Department on 5 June 1818.

In consequence of the passing of the Charter Act of 1833, the Governor-General of Fort William in Bengal became the Governor General of India. But the Governor-General and his Council also acted for same time as the Governor and his Council at Fort William. With the termination of monopoly in trade enjoyed, so far, by the East India Company, it remain henceforth only as a governing body. Separate series of consultations were started for the Government of India while the existing series continued for the most part to record the proceedings of the Government of Bengal. As, however, the Military Department was transferred to the Government of India in November[34] 1834 and the Bengal Military Consultations ceased from that time.

The year 1843 provides a landmark in the organisational history of the Secretariat Departments. By a Resolution dated 29 April 1843, the Secretariat of the Government of India was completely separated from that of Bengal. The General Department was redesignated as the Home Department with effect from 1 May 1843 (see Appendix-III). But no changes were made in the organisational set up of the Military Department.

The East India Company was extending its rule in every direction and it badly needed roads, bridges, embankments, barracks and cantonments etc., to facilitate the swift movement of its troops in order to consolidate its possession and further penetrate into the interior of the country. There were no doubt, some works called military works, which were executed exclusively for military purposes, but even the public or civil works were not only confined to the benefit of civil population only but were also used for military purposes. This rendered the distinction between military works and public works difficult. As such the subject was frequently transferred from the Military Department to the civil departments. The military works came under the purview of the Military Boards at the various Presidencies which were controlled by the Supreme Government. In order to streamline the public works administration, the Public Works Department was created[35] on 7 February 1855 which took over public works and the military works remained with the Military Board until its abolition[36] on 30 April 1855. From 1 May[37] 1855, the Military Works were also transferred to the Public Works Department.

The Government of India Act, 1858 changed the structure of the Government of India, and the control of the Government was transferred from the East India Company to the British Crown. The Governor General of India received the additional title of "Viceroy". The Act also abolished the "Board of Control" and the "Court of Directors" in London and in their place was created the Office of the Secretary of State for India. The Secretary of State for India exercised all the functions of the above two bodies, and was assisted in his work by a Council of fifteen members known as the "Council of India". It may be worthwhile to mention here that while the Secretary of State was supreme in matters concerning the administration of all Indian troops, British or Native, the decision[38] in certain matters, like terms of service and organisation of British troops were taken at the House Guards (the Army Headquarters in England) and the War Office and conveyed to the India Office and these decisions were communicated to the Military Department of the Government of India which proclaimed them in General Orders.

On 1 October 1889, all the work relating to studs and all matters connected with the improvement of the breed of horses and cattle previously being dealt with in the Military Department were tansferred[39] to the Revenue and Agricultural Department. The work connected with "Kheddah" which was also previously dealt with in the Military Department was transferred[40] to the charge of the Government of Burma in

August 1902. In 1903, the work concerning the horse breeding was transferred back to the Military Department.

The Bengal and Bomaby Government maintained separate fleets[41] of vessels of war. The Bombay fleet was the more important of the two and was subsequent to 1830 denominated as "the Indian Navy", the other fleet being designated the "Bengal Marine". In 1863, the Indian Navy ceased to exist as a war force and the Naval defence of India became the responsibility of the Home Government for which India contributed annually in the naval estimates. Separate marines were, however, maintained by the Government of Bengal and Bombay whose functions were mainly, the transport of troops and stores and carrying out the marine surveys. In 1877, these two marines were combined into the Indian Marine (in 1892 Royal Indian Marine) under the direct control of the Government of India in the Military Department.

The Afghan War of 1878-80,[42] involving the employment of a considerable army and a strain upon the military resources, proved a fruitful lesson in every branch of the art of war and that of the army organisation. Many defects were observed and the Army Organisation Commission was appointed in 1879 in compliance with Military Department Resolution No. 201 S.B., dated 7 July 1879. Sir Ashley Eden was appointed as the President and Captain E.H.H. Collen, of Bengal Staff Corps, the Secretary of the Commission. The Scope of the Commission was to suggest means for the reduction of the military expenditure and to test how for the existing system had been found adapted to the requirements of troops on active service. The Commission made a most exhaustive and comprehensive inquiry which eventually gave rise to many important reforms. Consequently, on 1 January[43] 1882, the execution of military works in connection with the Bengal Army was transferred from the Public Works Department to the Military Department and a separate Military Service consisting of Royal Engineer Officers was constituted for this purpose. In 1890, the same system was applied to Madras and Bombay armies.

Another important recommendation of the Commission

was the abolition of the system of Presidency Army and unification of the army under single authority of the Supreme Government. Thus, the Presidency Armies were abolished[44] with effect from 1 April 1895 by a General Order No. 981, dated 26 October 1894 of the Government of India in Military Department (see Appendix-IV). This order divided the Army of India into four following Commands :

1. Punjab (including the North-West Frontier and the punjab Frontier force).
2. Bengal.
3. Madras (including Burma).
4. Bombay (including Sind, Quetta and Aden).

These were placed under the command of the Lieutenant Generals who were under the direct control of the Commander-in-Chief and Government of India.

Towards the close of 1905, the controversy which started between the Commander-in-Chief, Lord Kitchener, and the then Viceroy, Lord Curzon, led to certain important changes in the administration of the army. Thus, in pursuance of Military Department Notification No. 203, dated 16 March 1906, the Military Department was abolished[45] on 19 March 1906, and it was replaced by two separate departments, *viz.,* the Army Department and the Military Supply Department (see Appendix-V). The Commander-in-Chief was made the head of the Army Department and the Military Supply Department was given over to the Military Member of the Viceroy's Executive Council. The Army Department was to conduct all business[46] connected with the army, except such functions as were allotted to the Military Supply Department. It was also given the charge of the Military cantonments. The Military Supply Department, on the other hand was given charge of all army contracts, the purchase of the army stores and ordance, the custody of all army stores and ordnance etc., the management of military works, the clothing and manufacturing section, the Indian Medical Service, the Royal Indian Marine the Marine Survey and damages to navigation.

In consequence of the abolition of the Military Department, the Military Accounts Department, which was formerly under the Military Department, was made subordinate to the Finance Department. Further, with the object of making financial control over military expenditure more efficacious, a special branch known as Military Finance Branch was created[47] on 13 April 1906.

However, the new division of functions was not found satisfactory and therefore, the Military Supply Department was abolished[48] on 1 April 1909 and its functions were taken over by the Army Department. On 1 October 1913, the Military Finance Branch was also abolished and its work was transferred[49] to the newly created Office of the Financial Adviser, Military Finance.

The First World War which lasted from 1914-1918 brought about several important changes in the Government of India. The Indian Munitions Board was created on 1 March 1917, especially for duration of the war. Its functions were to control and develop Indian industries with special reference to the needs created by the war, to regulate contracts, to limit and co-ordinate demands for articles not manufactured or produced in India, and to apply the manufacturing resources of India to war purposes. The Board also took over the administrative control of Ordnance Factories from the Army Department. The Great War also revealed many defects in the organisation of the army and the military administration in India. The lessons of the war were too clear to be ignored, and when the war came to an end, the military advisers of the Government immediately embarked upon a definite policy of reorganisation and reforms of the army. Thus, in early 1919, a Committee was appointed[50] to look into the army administration and suggest measures for its reorganisation in order to make a strong army in India. Lord Esher was appointed its President. The terms of reference of the Committee were as enumerated below :

1. To enquire into and report, with special reference to post-bellum conditions, upon the administration and, where necessary, the Organisation of the Army in India,

including its relations with the War Office and the India Office, and the relations of the two offices to one another.

2. To consider the position of the Commander-in-Chief of his dual capacity as head of the Army and Member of the Executive Council, and to make recommendations.

3. To consider and report upon any other matters which they may decide are relevant to the enquiry.

The committee presented their report on 22 June 1920. It may be worthwhile to point out here that the recommendations of Committee were largely responsible for improving the terms of service of the Indian ranks of the army in India, and these improvements were made on firm basis.

The process of the reorganisation was, in its more technical and specific aspect, complicated and laborious. It continued from 1921-1922 and at the close of 1922, the results thus achieved were subjected to the scrutiny of the Inchcape's Committee. The Inchcape or Retrenchment[51] Committee recommended large reductions in the military expenditure. The Committee also suggested that in carrying out their proposals the military advisers to the Government should be given a certain discretion to ensure to retain the essential feature of the organisation of the modern army and the capacity of its expansion in case of war. The War also added the Royal Air Force to the defence service of the country which gave more striking power to the army.

The beginning of Air Force in India* may, in fact be traced back to the formation of flying school at Sitapur in 1914. On the outbreak of Warld War I, this school was broken up and its staff called "Indian Flying Corps" was devoted to active field service in Egypt and Mesopatamia. However, in 1915 the Indian Flying Corps was merged with the Royal Flying Corps which had been initially formed in England. This step was considered

*The records of the Indian Air Force have not been transferred to the National Archives of India.

necessary as it was believed that with separate existence, the Indian Air Force would not be able to keep pace with the rapid technical development which was then taking place in Europe. As was expected, during the following years the Indian Air Force marched from strength to strength with the addition of more and more squadrons. But on the termination of World War I, the Air Force in India had also to share the effects of the post-war financial stringency. As a result a few of its squadrons were dispensed with. In 1922 the Indian Air Force was re-organised and certain reforms were carried out as a result of an Inquiry conducted in the state of its functioning. The Royal Air Force in India was not affected by the recommendations of the Inchcape Committee (1922-23) due to the recognition of the importance of the Air Force as a part of the defence services of India.

Still another change on account of the World War, was that in February 1917,[52] the work relating to 'Acetone' dealt within the Commerce and Industry was taken over by the Army Department.

Under the Reforms of 1919, the military expenditure was excluded from the control of the Indian Legislature but the representatives of the people could exercise an indirect influence on the military administration and army budget by taking prior permission of the Government for expressing their view on the matter.

The administrative control of the Ordnance Factories which was being dealt in the Indian Munition Board was transferred back to the Army Department with effect from 1 March 1920, when the Board was reconstituted as the Board of Industries and Munitions.

As a result of the recommendations of the Inchcape Committee, certain regrouping of Secretariat Departments took place in 1923 for economy in expenditure. But no change was made in the functioning of the Army Department (for the functions allotted to Army Department, please see Appendix VI).[53]

The Indian Air Force Act (Act XIV of 1932) became effective from 8 October 1932 by which the Indian Air Force was created as a definite branch of Indian Army.[54]

The constitutional reforms introduced under the Government of India Act of 1935 necessitated several changes in the Secretariat of the Government of India. The name of the Army Department was changed to 'Defence Department' with effect from 1 January[55] 1936.

The ecclesiastical business on the abolition of the Industries and Labour Department was also transferred[56] to the Defence Department on 8 November 1937.

The Second World War, which commenced on 3 September 1939, led to a tremendous increase in work, resulting in several changes in the Secretariat. A new department known as the Department of Defence Co-ordination was created[57] on 22 February 1939, to coordinate the work of all departments concerned with war preparation. In particular, it was to deal with emergency legislation, problems relating to transport and arrangements for supply in time of war to meet the needs of the Defence Services and the civil population generally. This Department ceased to exist with effect from 20 July 1942 and its work was merged in the Defence Department.

During the war, the subject "Civil Defence" also assumed an importance and hence on 24 October 1941, Department of Civil Defence[58] was created. This Department dealt with all the matters relating to Civil Defence of the country and control of the European manpower. But on 7 September 1943, this Department was also amalgamated[59] with the Defence Department.

As a result of the Cripps Mission, a new Defence Department was set up on 20 July 1942 under the Indian Defence Member, and the old Defence Department was redesignated as the War Department.[60] The new Defence Department dealt with the following items of work :

1. All questions concerning Defence which involved Co-ordination of policy and action between the civil

departments of the Government of India and the work of the War Member.

2. War legislation including the Defence of India Act and rules made thereunder.
3. Demobilisation and post-war reconstruction as far as the defence forces and labour forces were concerned.
4. Manpower, including the administration of the National Service (European British subjects) Act.
5. Amenities for and welfare of troops.
6. National Defence Council.
7. Local Self-Government in cantonments areas, the constitution and powers within such areas of cantonments authorities, the regulation of house accommodation in such areas, and, within British India, the delimitation of such areas.
8. Acquisition, custody and relinquishment of land vested in the Crown for purposes of defence.
9. Co-ordination of the provision, storage, location, transport, etc., of petroleum products of all kinds including those required by the defence forces.
10. Prisoners of War.
11. War Resources Committee.
12. Estates of deceased military officers (Regimental Debt Act).
13. Control and Supply of printing stationery and forms.
14. Medal Section and Indian Army List.
15. Canteens organisations (Q.M.G.).
16. The prince of Wale's Indian Military College, the King George's Indian Military Schools and the Lawrence Military Schools.

The following subjects[61] came under the purview of the War Department :

1. All questions which required the orders of the

Government of India were submitted to the department for decision and issue of orders.

2. All matters requiring the orders of His Majesty's Government were submitted to this Department which referred them to the Secretary of State for India.
3. The Department was the sole official channel of communication between the Defence Service Headquarters on the one hand and Provincial Governments and Administrations on the other hand.
4. It also dealt with all political matters arising out of the administration of the Defence Forces. It also defended the interest of the Forces in the Central Legislature.
5. The War Department was responsible for the substance of all regulations published in India for the Royal Indian Navy, the Army in India and the Indian Air Force.
6. The War Department exercised ultimate control over the entire clerical and subordinate establishments of the War Department itself, Naval Headquarters, General Headquarters and Air Headquarters.

A major reorganisation took place in the Central Government Secretariat soon after the War, when the Defence Department was abolished[62] on 16 January 1946 and major portion of its work was absorbed in the War Department (for the functions allotted to the War Department in September 1946, *i.e.,* when the interim-Government was formed, before the transfer of power by the British, please see Appendix VII).

The name of the War Department was changed[63] to Defence Department with effect from 15 October 1946 by a Resolution No. 2599-A, dated 12 October 1946 of the Government of India in the War Department.

With the attainment of Indian Independence on 15 August 1947, the British rule in India almost ended after two centuries, and a new era commenced in the history of the country. The Indian Independence Act of 1947, while recognising the Independence of India, divided the country into two dominions, *viz.* India and Pakistan. With the setting up of a popular government in India, the various "Departments" of the Central Government Secretariat were designated as "Ministries". Thus the Defence Department was designated as the "Ministry of Defence" with effect from 29 August 1947 (for functions allotted to the Ministry of Defence in 1948, *i.e.,* soon after independence, please see Appendix VIII).

After independence, each Service was placed under its Commander-in-Chief *i.e.,* instead of a single Commander-in-Chief, there were three Commanders-in-Chief, one each for the Army, Navy and Air Force. Under the new Constitution, the Supreme Command of the Armed Forces of the Indian Republic vests in the President. In 1955[64] the title of "Commander-in-Chief" was abolished and the three Services Chiefs were designated as the Chief of the Army Staff, the Chief of the Naval Staff and Chief of the Air Staff respectively.

It may be mentioned here that the system of recording "Proceedings" which was adopted in 1860 was changed to the present "filling" system in the Central Government in 1923. However, the Home Department and Education, Health and Lands Department started the file system in 1921 and 1923 respectively. But it has been observed that this file system was not adopted by the Army/Defence/War Departments which continued the old "Proceedings" system and in addition to the Proceedings numbers, the files bear the case number, instead of the file number.

REFERENCES

1. The Army in India and its Evolution, Superintendent, Government Printing, India, Calcutta, 1924, p. 3.
2. Secret Committee Minute No. 1, dated 22 August, 1756, on board of the *Phoenix Schooner* at Falta.
3. Public General Letters from the Court of Directors, dated 11 February 1756, No. 2, para 59.
4. Select Committee Proceedings, 7 May—27 December 1765, Volume No. 10, pp. 1-9.
5. The Central Administration of the East India Company (1733-1834) by B.B. Misra, Bombay, 1959, p. 67.

6. Home (Public), 9 September 1765, No. 2.
7. Secret Proceedings Volume (22 August—16 December 1768), No. 4, pp. 1-2.
8. Secret Proceedings Volume (March—December 1771), pp. 41, 47-48.
9. Public Letters from Court of Directors, dated 7 April 1773, para 60; Public Department, 6 December 1773, No. 7-9.
10. Public Department, 18 February, 1774, No. 7.
11. Public Department, Body Sheet, 3 April 1775, p. 117-118.
12. Public Department, 30 October 1776, No. 7-A.
13. Public Department, 23 September 1783, No. 16.
14. Secret Department, 10 December 1783, No. 2.
15. Secret Proceedings, 16 May—30 June 1786, Volume No. 75. pp. 2102-13; Public Department, 2 May 1786, No. 2. para 17; A Guide to the India Office Records (1600-1858), by William Foster, London, 1919, p. 48.
16. Public Department, 10 April 1789, Nos. 22-22A.
17. Public Department, B.S. Volume, 28 September 1785, p. 19.
18. Public Proceedings Volume, 11 May 1786, pp. 1102-3 and 1127 Military General Letters from Court, No. 3, dated 21 September 1785, para 18.
19. Military Department, 2 August 1786, No. 28.
20. Military Department, 3 June 1793, No. 41.
21. Public General Letters from Court of Directors, 21 September 1785; Medical Board Proceedings, 29 May 1786.
22. Military General Letters from Court of Directors, 15 January 1796, para 57; Medical Board Proceedings, 27 June 1796.
23. Military General Orders by G.G. January-April 1858, No. 158.
24. Fosters, *op. cit.,* p. 52.
25. General Department, Marine, 23 May 1838, No. 1.
26. Home Department, Public 'A' October 1867, Nos. 86-91.
27. Public Department, Ecclesiastical, 1 November 1815, Nos. 1-5.
28. Military General orders dated 22 December 1809.
29. Military Department, 29 March 1816, Nos. 120-121.

30. Military General Orders dated 10 March 1817.
31. Military Department, 19 August 1817, No. 3.
32. Military Department, 23 May 1823, No. 171.
33. Public Department, 5 June 1818, No. 1.
34. Foster, *op. cit.,* p. 52.
35. Home (Public) 9 February 1855, No. 45.
36. Military Department, 9 February 1855, No. 2.
37. *Ibid.*
38. The Military System of India (1850-1900) by K.M.L. Saxena, pp. 25-26.
39. See Civil Veterinary Administrative Branch in Part IV of the guide.
40. Revenue and Agricultural Department, Forests 'A' September, 1902, No. 3.
41. "Royal Commission on Decentralisation, General Memorandum on the development of British Administration in India and on the origin and functions of the India Governments" by W.S. Meyer, Simla, 1907.
42. The Imperial Gazetteer of India, Volume IV, p. 347.
43. Public Works Department, General 'A' December 1881, No. 4.
44. Gazette of India, 27 October 1894 (Part-I), p. 583.
45. Army Department 'A' July 1906, Nos. 1357-1366.
46. Home Department Public 'A' September 1907, Nos. 213-218.
47. See also Military Finance Branch in Part-IV of the Guide.
48. Army and Marine Department, Summary of Important events and measures during the viceroyalty of Lord Minto from 1 June 1908 to 31 May 1909.
49. Finance Department, Salaries, Establishment, 'A' November 1913, Nos. 161-66.
50. Report of the Army in India Committee (1919-1920).
51. The Army in India and its Evolution. *op. cit.*
52. Commerce and Industry Department, Acetone, "Field", February 1917, No. 5.

53. Home Department, Public, File No. 172 of 1923, Serial Nos. 1-15.
54. Legislative Department, File No. 303/31C&G.
55. Home Department, Public, File No. 18/8 of 1935.
56. Home Department, Public, File No. 286 of 1937.
57. Home Department, Public, File No. 96 of 1939.
58. Home Department, Public, File No. 208 of 1941.
59. Home Department, Public (C), File No. 151 of 1943.
60. Home Department, Public (C), File No. 219 of 1942.
61. Secretariat of the Governor General (Public), File No. 176/42-G.G. (A).
62. Home Department, Public (C), File No. 320 of 1945.
63. Gazette of India, 12 October 1946, Part I, Section 3, p. 1500.
64. The organisation of the Government of India, the Indian Institute of Public Administration, October 1958.

APPENDIX—II

(I) CENTRAL GOVERNMENT RECORDS (1760-1858)

The following records series are available :-

(II) RECORDS SERIES AND THEIR FINDING AIDS

Series	*Year*	*Space (in metres)*
(1)	*(2)*	*(3)*
A. COMPANY PERIOD (1760-1859)		
1. Proceedings (2022 Volumes; manuscript)	1779-1859 Gaps : July 1779-April 1786, 1788 (March-April), 1797 (July), 1798 (Oct.), 1807 (May), 1808 (Feb.), 1853 (23 Feb., 6 May and 17 June), 1854 (8 Dec.), 1855 (28 Dec.), 1856 (15 Feb.) and 10 Oct.), and 1858 (2 April)	235.50
2. Original Consultations (1196 Bundles and 35 Carton Boxes; (manuscript)	1786-1859	507.50
3. Index to Proceedings (324 Volumes; manuscript)	1786-1859 Gaps : 1814 (M-W), 1850 Jan.-June) and 1858 (July-Sept.)	32.50
4. Letters from Court of Directors and Secretary of State for India (134 Volumes; manuscript)	1785-1859 *(i)* Gaps : 1786 and 1858 (Part I) *(ii)* Combined Volumes : 1790-94, 1795-97, 1798-1803, 1835-36, 1837-40, 1841-42, 1846-47, 1848-49, 1848-50, and 1851-53	10.20

(1)	(2)	(3)
5. Letters from Court of Directors (41 Bundles; manuscript)	1804-1858 Gaps : 1815, 1817, 1821, 1848, 1851-52 and 1854	15.50
6. Index to Letters from Court of Directors (7 Volumes; manuscript)	1821-1858 Combined Volumes : 1841-47 and 1848-50	0.25
7. Letters to Court of Directors and Secretary of State for India (103 Volumes; manuscript)	1790-1859 Combined Volumes : 1792-93, 1794-95 and 1798-99	10.25
8. Drafts of Letters to Court of Directors and Secretary of State for India (99 Volumes; manuscript)	1818-1859 Gaps : 1837 and 1845	5.20
9. Index to Letters to Court of Directors (7 Volumes; manuscript)	1809-1856 Gaps : 1810-18, 1820-24, 1826-38, 1841-46, and 1848-55	0.50
10. Letters from Court of Directors to Bengal (82 Volumes; manuscript)	1835-1854	5.00
11. Letters from Court of	1835-1854	6.25

(1)		*(2)*	*(3)*
Directors to Bengal, (25 Bundles; manuscript)			
12. Index to Letters from Court of Directors to Bengal (5 Volumes; manuscript)	(i) Gaps : (ii) Gaps :	1841-1854 1842-50 Combined Volumes : 1853-54	0.25

These communications relate exclusively to the Bengal army and were addressed to the Governor of Bengal, who during the period stated above was the same person as the Governor General of India in his ex-officio capacity.

13. Drafts of Bengal Letters to Secretary India House (One Volume; manuscript)		1854-1865 Combined Volume	0.05
14. Body Sheets (170 Volumes; manuscript)	Gaps :	1805-1859 1805 (Jan.-March) and July-December, 1806 (April-December), 1807-1824, 1834 (July-December), 1851-1852, 1853 (January-September), 1857, 1858 (Feb.-Dec. and 1859 (January-September)	10.50
15. Body Sheets (41 Carton Boxes; manuscript)		1786-1858	20.50
16. Ootacamand Proceedings (3 Volumes;		1834 These records relate to the Proceedings to Govern-	0.15

(1)	(2)	(3)
manuscript)	ment while the Governor General with his Council was staying at Ootacamand	
17. Ootacamand Original Consultations	1834-1855	2.75
18. Ootacamand Index to Proceedings (3 Volumes; manuscript)	1834	0.15
19. Ootacamand Abstract of Proceedings (One Volume; manuscript)	1855	0.05
20. Ootacamand Drafts of Letters (One Volume; manuscript)	1855	0.05
21. Java or Batavia Proceedings (10 Volumes; manuscript)	1813-1814	0.50
22. Correspondence (4 Volumes; manuscript)	1812-1817 Combined Volumes : 1812-1814 and 1816-17	0.20
23. Letter-Book (One Volume; manuscript)	1812-1815 Combined Volume	0.05

In 1602 the East India Company established a factory at Bantam, on the North-West Coast of Java. There were continuous conflicts between them and the Dutch and in 1758, after a chequered career, the English found themselves at Batavia, where they had fixed their seat more than once before. Java came into French possession on the beginning of nineteenth Century and as a sequel of the hostility between England and France it was annexed by the British Government in 1811. Although by a Convention of 13 August 1814, Java was restored to Holland, it was administered by the English until the end of 1816 before being formally handed over to the Dutch.

(1)	*(2)*	*(3)*
24. Up-Country Original Consultations (153 Bundles; manuscript)	1837-1859 The Up-Country papers relate to the Correspondence of the Governor General during his tour.	74.00
25. Up-Country Index to Proceedings (16 Volumes; manuscript)	1837-1859 *(i)* Gaps : 1841, 1844 and 1854-57 *(ii)* Combined Volumes : 1837-38, 1839-40, 1842-43, 1848-49, 1850-51, 1851-52 and 1858-59	1.50
26. Up-Country Body Sheets (One Volume; manuscript)	1843	0.05
27. Up-Country Rough Drafts (66 Volumes; manuscript)	1837-1859 Gaps : 1843-44 and 1855-57	4.00
28. Up-Country Diaries of Letters received (16 Volumes; manuscript)	1837-1858 Gaps : 1840-41 and 1852-54	
29. General Orders (Minutes of (Council*) (113 Volumes; manuscript)	1776-1859 Combined Volumes : 1787-88, 1788-89, 1789-92, 1817-18, 1837-40 and 1839-42	8.0
30. Drafts of General Orders (26 Volumes; manuscript)	1822-1844	4.0
31. General Orders	1827	0.05

(1)	*(2)*	*(3)*
Rough Drafts (One Volume; manuscript)		
32. Index to General Orders and Notifications (One Volume; manuscript)	1858	0.02
33. General Orders by Commander-in-Chief (103 Volumes; printed)	1816-1859 Combined Volumes : 1816-17	20.00
34. General Orders and General Orders by Commander-in-Chief (34 Volumes; printed)	1818-1859 Gaps : 1820, 1822, 1837, 1841-44, 1854 and 1857	4.0
35. General Orders by Commander-in-Chief (Adjutant General's Office) (46 Volumes; manuscript)	1774-1829 *(i)* Gaps : 1816-1827 *(ii)* Combined Volumes : 1774-77, 1777-78, 1779-82, 1780-81, 1781-83, 1783-85, 1786-87, 1787-88, 1788-89, 1789-90, 1793-94, 1794-95, 1796-97, 1797-98, 1798-99, 1799-1800, 1800-01, 1801-02, 1802-03, 1803-04, 1804-05, 1806-07, 1807-08, 1808-09, 1809-10, 1811-12, 1813-14, 1814-15 and 1828-29	3.0
36. General Orders by Commander-in-Chief (Home Department (2 Volumes; manuscript)	1796-1822 *(i)* Gaps : 1802-1819 *(ii)* Combined Volumes : 1796-1801 and 1820-22	0.10

(1)	*(2)*	*(3)*
37. General Orders by Commander-in-Chief (Finance Department) (37 Volumes; printed)	1831-1857 (i) Gaps : 1832-33 and 1839-41 (ii) Combined Volumes : 1833-38, 1839-44 and 1845-54	4.0
38. General Orders by Commander-in-Chief (Public Works Department) (25 Volumes; printed)	1831-1859 (i) Gap : 1851 (ii) Combined Volumes : 1831-41, 1855-57 and 1858-59	3.0
39. General Orders by Commander-in-Chief (Surgeon General's Office) (55 Volumes; printed)	1816-1858 Gaps : 1834-35 and 1838	4.0
40. Standing Orders and Regulations (4 Volumes; printed)	1830-1852 *(i)* Gap : 1850 *(ii)* Combined Volumes : 1830-39 and 1830-49	0.20
41. General Orders (King's Troops) (16 Volumes; manuscript and printed)	1817-1837 *(i)* Gap : 1819 *(i)* Combined Volumes : 1821-22, 1830-32 and 1833-35	1.0
42. General Orders (Queen's Troops) (15 Volumes; printed)	1838-1858 *(i)* Gap : 1846 *(ii)* Combined Volumes : 1838-39, 1841-42, 1843-44, 1847-48, 1849-50, 1850-51, 1853-54, 1853-55 and 1855-56	1.0
43. General Orders	1858-1859	0.08

(1)		(2)	(3)
(His Majesty's Forces) (2 Volumes; printed)		Combined Volume : 1858-59	

In addition to the East India Company's troops, Crown troops also served in India. The authority of the Company in respect of the latter was largely confined to financial control. The War Office in England exercised administrative control through the Commander-in-Chief. These volumes contain orders of the Commander-in-Chief relating to promotions, appointments, Court martial, etc. in the Crown army.

(1)		(2)	(3)
44. Diaries of Letters received (81 Volumes; manuscript)		1819-1850	5.20
45. Diary Sheets (One Bundle; manuscript)		1837-1855	0.25
46. Order Book (67 Volumes; manuscript)	Gaps :	1792-1813 1793-94 and 1802 These volumes contain letters written by the Secretaries under the orders of the Board	5.00
47. Rough Drafts (824 Volumes; manuscript)	Gaps :	1813-1850 1813 (January-March) and 1836 (August) This is a continuation of the foregoing series, the drafts representing the preliminary notes of the communications	44.00
48. Bengal Annual Military Statements and returns (57 Volumes; manuscript)	Gaps :	1760-1858 1895 and 1802-10 The first five volumes represent the following *viz.,* *(i)* General Military Registers, 1760-1793 and 1795-1810, *(ii)* General returns of the	2.00

(1)	*(2)*	*(3)*
	troops—31 July 1770-31—31 August 1775; *(iii)* and *(iv)* Lists of the Army, 1772-78 and 1778-85. The rest of the volumes are annual military statements dating from 1792.	
49. Medal Rolls		
(i) Arracan (3 Volumes; manuscript)	1831-1843 Combined Volumes : 1831-39 and 1840-43	0.15
(ii) Arracan, Ava and Assam (5 Volumes; manuscript)	1826-1834 *(i)* Gap : 1828-30 *(ii)* Combined Volume : 1826-27	0.75
(iii) Ava (One Volume; manuscript)	1831-1845 Combined Volume	0.05
(iv) Ava prize Proceedings (One Volume; manuscript)	1832-1838 Combined Volume	0.50
(v) Carnatic and Mysore (2 Volumes; manuscript)	1794	0.15
(vi) Egypt and Ceylon (3 Volumes; manuscript)	1811	0.05
(vii) Egypt and Seringapatam (2 Volumes; manuscript)	1807-1822 Combined Volumes	0.20
(viii) French Island (One Volume; manuscript)	1812-1814 Combined Volume	0.05
(ix) Java (3 Volumes; manuscript)	1816-1820 Combined Volumes : 1816-20, 1817-20 and 1818-20	0.25

(1)	(2)	(3)
(x) Nepaul (Nepal) (One Volume; manuscript)	1816-1819 Combined Volumes	0.10
(xi) India (Nepaul (Two Volumes manuscript)	1824-1830 and 1854-1855 Combined Volumes	0.10
(xii) Accounts of Nepal Medals (One Volume; manuscript)	1817-1837 Combined Volume	0.05
(xiii) Seringapatam (One Volume; manuscript)	1808-1822 Combined Volume	0.15
(xiv) Medal Roll Drafts (7 Volumes; manuscript)	1843-1855 *(i)* Gaps : 1846-49 and 1852 *(ii)* Combined Volumes : 1854-55	1.00
(xv) Accounts of Medal Rolls (2 Volumes; manuscript)	1811-1844 *(i)* Gap : 1818 *(ii)* Combined Volume : 1811-17 and 1819-44	0.10
(xvi) Medal Correspondence Book (One Volume; manuscript)	1811-1818 Combined Volume	0.05
(xvii) Bhurtpore Prize Rolls (One Volume; manuscript)	1826	0.15
(xviii) Assam and Arracan Medal Rolls Correspondence (One Volume; manuscript)	1835-1841	0.05
(xix) Cabool Medal Account Book	6 November 1843- 11 January 1847	0.20

(1)	*(2)*	*(3)*
Correspondence (One Volume; manuscript)	Combined Volume	
(xx) Candhar, Gaznee and Cabool (One Volume; manuscript)	1844	0.05
(xxi) Kandhar, Kabool, Ghaznee, Maharajpur and Punniar (One Volume; manuscript)	1846	0.10
(xxii) Medal Correspondence (One Volume; manuscript)	1847	0.10
(xxiii) Medal Correspondence; Kandhar, Kabool, Ghaznee, China and Jalalabad (2 Volumes; manuscript)	1848-1849 Combined Volumes	0.15
(xxiv) Punjab Medal Correspondence (2 Volumes; manuscript)	1849-1852 Combined Volumes	0.15
50. Death Reports and Promotions Rolls (16 Volumes; manuscript)	1836-1858 Gaps : 1844, 1847-49, 1854 and 1857 Two of these volumes contain only *(i)* Native Promotion Rolls 1841 and *(ii)* Rolls of Promotions, 1856-58	1.00

(1)	(2)	(3)
51. Passenger List Books (21 Volumes; manuscript and printed)	1797-1850 Gaps : 1813-14, 1818-19, 1829-31 and 1839-40	1.00

These volumes generally contain reports of the departure of officers and troops and men from Bengal to Europe and other places by sea; there are only a few reports of arrival during the period 1797-1826. The volumes from 1827 onwards are sometimes called passenger and Pilot's Certificate Report Books and are printed.

52. Furlough Book (One Volume; manuscript)	1802-1825 Combined Volume This volume contains names of military officers with the date of their departure and on return from furlough	0.05
53. Furlough Papers (51 Volumes; manuscript)	1832-1859 Gaps : 1833 and 1836	4.00

These contain letters from the Adjutant General to Government recommending furlough to officers and Certificates permitting officers to return to duty on the expiry of their leave.

54. Service Certificate Book (16 Volumes; manuscript)	1810-1856 Gaps : 1853-54	1.20
55. Proceedings of Medical Board on sick and wounded officers (4 Volumes; manuscript)	1858-1859	0.20

B. CROWN PERIOD (1860-1942)

1. Proceedings	1860-1930	147.50

(1)	*(2)*	*(3)*
(1653 Volumes; printed)	Gaps : 1866 (March), 1906 (April) and 1921 (October)	
2. Proceedings (1309 Bundles; mostly printed)	1860-1942	459.00
3. Confidential Proceedings (14 Bundles; printed)	1914-1936 Gaps : 1933-34	3.50
4. Notes (24 Bundles; printed)	1884-1942 Gap : 1924	6.00
5. Confidential Notes (One Bundle; printed)	1914-1924	0.25
6. Index to Proceedings (260 Volumes; printed)	1860-1940 Gaps : 1860 (April-June), 1866 (January-June), 1870 (A-B, C-E and S-Z), 1871 (A-B, F-L, P-R and November), 1874 (C-D), 1875 (Q-Z), 1876 (D-Z), 1879 and 1890 (Q-N)	20.00
7. Index to the important decisions etc. to the Military Department (One Volume; printed)	1881	0.05
8. Index to Questions, Resolutions, etc. in the	1921-1941 Combined Volumes : 1921-31 and 1932-36	1.00

(1)		*(2)*	*(3)*
Central Legislature Concerning Army/Defence Departments (18 Volumes; printed)			
9. Index and Contents (65 Volumes; printed)	Gaps :	1860-1883 Mostly Yearly Volumes 1860 (January-May), August and December) 1861 (January-February, May, August-September and December), 1862 (April and July-October), 1863 (April, June-August and October-December), 1864-65, 1866 (January-August and October-December), 1867 (January, May-July and October-November, 1868 (February, May-July and September-December), 1869 (March-April and June-October), 1870 (February, April, July and September-October), 1871 (January, April-May and July-December), 1872 (April, June and August-December) 1873-1881, 1882 (March, May-October and December and 1883 (January-August and October-December)	2.75
10. Abstracts of Tabular		1879-1922	8.10

(1)	*(2)*	*(3)*
Statements of Proceedings (89 Volumes; printed)	Gaps : 1879 (January-March) 1901 (January) and 1920 (January-June)	
11. Despatches from Secretary of State for India (241 Volumes; printed)	1860-1929 Combined Volume : 1924-29	23.00
12. Despatches from Secretary of State for India (19 Bundles; printed)	1890-1929 Gaps : 1895, 1912 and 1914-16	4.75
13. Military (Stores) Despatches from Secretary of State for India (7 Volumes; printed)	1888-1897 Gaps : 1890-92	0.50
14. Military (Stores) Despatches from Secretary of State for India (One Bundle; printed)	1908-1909	0.25
15. Military Financial Despatches from Secretary of State	1862-1888 *(i)* Gaps : 1863-65, 1877, 1878 (May-December) and 1879-84 *(ii)* Combined Volume :	2.75

(1)	(2)	(3)
for India (26 Volumes; printed)	1862-66	
16. Index to Despatches from Secretary of State for India (14 Volumes; printed)	1860-1905 Combined Volumes : 1864-66, 1866-68, 1867-70, 1870-72, 1871-76, 1877-85, 1884-90, 1891-95, 1896-1900 and 1901-05	1.25
17. Heading File of Despatches from Secretary of State for India (16 Volumes; printed)	1906-1926 *(i)* Gaps : 1918, 1920 and 1922-23 *(ii)* Combined Volumes : 1907-09 and 1924-26	4.00
18. Countermark File of despatches from secretary of State for India (29 Volumes; printed)	1902-1920 Gaps : 1904, 1906, 1910 and 1919	10.00
19. Despatches to Secretary of State for India (247 Volumes; printed)	1860-1929 *(i)* Gaps : 1868 (Part I) and 1884 (January-June) *(ii)* Combined Volume : 1924-25, 1926-27 and 1928-29	28.50
20. Despatches to Secretary of State	1886-1929 Gaps : 1912-13, 1914-15 and 1916	20.00

(1)	*(2)*	*(3)*
for India (65 Bundles; manuscript)		
21. Drafts of Despatches to Secretary of State for India (30 Volumes; manuscript)	1860-1874 Gaps : 1861-62, 1969, and 1873	2.50
22. Heading File of Despatches to Secretary of State for India (17 Volumes; printed)	1908-1926 *(i)* Gaps : 1909, 1918-19 and 1925 *(ii)* Combined Volume : 1911-15	4.00
23. Countermark File of Despatches to Secretary of State for India (24 Volumes; printed)	1903-1919 *(i)* Gap : 1918 *(ii)* Combined Volume : 1911-15	9.00
24. Index to Despatches to Secretary of State for India (21 Volumes; printed)	1862-1919 *(i)* Gap : 1907 *(ii)* Combined Volume : 1864-66, 1867-69, 1870-72, 1874-76, 1877-83, 1884-91, 1891-95, 1896-1900 and 1909-19	1.25
25. Despatches to Under Secretary of State for India (21 Volumes; printed)	1873-1911 *(i)* Gap : 1899 *(ii)* Combined Volumes : 1878-84, 1885-90 and 1910-11	2.75

(1)	*(2)*	*(3)*
26. Despatches to Under Secretary of State for India (8 Bundles; printed)	1885-1911	2.00
27. Drafts of Bengal Letters to Military Secretary, India House	1868-1869 Combined Volume :	0.05
28. Body Sheets (14 Volumes; printed)	1861-1877 Gaps : 1862, 1804 and 1875	0.75
29. Up-Country Proceedings (9 Bundles; manuscript)	1860-1871	8.00
30. Up-Country Index to Proceedings (15 Volumes; manuscript)	1860-1870 *(i)* Gap : 1862 *(ii)* Combined Volume : 1860-61	1.50
31. Up-Country Despatches from Secretary of State for India (One Volume; manuscript)	1869	0.05
32. Up-Country Despatches to Secretary of State for India (One Volume; manuscript)	1869	0.05
33. Up-Country Body Sheets	1867-1870	0.25

(1)	(2)	(3)
(11 Volumes; printed)		
34. Up-Country Rough Drafts (58 Volumes; manuscript)	1860-1870 Gaps : 1861-62	3.50
35. General Orders (70 Volumes; manuscript and printed)	1860-1920 Gap : 1873	4.5
36. General Orders By Commander-in-Chief (86 Volumes; printed)	1866-1903	8.0
37. General Orders (Queen's Troop) (6 Volumes; printed)	1860-1863	0.50
38. Standing Orders and Regulations (2 Volumes; printed)	1861-1863 Combined Volume	0.1
39. Standing General Orders (39 Volumes; printed)	1863-1892 Gap : 1891	2.1
40. Circulars and General Orders (5 Volumes; printed)	1860-1881 Gaps : 1863-79	0.20
41. Rough Drafts of Telegraphic Messages (10 Volumes; manuscript and printed)	1863-1870	0.50

(1)	*(2)*	*(3)*
42. Death Reports and Promotions Rolls (One Volume; manuscript)	1864-1865 Combined Volume	0.05
43. Service Certificate Book (4 Volumes; manuscript)	1860-1863	0.20
44. Furlough Papers	1861-1863 Combined Volume	0.05
45. Diary of Letters received (One Volume; manuscript)	1864	0.05
46. Report of the Committee on the obligations devolving on the Army in India, its strength and cost. (3 Volumes) printed)	1912 Volume I. Contains Minority Report, Volume III. contians Minutes of Evidence and Volume VI. contain Appendices I-VIII	0.15
47. Mutiny Medal Rolls. (One Volume; manuscript)	1867-1868 Combined Volume	0.10
48. Mutiny Medal Receipts (4 Volumes; manuscript)	1863-1869 *(i)* Gaps : 1864-66 *(ii)* Combined Volume : 1867-68	0.20
49. 1914-Star Index to the Claims of the Supply and Transport Corps.	1914	0.10

(1)	(2)	(3)
(2 Volumes; printed)		
50. Annual Reports (Ordnance Department) (2 Volumes; manuscript)	1859-1865 *(i)* Gaps : 1862-63 *(ii)* Combined Volumes : 1859-61 and 1864-65	0.10
51. Register of Papers Recorded (One Volume; printed)	1875	0.05

C. POST-INDEPENDENCE PERIOD (1947-1951)

1. Files (8 Bundles; manuscript and printed)	1947-1951 Gaps : 1948	2.00

(These are not strictly according to the File System as adopted in 1923 in most of the departments. Most of these bear Proceedings numbers alongwith the Case numbers).

(ii) GOVERNMENT OF MADRAS RECORDS (1757-1895)

A. COMPANY PERIOD (1757-1859)

1. Abstract of Proceedings (6 Bundles; manuscript)	1840-1855 Gaps : 1841-44 and 1846-49	1.50
2. Letters from Court of Directors and Secretary of State for India (67 Volumes; manuscript)	1787-1859 *(i)* Gaps : 1797 and 1798 *(ii)* Combined Volumes : 1787-88, 1788-96, 1798-99, 1801-02, and 1805-06	5.00
3. Letters from Court of Directors and Secretary of	1814-1859	6.50

(1)	(2)	(3)
State for India (26 Bundles; manuscript)		
4. Index to Letters from Court of Directors and Secretary of State for India (9 Volumes; manuscript)	1846-1859 Combined Volumes : 1853-55 and 1856-59	0.25
5. Letters to Court of Directors and Secretary of State for India (81 Volumes; mostly manuscript)	1796-1859 *(i)* Gap : 1799 *(ii)* Combined Volumes : 1796-98 and 1800 and 1827-28	2.50
6. Index to Letters to Court of Directors and Secretary of State for India (12 Volumes; mostly manuscript)	1846-1858 Combined Volume : 1851-52	2.00
7. General Orders (32 Volumes; printed)	1820-1859 Combined Volumes : 1820-23, 1824-25, 1826-28, 1831-32 and 1833-34	4.00
8. Annual Military Statements (52 Volumes; manuscript)	1796-1857	5.00
9. Records of the old Madras Army	1757-1759	0.05

(1)	*(2)*	*(3)*
(In all 7 papers; manuscript)		

B. CROWN PERIOD (1860-1895)

(1)	*(2)*	*(3)*
1. Despatches from Secretary of State for India (21 Volumes; manuscript and printed)	1860-1891 *(i)* Gap : 1884 *(ii)* Combined Volumes : 1867-68, 1869-70, 1870-71, 1872-73, 1874-75, 1876-77, 1878-79, 1880-81, 1882-83, 1886-87, 1888-89 and 1890-91	2.00
2. Index to Despatches from Secretary of State for India (16 Volumes; printed)	1862-1889 *(i)* Gaps ; 1864, 1867, 1871-72, 1878, 1880-81 and 1888 *(ii)* Combined Volumes : 1862-63, 1865-66 and 1868-70	0.75
3. Despatches to Secretary of State for India (77 Volumes; printed)	1860-1894 Gaps : 1867 and 1869-71	6.20
4. Index to Despatches to Secretary of State for India (21 Volumes; printed)	1863-1895 Gaps : 1864, 1866-68, 1880, 1882-83 and 1889-93	1.20
5. General Orders (26 Volumes; printed)	1864-1872	3.00
6. General Orders by Commander-in-Chief and General Orders Books (9 Volumes; printed)	1886-1894 Gaps : 1890 and 1892	0.25

(1)	(2)	(3)
(iii) GOVERNMENT OF BOMBAY RECORDS (1797-1894)		
A. COMPANY PERIOD (1797-1859)		
1. Abstract of Proceedings (26 Bundles; manuscript)	1835-1859	6.50
2. Letters from Court of Directors and Secretary of State for India (58 Volumes; manuscript)	1797-1859 Volume for 1797 also contains Letters to Madras *(i)* Gaps : 1798-1800 and 1804 *(ii)* Combined Volumes : 1802-03, 1805-06, 1808-09 and 1830-31	2.50
3. Letters from Court of Directors and Secretary of State for India (26 Bundles and 3 Carton Boxes; manuscript)	1810-1859	7.00
4. Letters to Court of Directors and Secretary of State for India (51 Volumes; manuscript)	1805-1859 *(i)* Gap : 1818 *(ii)* Combined Volumes : 1805-07, 1808-09, and 1826-29	3.00
5. General Orders (53 Volumes; printed)	1820-1859 Combined Volumes : 1820-22, 1823-24, 1825-26, 1827-28, 1829-30, 1831-32, 1833-34, 1840-41, 1843-44 and 1845-46	3.20
6. Annual Military	1807-1859	0.50

(1)	(2)	(3)
Statements (47 Volumes; manuscript)	Gaps : 1818 and 1826-27	
7. Records of the Old Bombay Army		
(i) Adjutant General's Correspondence and Miscellaneous papers (102 Volumes; manuscript)	1819-1859	2.00
(ii) Quarter Master General's Correspondence (20 Volumes; manuscript)	1839-1859	0.50
B. CROWN PERIOD (1860-1894)		
1. Despatches from Secretary of State for India (22 Volumes; manuscript)	1860-1891 Combined Volumes : 1873-75, 1876-77, 1878-79, 1880-81, 1882-84, 1885-87, 1888-89, and 1890-91	1.20
2. Despatches to Secretary of State for India (60 Volumes; manuscript)	1860-1892	5.20
3. General Orders (31 Volumes; printed)	1860-1877 Gap : 1873	1.50
4. General Orders by Commander-in-Chief and General Orders	1880-1894 Gaps : 1881-84 and 1892-93	0.50

(1)	(2)	(3)
Books (9 Volumes; printed)		
5. Records of the Old Bombay Army		
(i) Adjutant General's Correspondence and Miscellaneous papers (94 Volumes; manuscript)	1860-1893	1.50
(ii) Quarter Master General's Correspondence (26 Volumes; manuscript)	1860-1890	0.75
(iii) Correspondence Relating to the Royal Artillery (8 Volumes; manuscript)	1864-1868	0.50

(iv) GOVERNMENT OF THE PUNJAB RECORDS (1854-1859)

(1)	(2)	(3)
1. Abstract of the Proceedings (15 Volumes; manuscript)	1854-1859	0.75

(III) Records created in the Branches/Sections.

1. ESTATES BRANCH (1824-1878)

The Estates Branch dealt with all the business connected with the estates of the deceased European Commissioned and non-commissioned officers and soldiers of the East India Company's service in Bengal.

The following records of this Branch are available :

Series	*Years*	*Space (in metres)*
(1)	*(2)*	*(3)*
A. COMPANY PERIOD (1825-1859)		
1. Proceedings 38 Volumes; manuscript)	1846-1859 Gaps : 1847, 1852, 1854 (April) and 1859 (May-Dec.)	2.00
2. Original Consultations (98 Bundles; manuscript)	1843-1859	24.50
3. Estates Correspondence (118 Bundles; manuscript)	1826-1859	29.50
4. Index to the Proceedings (One Volume; manuscript)	1846 (June-August)	0.05
5. Rough Draft Files (46 Volumes; manuscript)	1847-1859 Gaps : 1847 (January-June), 1848 (July-December), 1849, 1850 (July-December), 1851, 1853 1854 (April-December), 1855 (August-December), 1856 (January, March and September-December), 1857 (January-April), 1858 (January-May) and 1859 (January-April)	15.00
6. Index to Letters of Administration Obtained in Respect of estates (One Volume; manuscript)	1844-1859 Combined Volume	0.05
7. Deposit Number Book	1851-1854 Volumes II and III	0.10

(1)	(2)	(3)
(2 Volumes; manuscript)	These are indexes to Estate Correspondence	
8. Body Sheets (3 Bundles; manuscript)	1853-1858	0.75
9. Index to Register of Estate (One Volume; manuscript)	1824-1832 Combined Volume	0.05
10. Index to Register of Estates (Officers and Soldiers) (3 Volumes; manuscript)	1833-1851 Combined Volumes: 1833-40, 1841-47 and 1848-51	0.15
11. Index to Register of Estates (Officers) (3 Volumes; manuscript)	1852-1860 Combined Volumes : 1852-54, 1855-57 and 1858-60	0.15
12. Index to Register of Estates (Soldiers) (4 Volumes; manuscript)	1852-1859	0.20
13. Officers Registers (6 Volumes; manuscript)	1841-1859 Combined Volumes : 1841-47, 1846-47, 1848-51, 1852-54, 1855-57 and 1858-59	0.75
14. Soldiers' Registers (4 Volumes; manuscript)	1852-1859 Combined Volumes : 1852-54, 1855-56 and 1857-58	0.20
15. Register of Officer's and Soldiers' Wills (One Volume; manuscript)	1824-1832	0.05
16. Register of	1833-1836	0.05

(1)	(2)	(3)
Officers' Wills (One Volume; manuscript)		
17. Register of Soldiers' Wills (13 Volumes; manuscript)	1836-1856 Combined Volume : 1836-40, 1837-39, 1839-40, 1842-44, 1844-46, 1835-48, 1848-49, 1848-50, 1850-51, 1851-52, 1853-54 and 1854-56	1.75
18. Drafts Office Memos (One Volume; manuscript)	1853-1865 Combined Volume	0.05
19. Drafts of letters to the Treasurer (One Volume; manuscript)	1855	0.05
20. Drafts of letters to the Sub-Treasurer (3 Volumes; manuscript)	1858-1859	0.15
21. Diaries of Letters received (7 Volumes; manuscript)	1855-1859	0.50
22. General Distribution of Returns Register (9 Volumes; manuscript)	1826-1856 Gaps : 1831-32, 1840-41, 1844-47 and 1854	1.10
23. General Distribution Register (7 Volumes; manuscript)	1840-1860 Combined Volumes : 1840-41, 1844-45, 1846-47 1848-49, 1849-50, 1856-57 and 1856-60	1.00
24. Number Book (4 Volumes; manuscript)	1851-1855 Combined Volumes : 1851-54 and 1852-54	0.20
25. Casualty List of	1852-57	0.05

(1)	*(2)*	*(3)*
Officers and Soldiers (One Volume; manuscript)	Combined Volume	
26. Transfer Bill (One Volume; manuscript)	1859-1860	0.05
B. CROWN PERIOD (1960-1878)		
1. Proceedings (11 Bundles; manuscript)	1860	2.75
2. Estates Correspondence (13 Bundles; manuscript)	1860	3.75
3. Officers Registers (7 Volumes; manuscript)	1859-1874 Combined Volumes : 1859-60, 1861-62, 1863-64, 1865-67, 1867-69, 1868-69, and 1870-74	0.75
4. Soldiers Registers (6 Volumes; manuscript)	1860-1878 Combined Volumes : 1863-64, 1865-76, and 1875-78	0.25
5. Register of Soldiers Wills (One Volume; manuscript)	1857-1874 One Combined Volume	0.05
6. Rough Drafts files (One Volume; manuscript)	1860 (May-August)	0.05
7. Diaries of letters received (9 Volumes; manuscript)	1860-1875 Combined Volumes : 1863-64, 1865-66, 1867-72, 1870-72 and 1873-75	0.75

Index